Elements of Data Compression

Elements of Data Compression

Adam Drozdek

Duquesne University

BROOKS/COLE

THOMSON LEARNING

Australia • Canada • Mexico • Singapore • Spain • United Kingdom • United States

BROOKS/COLE

™

THOMSON LEARNING

Publisher: *Bill Stenquist*
Sponsoring Editor: *Kallie Swanson*
Marketing Team: *Christopher Kelly, Samantha Cabaluna*
Editorial Assistant: *Carla Vera*
Production Coordinator: *Kelsey McGee*
Permissions Editor: *Sue Ewing*
Production Service: *The Book Company*
Manuscript Editor: *Frank Hubert*

Media Editor: *Burke Taft*
Interior Design: *Devenish Design*
Cover Design: *Denise Davidson*
Cover Illustration: *George Abe*
Interior Illustration: *Lotus Art*
Print Buyer: *Vena M. Dyer*
Typesetting: *Omegatype Typography, Inc.*
Cover Printing, Printing and Binding: *Webcom*

For more information about this or any other Brooks/Cole product, contact:
BROOKS/COLE
511 Forest Lodge Road
Pacific Grove, CA 93950 USA
www.brookscole.com
1-800-423-0563 (Thomson Learning Academic Resource Center)

Printed in Canada

10   9   8   7   6   5   4   3   2   1

Library of Congress Cataloging-in-Publication Data

Drozdek, Adam.
    Elements of data compression / Adam Drozdek.
       p.   cm.
    Includes bibliographical references and index.
    ISBN 0-534-38448-X
    1. Data compression (Computer science)   I. Title.
QA76.9.D33 D76 2002
005.74'6—dc21
2001025899

To Ewa, Zuzanka, and Kamil

Contents

Preface

The data compression field has always been an important part of computer science, and it is becoming increasingly popular and important today. Although computers become faster and data storage becomes less expensive and more efficient, the increased importance of sound and video necessitates the use of at least a small measure of data compression due to vast storage and transmission requirements. The question in many applications is now no longer whether to compress data, but what compression method should be applied.

In spite of this growing interest in data compression, there is only a handful of data compression books on the market. Many are technical monographs aimed primarily at professionals, and they require a fair knowledge of data compression to be intelligible. There is a need for a textbook addressed primarily to undergraduate students (juniors and seniors) of computer science and electrical engineering who already have some data structures and discrete mathematics background.

This is why *Elements of Data Compression* was written. The goal is to present elementary-level representative method of text, audio, and video compression with the emphasis on presenting these methods with pseudocode, tables, diagrams, and many worked out examples. By necessity, only representative methods are discussed. A truly comprehensive presentation is not possible here because of the immense number of papers and contributions: J. A. Storer compiled a 70-page data compression bibliography which, as he says at its preamble, "represents only a very small fraction of the existing data compression research" (*Image and Text Compression*, Kluwer, 1992).

This book also provides necessary theoretical foundations for data compression methods, in particular: (a) basic concepts of information theory, (b) problems of sampling and quantization, (c) transforms, and (d) filters. This is not a simple task because these domains are very extensively researched, and in many cases, they rely on a fairly sophisticated mathematical apparatus. To maintain an accessible level, the book includes only the material indispensable to understand these topics, which in turn are needed to have a fair grasp of particular data compression methods. For example, some information concerning matrices is included in the chapter that discusses transforms. The last two chapters also present additional material. Chapter 12 presents

Fourier analysis, which allows for better understanding of Fourier and cosine transforms and for proving the sampling theorem, and Chapter 13 introduces the reader to the problem of wavelets.

I hope that readers will benefit from studying this book and that their knowledge of such an important and interesting domain as data compression will be significantly enhanced.

Acknowledgments

I would like to thank the following reviewers, whose comments and advice helped me to improve this book:

Krzysztof Diks	Warsaw University
Przemyslaw Korohoda	University of Mining and Metallurgy, Cracow
Eve Riskin	University of Washington
Eli J. Weissman	DeVry Institute of Technology, Long Island
David G. Dent	Rutgers University

However, the ultimate content is my responsibility and I would like to hear any comments from the readers; my e-mail address is drozdek@duq.edu.

Adam Drozdek

Elements of Data Compression

Chapter 1

Information and Coding

The process of communication or the process of information transmission is one of the most important tenets of life in general and of the human condition in particular. The process has been analyzed for centuries, and it can be scrutinized from a variety of perspectives. For example, we can be interested in the meaning of information—that is, in its semantic aspect. We can focus on the social ramifications of the communication process, on the way information is generated and absorbed, and so on. From an engineering point of view, the most important aspect is syntactic, in which the meaning of information is suspended and only the form in which it is vested is analyzed to know how information can be coded when readying it for transmission and how it can be decoded upon receiving it.

A diagram representing the transmission process is shown in Figure 1.1. A source of information, whether it is a human being, another being, or an inanimate entity such as a sensor, generates some information to send to a receiver. Sending can be as simple as speaking to someone next to us or as complex as transmitting messages from a space shuttle. Sometimes video or audio signals are transmitted directly over the communication channel. Signals of this kind are called *analog signals*. In many situations, however, the message has to be transformed into a form that makes the transmission possible. For instance, readings of a sensor may need to be transformed into a binary form and then transmitted. Since the readings are made continuously and the message is transmitted in digital form, an *analog-to-digital* conversion must be performed before sending the transformed message through the channel. This in turn requires using proper *sampling* and *quantization*—that is, knowing how frequently to take samples from the sensor's readings and into how many levels to divide possible readings. Moreover, the transformed message may make the transmission too lengthy; therefore, if possible, it is compressed so that the compressed form retains the same

Figure 1.1   Basic elements of the communication process

information as the original form, or if some information is lost, the information left is sufficient for adequate communication. The reversal of these two processes is on the receiving side. First, the signal is decompressed and then converted by *digital-to-analog* conversion into a form intelligible to the user.

Some sources are *discrete*; that is, the number of possible symbols they can emit is finite or countable. In this way, for two neighbor values v and w, it is impossible to find a value that is between v and w. For continuous sources, it is always possible to give a value between any two nonidentical values. An example of a discrete source is a keyboard, which has a limited number of keys and an interval between two symbols being typed. An example of a continuous source is a barometer.

Figure 1.1 shows that a transformed msg_1 (i.e., $signal_1$) is on one side of the channel and $signal_2$ is on the other side. If $signal_1 = signal_2$ (i.e., if the transmitted signal is the same as the received signal), then we are using a *noiseless channel*. However, if these two signals are not the same, the channel is called *noisy*. In the case of noisy channels, there is a need to detect the fact that a signal is distorted during transmission to rectify the problem either by retransmitting the signal or by fixing it on the receiving side. Codes that enable us to recover the original signals are called *error-correcting codes*.

Some of these aspects conflict with each other, and a proper balance has to be found to make communication feasible: Information should be transmitted with as little damage as possible, but also as rapidly as possible. Error treatment of information is roughly proportional to the size of signal transmitted. The more we send, the better is the chance to remove all errors. Natural languages are very good examples of that idea. We are able to recover meanings of English messages even if their grammar is faulty, some parts are missing, or some parts are distorted. It is because there is a great deal of redundancy in English: The same could be said with fewer letters and words, but in such a case, each error has more impact on the intelligibility of messages than without using such compression. On the other hand, transmission speed is inversely proportional to the size of messages; thus, the shorter the message, the quicker transmission can be. Hence, error correction is improved by, among other things, increasing the size of messages and data compression by downsizing them. These criteria are difficult to reconcile; therefore, error correction is used in conjunction with data compression.

In this book, we are interested in the data compression aspect of transmitting information; however, the discussion of different compression algorithms should not be divorced from some theoretical aspects of information theory. A discussion of some basic concepts of this theory is given in this chapter.

1.1   Information and Entropy

The flow of information enables people to interact. Therefore, it is not surprising to ask about what information is and how it can be measured. We intuitively feel that the sentence "tomorrow there will be a sunrise" carries less information than "I won a million," although the second sentence is shorter than the first. The reason is that the first sentence states a fact, which is a matter of course and not surprising, whereas the second tells us something that happens very seldom, if ever, and is very unexpected. Hence, this element of surprise, unexpectedness, or uncertainty is relevant to the amount of information of some utterance.

Another intuition is that the amount of information about unrelated events should be the sum of amounts of the information concerning the individual events. For example, the sentences "it's raining today" and "I don't have to water my garden now" are interrelated in that they convey information which is to a large extent overlapping. Hence, the combined amount of information is smaller than it is when the sentences are unrelated, as for these two sentence: "it's raining today" and "this book has one missing page."

These intuitions became a basis of information theory proposed by Claude E. Shannon in 1948.

Let us assume that there exists a set of events $S = \{x_1, \ldots, x_n\}$. The set S is called an *alphabet* if each x_i is a symbol (*letter*) used to create messages. Let us also assume that we know the probability of occurrence of each event, $p(x_i) = p_i$. These probabilities, $P = \{p_1, \ldots, p_n\}$, are such that each $p_i \geq 0$, and they all add up to 1, $\sum_{i=1}^{n} p_i = 1$. In the case of a *memoryless source*—that is, when successive source letters are sent independently (the source does not remember what it already sent when sending a particular letter, i.e., there is no dependence between successive events)—the following definition will be used.

Definition 1.1   The function

$$I(x_i) = -\log_k p_i$$

is called the amount of *self-information* associated with the event x_i.

This function is a measure of information (surprise or unexpectedness) of the occurrence of the event x_i. The negative logarithm is chosen because of its convenient properties (Figure 1.2). The change of the function I is inversely proportional to the

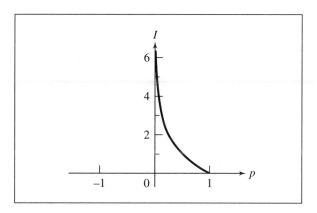

Figure 1.2   The self-information function I

changes of probability—the less probable an event is, the more information it contains—and it is equal to 0 when probability is equal to 1 because receiving a message that we expect with certainty gives us, in effect, no new information. This is in line with our intuition that rare events are more informative than unsurprising events.

A unit of information (uncertainty) is called a *bit* if we use logarithms to the base 2 or *nats* if we use natural logarithms. The number of nats is 0.693 times the number of bits. In this book, a two-base logarithm will be used, defined as $\lg x = \log_2 x$.

Example 1.1   For a binary source $S = \{x_1, x_2\}$ and corresponding probabilities $P = \{\frac{1}{2}, \frac{1}{2}\}$, $I(x_1) = I(x_2) = -\lg \frac{1}{2} = 1$ bit. That is, choosing one of two equally probable alternatives requires 1 bit of information; in other words, the information associated with one of two equiprobable events is 1 bit, as in tossing an unbiased coin. However, if for the same two events, $P = \{\frac{1}{4}, \frac{3}{4}\}$, then $I(x_1) = 2$ bits, and $I(x_2) = -\lg \frac{3}{4} = 0.415$ bits.

The function I focuses on one event or letter at a time. In most situations, however, and certainly in the context of data compression, we have to look at the entire set of all possible letters to measure information content over the entire set. An important concept introduced by Shannon is a measure of uncertainty or entropy associated with a set of events.

Definition 1.2   The function

$$H(p_1, \ldots, p_n) = H(S) = -\sum_{i=1}^{n} p_i \lg p_i$$

is called an *entropy* associated with a set of n independent events $S = \{x_1, \ldots, x_n\}$ and with the set of probabilities of their occurrence $P = \{p_1, \ldots, p_n\}$.

Entropy is the average self-information—that is, the mean (expected or average) amount of information for an occurrence of an event x_i. If in some experiment conducted for some time, a variable X acquires values from S, then the average probability associated with X is approximately $H(p_1, \ldots, p_n)$. It is important to note that this uncertainty depends only on the probabilities and not on the values or the nature of events.

Entropy can also be interpreted as the minimum average number of yes/no questions necessary to determine a specific value of a variable X. If there are seven values, $a, b, c, d, e, f,$ and g, then we can draw a tree as in Figure 1.3 that corresponds to

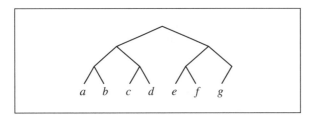

Figure 1.3   A simple decision tree

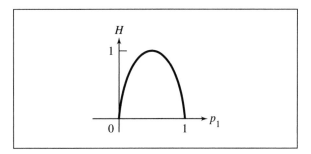

Figure 1.4 **An entropy function $H(S)$ for a binary source S**

questions which basically divide subsets into halves: First, is it a, b, c, or d? If yes, then is it a or b? If no, then is it c? The answer to the last question is final.

In the context of coding messages, entropy represents the lower bound on the average number of bits per one input value—that is, on the average codeword length used to code an input.

Example 1.2   For a binary source, the set of probabilities $P = \{p_1, p_2\} = \{p_1, 1 - p_1\}$, and
$$H(p_1, p_2) = -p_1 \lg p_1 - p_2 \lg p_2 = -p_1 \lg p_1 - (1 - p_1) \lg (1 - p_1) = H(p_1)$$

Figure 1.4 shows a plot of this function in terms of p_1. The plot indicates that H has a maximum (1 bit) when $p_1 = .5$ and minimum when p_1 is either 0 or 1.

Example 1.3   If $S = \{x_1, x_2, x_3\}$, $P = \left\{\frac{1}{2}, \frac{1}{4}, \frac{1}{4}\right\}$, then

$$H(p_1, p_2, p_3) = -\frac{1}{2} \lg \frac{1}{2} - \frac{1}{4} \lg \frac{1}{4} - \frac{1}{4} \lg \frac{1}{4} = \frac{1}{2} + \frac{1}{2} + \frac{1}{2} = 1.5 \text{ bits/event}$$

1.1.1   Characteristics of Entropy

The entropy function H has several useful properties that can now be discussed.

1. The function H is continuous on the interval $[0, 1]$ whereby small changes of probabilities are associated with small changes in the amount of information. Since all independent variables p_i are continuous, the logarithm is continuous on $(0, 1]$ and so are addition and multiplication; thus, H is continuous in each variable p_i. To preserve continuity also for zero probabilities, assume that $0 \lg 0 = 0$ because $\lim\limits_{x \to 0} x \lg x = 0$.

2. Symmetry of H means that the order of arguments of H does not matter. Or for each permutation $\sigma: \{1, \ldots, n\}^{\{1, \ldots, n\}}$, $H(p_1, \ldots, p_n) = H(p_{\sigma(1)}, \ldots, p_{\sigma(n)})$. This fact is obvious from the symmetry of addition.

3. The function H has the lower and the upper limits:
$$0 = H(1, 0, \ldots, 0) \le H(p_1, \ldots, p_n) \le H\left(\tfrac{1}{n}, \ldots, \tfrac{1}{n}\right) = \lg n$$

That is, if the events are equally likely, the uncertainty is the highest since the choice of an event is not obvious. If one event has probability 1 and others probability 0, then the choice is always the same, and all uncertainty disappears. A proof that $H(1, 0, \ldots, 0)$ is the lower bound and $H(\frac{1}{n}, \ldots, \frac{1}{n})$ the upper bound of function H is given in Section 1.3.

4. Grouping axiom. If in the set $S = \{x_1, \ldots, x_n\}$, values $x_1, \ldots, x_i$ are put together to form a group S_i, then the amount of information does not change after making this separation and is equal to the information associated with the set $S - S_i$ plus the information about choosing the set S_i, which is $p_{sum} = p_1 + \ldots + p_i$, multiplied by the information about choosing a value x_i if the group S_i is chosen, or

$$H(p_1, \ldots, p_i, p_{i+1}, \ldots, p_n) =$$

$$H(p_1 + \ldots + p_i, p_{i+1}, \ldots, p_n)$$

$$+ (p_1 + \ldots + p_i) H\left(\frac{p_1}{p_1 + \ldots + p_i}, \ldots, \frac{p_i}{p_1 + \ldots + p_i}\right)$$

See Figure 1.5 for the case of grouping six values.

Since the left side of this equation is

$$H(p_1, \ldots, p_i, p_{i+1}, \ldots, p_n) = -\sum_{j=1}^{n} p_j \lg p_j = -\sum_{j=1}^{i} p_j \lg p_j - \sum_{j=i+1}^{n} p_j \lg p_j$$

and the right side is

$$H(p_{sum}, p_{i+1}, \ldots, p_n) + p_{sum} H\left(\frac{p_1}{p_{sum}}, \ldots, \frac{p_i}{p_{sum}}\right) =$$

$$-p_{sum} \lg p_{sum} - \sum_{j=i+1}^{n} p_j \lg p_j - p_{sum} \sum_{j=1}^{i} \frac{p_j}{p_{sum}} \lg \frac{p_j}{p_{sum}}$$

it is enough to show that

$$-\sum_{j=1}^{i} p_j \lg p_j = -p_{sum} \lg p_{sum} - p_{sum} \sum_{j=1}^{i} \frac{p_j}{p_{sum}} \lg \frac{p_j}{p_{sum}} \tag{1.1}$$

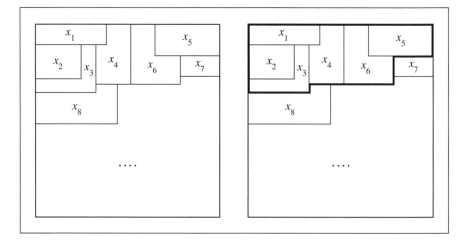

Figure 1.5   Illustration of the grouping axiom

After we notice that

$$P_{sum} \sum_{j=1}^{i} \frac{p_j}{P_{sum}} \lg \frac{p_j}{P_{sum}} = \sum_{j=1}^{i} p_j \lg \frac{p_j}{P_{sum}}$$

$$= \sum_{j=1}^{i} p_j \lg p_j - \sum_{j=1}^{i} p_j \lg P_{sum}$$

$$= \sum_{j=1}^{i} p_j \lg p_j - P_{sum} \lg P_{sum}$$

we can see that (1.1) is in fact true, which concludes the proof.

5. Null set property. Adding an event with probability 0 to a set of events does not affect entropy, or

$$H(p_1, \ldots, p_n, 0) = H(p_1, \ldots, p_n)$$

6. The function $f(n) = H(\frac{1}{n}, \ldots, \frac{1}{n})$ grows monotonically; that is, $f(n) < f(n + i)$ for any $i > 0$ and $n > 0$. The amount of information grows with the number of equiprobable events. The proof is immediate from monotonicity of logarithm since $f(n) = \lg n$.

1.2   Noiseless and Memoryless Coding

Consider a source with alphabet $S = \{x_1, \ldots, x_n\}$ and probabilities $P = \{p_1, \ldots, p_n\}$ for which letters x_i are encoded as strings or *codewords*, $C = \{c_1, \ldots, c_n\}$. A *code* is a mapping from S onto C—that is, a way of assigning a codeword c_i to each letter x_i. A code is called a *binary code* if codewords are composed of 0s and 1s. Assume that the source has no memory (i.e., letters are transmitted independently). In data compression, we are interested in minimizing the expected (average) cost

$$L_{avg} = \sum_{i=1}^{n} p_i l_i$$

where l_i is the length of codeword c_i encoding letter x_i.

Definition 1.3   A code is *uniquely decodable* if there is only one way of splitting a codeword sequence $c_{i_1} c_{i_2} \ldots c_{i_k}$ into separate codewords. That is, if $c_{i_1} c_{i_2} \ldots c_{i_k} = c_{j_1} c_{j_2} \ldots c_{j_3}$, then for each s, $i_s = j_s$ (i.e., $c_{i_s} = c_{j_s}$).

Definition 1.4   A code has a *prefix* (or *irreducibility* or *self-punctuating*) *property* if no codeword can be obtained from another codeword by adding more 0s or 1s, or no codeword is a prefix of another codeword.

It is clear that prefix codes are a subclass of uniquely decodable codes. The prefix property means that when scanning a stream of codewords, no look ahead is needed to disambiguate them. Since decoding does not require any look ahead, then after reading a 0 or 1, it is possible to determine whether it is the last symbol of a codeword encoding a letter of the original message. Hence, since no codeword is a prefix of any other codeword, no special punctuation is required to separate two codewords in an encoded message.

Definition 1.5   An *optimal code* is one that has the lowest possible value of L_{avg} for a given probability distribution P. In practice, such a code may not be unique and codeword lengths $l_1, \ldots, l_n$ may not be unique.

In an optimal encoding system, there should not be any unused codewords either as stand-alone encodings or as prefixes for longer codewords since this would mean that longer codewords are created unnecessarily. Consider the following four sets of codewords for the letters *A, B,* and *C:*

letter	$code_1$	$code_2$	$code_3$	$code_4$
A	0	0	00	00
B	1	11	01	01
C	01	01	10	1

It is very convenient to associate codewords with nodes of a binary tree in which each left branch is marked with 0 and right branch with 1. By scanning the tree from the root to a node, all the 0s and 1s encountered along the way are put together to form codewords. Trees associated with the four codes $code_1, \ldots, code_4$ are shown in Figure 1.6. The first code allows us to decode 01 as either *AB* or *C;* therefore, $code_1$ is not uniquely decodable. The second code does not have this ambiguity, but it requires performing a look ahead, as in 0111: The first 0 can be decoded as *A*; the following 1 may indicate that *A* was improperly chosen, and 01 should have been decoded as *C*, or that *A* may be a proper choice, if the third symbol is 1; since 1 is found, *AB* is chosen as the tentatively decoded string, but the fourth symbol is another 1. Hence, the first turn was wrong, and *A* has been ill-chosen; the proper decoding is *CB*. This example indicates that $code_2$ is uniquely decodable, but it is not a prefix code. Both $code_3$ and $code_4$ can be unambiguously decoded as read, and thus, they are prefix codes, but

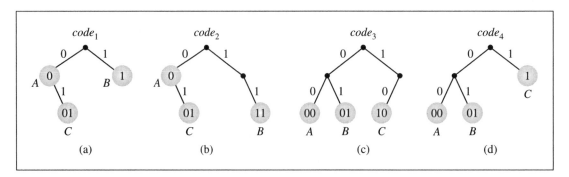

Figure 1.6   Four different codes for three letters A, B, and C

$code_3$ is not optimum since reducing the codeword for letter C from 10 to 1 reduces L_{avg} without undermining the prefix property. Note also that the prefix property manifests itself in code trees in that codewords are only in leaves of the trees, as in Figure 1.6c–d, and never in nonleaves, as in Figure 1.6a–b.

1.2.1 The Kraft Inequality

Our goal is to design an optimum code with prefix property. First, we have to know in what situations this is possible to avoid looking for such a code when it cannot be found. Some information concerning this possibility can be garnered from a theorem proven by Leon G. Kraft in his 1949 master's thesis.

Theorem 1.1 *(Kraft's Theorem).* There exists a prefix binary code with codewords $\{c_1, \ldots, c_n\}$ with corresponding lengths $\{l_1, \ldots, l_n\}$ iff

$$\sum_{i=1}^{n} 2^{-l_i} \leq 1$$

Proof. Let us put all codewords in a binary tree and then extend this tree to make it a complete binary tree with $2^{l_{max}}$ nodes (leaves) on the last level $l_{max} + 1$, where $l_{max} = \max\{l_1, \ldots, l_n\}$. For example, a tree with five levels is shown in Figure 1.7. Dashed lines indicate links added to the tree to make it complete. If a codeword of length l_i is chosen, then because of the prefix property, $2^{l_{max}-l_i}$ leaves become inaccessible because if they were accessible, the prefix property would be violated. In Figure 1.7, codeword 00 of length 2 makes inaccessible $2^{4-2} = 4$ leaves, and codeword 010 of length 3 makes inaccessible $2^{4-3} = 2$ leaves. Therefore,

$$\sum_{i=1}^{n} 2^{l_{max}-l_i} \leq 2^{l_{max}} \quad \text{or} \quad \sum_{i=1}^{n} 2^{-l_i} \leq 1$$

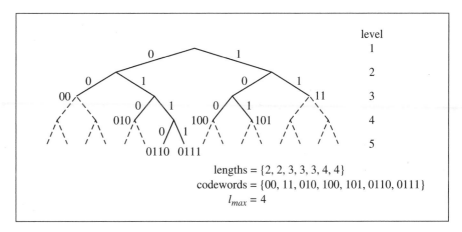

lengths = {2, 2, 3, 3, 3, 4, 4}
codewords = {00, 11, 010, 100, 101, 0110, 0111}
$l_{max} = 4$

Figure 1.7 Creating codes in accordance to Kraft's inequality

The second part of the proof consists in constructing a prefix code under the assumption that the Kraft inequality is true. We begin with a complete binary tree of $l_{max} + 1$ levels and $2^{l_{max}}$ leaves. Assume that the lengths are put in nondecreasing order, $l_1 \leq, \ldots, \leq l_{n-1} \leq l_n = l_{max}$. Now select any node on level $l_1 + 1$ and construct the codeword by going from the root to this node and concatenating 0s and 1s found along the way. Since this node now becomes a leaf, it eliminates from the tree $2^{l_{max} - l_1}$ leaves below the one just chosen. Then, select a node on level $l_2 + 1$ and the codeword corresponding to this node, which eliminates from the tree $2^{l_{max} - l_2}$ leaves below the second chosen node. Continue until l_{max} is processed. But can we run out of nodes for some $k < n$? Note that for a node on level $l_k + 1$, the number of eliminated leaves

$$2^{l_{max} - l_1} + \ldots + 2^{l_{max} - l_k} = 2^{l_{max}} \sum_{i=1}^{k} 2^{-l_i} \leq 2^{l_{max}} \sum_{i=1}^{n} 2^{-l_i} = 2^{l_{max}}$$

from among all $2^{l_{max}}$ leaves in the original complete binary tree. Therefore, there are always some nodes available on a level $l_j + 1 \geq l_k + 1$ for constructing other codewords.

Figure 1.7 shows an example with the set of lengths {2, 2, 3, 3, 3, 4, 4}.

Let us look carefully at what this theorem claims.

1. The theorem makes certain assumptions about the lengths of codewords rather than about the form of these words and says that a prefix code corresponding to these lengths can be constructed. The proof of the theorem was constructive by showing how such a prefix code can be found. However, it is possible that many prefix codes can be constructed and still satisfy the theorem's conditions. For example, Figure 1.8 shows two sets of codewords constructed for the same set of lengths {2, 3, 3, 3, 4}. Also, a prefix code can be transformed into another prefix code by changing 0s to 1s and 1s to 0s.

2. The theorem guarantees finding a prefix code for a given set of lengths but does not change the lengths whereby the constructed code may not be optimal. For example, in Figure 1.8a, the codeword 00 could be shortened to 0 and 1000 to 100, and the resulting set of codewords would serve its purpose just as well as the

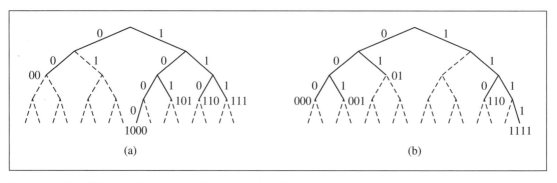

Figure 1.8   Two different codes generated for the same lengths

original set or even better since two codewords are shorter and require less processing for coding, transmission, and decoding. But the theorem cannot do anything about it because it begins with the set of lengths $\{2, 3, 3, 3, 4\}$, although the set $\{1, 3, 3, 3, 3\}$ would give a better result.

3. Very closely associated with the last problem is the question, why or rather when inequality? When does the Kraft inequality become an equality? Consider the set of lengths $\{2, 3, 3, 3, 4\}$. This renders

$$\frac{1}{2^2} + \frac{1}{2^3} + \frac{1}{2^3} + \frac{1}{2^3} + \frac{1}{2^4} = \frac{11}{16} < 1$$

And now the set of lengths $\{1, 3, 3, 3, 3\}$, which gives us

$$\frac{1}{2^1} + \frac{1}{2^3} + \frac{1}{2^3} + \frac{1}{2^3} + \frac{1}{2^3} = \frac{8}{8} = 1$$

The Kraft inequality turns into equality in the case of codewords that cannot be shortened. This should be obvious because longer codewords cause less leaves to be eliminated in constructing the code tree as shown in the proof of the Kraft inequality.

4. The theorem says that for some codeword lengths a prefix code can be found, but to be sure, there is a possibility that for the same set of lengths a nonprefix code can be constructed as well; that is, if a code satisfies the Kraft inequality, it does not necessarily have to be a prefix code.

5. The theorem refers to prefix codes only. However, as proven by Brockway McMillan, the inequality can refer to any uniquely decodable code. This means that our concentration on prefix codes is well justified, and nothing is gained by discussing uniquely decodable codes in general since if a nonprefix uniquely decodable code exists for a certain set of lengths, then so does a prefix code. But unlike nonprefix codes, prefix codes can be decoded quickly by looking only once at each code symbol.

1.2.2 Fundamental Theorem of Discrete Coding

The Kraft inequality allows us to decide whether a prefix code exists if lengths of prospective codewords are given. But we would like to find out something more about such a code. From the standpoint of data compression, it is important to know a performance measure. One possible measure is the compression ratio, where

$$\text{compression ratio} = \frac{\text{length(output)}}{\text{length(input)}} \cdot 100\%$$

which specifies the percentage of its original size that the compressed file occupies. For example, 75% compression ratio means that the compressed file is three-fourths the size of the uncompressed original file. Another measure is

$$\text{compression rate} = 1 - \text{compression ratio} = \frac{\text{length(input)} - \text{length(output)}}{\text{length(input)}} \cdot 100\%$$

which specifies the percentage of saved space. For example, 25% compression rate means that the uncompressed file was reduced by one-fourth of its original size.

If a certain compression ratio is accomplished and this is not considered satisfactory, then can we expect any improvement? How hard should we try to improve the compression ratio reached thus far? The concept of entropy becomes very practical in this respect because the source entropy imposes a limit on compression that can be approached, but not surpassed. A theorem to follow says that the average codeword length is within one digit of the lower bound, and the lower bound is the source entropy. This theorem endows the concept of entropy with very practical significance. But first we need to prove the following.

Theorem 1.2   For $x > 0$,

$$\ln x \leq x - 1$$

Proof. This is obvious if we plot functions $\ln x$ and $x - 1$, as in Figure 1.9, which indicates that the two functions are equal only at 1. To prove it analytically, let us use an auxiliary function $f(x) = \ln x - (x - 1)$. The first derivative, $f'(x) = \frac{1}{x} - 1$, which equals 0 for $x = 1$. The second derivative, $f''(x) = -\frac{1}{x^2}$, which equals -1 for $x = 1$. Because the second derivative is negative at $x = 1$, the function f has a unique maximum at that point. It follows that the inequality $\ln x - (x - 1) \leq 0$, that is, $\ln x \leq x - 1$.

Because $\ln x = \frac{\lg x}{\lg e}$, we derive immediately from Theorem 1.2 the inequality

$$\lg x \leq (x - 1)\lg e \tag{1.2}$$

Theorem 1.3   (a) For any prefix binary code with the average codeword length $L_{avg} = \sum p_i l_i$

$$L_{avg} \geq H(S)$$

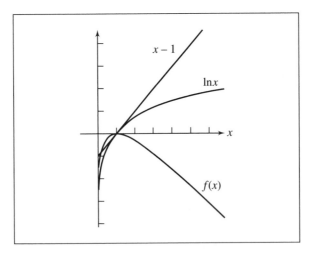

Figure 1.9   Plots of functions $x - 1$ and $\ln x$

(b) There exists a prefix binary code for which

$L_{avg} < H(S) + 1$

Proof (a). $H(S) - L_{avg} = -\sum p_i \lg p_i - \sum p_i l_i$

$$= -\sum p_i(\lg p_i + \lg 2^{l_i})$$

$$= -\sum (p_i \lg p_i 2^{l_i})$$

$$= \sum p_i \lg \frac{1}{p_i 2^{l_i}}$$

$$\leq \sum p_i \left(\frac{1}{p_i 2^{l_i}} - 1\right) \lg e \qquad \text{from inequality (1.2)}$$

$$= \lg e \sum (2^{-l_i} - p_i)$$

$$= \lg e \left(\sum 2^{-l_i} - \sum p_i\right)$$

$$\leq \lg e(1 - 1) = 0$$

from Kraft inequality and $\sum p_i = 1$

Note that if $-\lg p_i = l_i$, then $L_{avg} = H(S)$, which requires that $-\lg p_i$ is an integer; this in turn is possible only when p_i is an inverse of a power of 2. This happens rather infrequently; therefore, the average length of codewords is usually larger than the source entropy (i.e., the ideal average).

Proof (b). Let us define the *Shannon length* $l_i = \lceil -\lg p_i \rceil$ for each i (i.e., $l_i \geq -\lg p_i$), which gives $p_i \geq 2^{-l_i}$. After summing it over i's, we obtain

$$\sum 2^{-l_i} \leq \sum p_i = 1$$

which is the Kraft inequality that guarantees the existence of the prefix code for these lengths. Also,

$l_i < -\lg p_i + 1$

or after multiplying it by p_i

$p_i l_i < p_i(-\lg p_i + 1)$

which again, when summed over i's, renders

$$L_{avg} = \sum p_i l_i < \sum p_i(-\lg p_i + 1) = -\sum p_i \lg p_i + \sum p_i = H(S) + 1$$

Example 1.4

Consider a source alphabet $S = \{a, b, c\}$ and probabilities $P = \{.1, .45, .45\}$. The entropy of the source $H(S) = -.1 \lg .1 - .45 \lg .45 - .45 \lg .45 = 1.369$ (see section 1.4). The Shannon lengths of codewords are $\lceil -\lg .1 \rceil = 4$, and $\lceil -\lg .45 \rceil = 2$ so that $L_{avg} = .1 \cdot 4 + .45 \cdot 2 + .45 \cdot 2 = 2.2$ bits/letter. However, if we chose for lengths of prospective codewords the numbers 2, 2, and 1, then these three lengths would still satisfy Kraft's inequality; that is, a prefix code would exist for these lengths, and the average length would be substantially reduced since now $L_{avg} = .1 \cdot 2 + .45 \cdot 2 + .45 \cdot 1 = 1.55$. Hence, the way of constructing prefix codes suggested by the proof of this theorem does not lead to best compression. However, although the average 1.55 is superior to the average 2.2, there is still some room for improvement because the lower bound is 1.369 bits/letter.

The preceding theorem can be strengthened so that sequences of source letters can be coded instead of individual letters. In this way, the problem indicated in Example 1.4 can be overcome: If coding individual letters of the source renders an average length much larger than the entropy of the source, then the average can be improved by coding blocks or sequences of letters rather than single letters, at the cost of increased complexity of the code.

Theorem 1.4

(*Shannon's Fundamental Theorem of Discrete Noiseless Coding*). For a source S with entropy $H(S)$, it is possible to assign codewords to sequences of k letters of the source so that the prefix condition is satisfied and the average length L_k of the codewords per source letter satisfies

$$H(S) \le \frac{L_k}{k} < H(S) + \frac{1}{k}$$

Proof. A sequence of $s = x_{i_1} x_{i_2} \ldots x_{i_k}$ of k letters from n letters of the original source with alphabet $S = \{x_1, x_2, \ldots, x_n\}$ has a probability $p(s) = p(x_{i_1}) \cdot \ldots \cdot p(x_{i_k})$ since the source is memoryless (i.e., letters are sent independently). Now we view the source as using an alphabet composed of supersymbols, each supersymbol being a sequence of k letters of the original source. The entropy of the new source alphabet $S_k = \{s_1, s_2, \ldots, s_{n^k}\}$ of all sequences of k letters is $kH(S)$ (see Exercise 1.7); hence, by the Theorem 1.3,

$$kH(S) \le L_k < kH(S) + 1$$

from which the fundamental theorem follows. Note that with the increase of the length k of sequences in the new source alphabet, the average length of codeword per letter converges to the entropy of the original source, or $\lim_{k \to \infty} \frac{L_k}{k} = H(S)$ since $\lim_{k \to \infty} \frac{1}{k} = 0$.

Example 1.5

Let us use the source from Example 1.4. The source alphabet has three letters, $S = \{a, b, c\}$, that are sent with probabilities $P = \{.1, .45, .45\}$. We create a new source alphabet $S_2 = \{aa, ab, ac, ba, bb, bc, ca, cb, cc\}$ of pairs of letters sent with probabilities $\{.01, .045, .045, .045, .2025, .2025, .045, .2025, .2025\}$ and the entropy $H(S_2) = 2H(S) = 2.738$. The Shannon lengths of codewords for the supersymbols equal $\lceil -\lg .01 \rceil = 7$, $\lceil -\lg .045 \rceil = 5$, $\lceil -\lg .2025 \rceil = 3$. The average length per supersymbol $L_2 = .01 \cdot 7 + 4 \cdot .045 \cdot 5 + 4 \cdot .2025 \cdot 3 = 3.4$ so that $\frac{L_2}{2} = 1.7$ bits/letter, which is much closer to the optimal 1.369 than the average length for the original source, 2.2.

1.3   Appendix: Bounds of the Entropy Function H

We now prove that the function H has the lower and the upper limits:

$$0 = H(1, 0, \ldots 0) \le H(p_i, \ldots, p_n) \le H(\tfrac{1}{n}, \ldots, \tfrac{1}{n}) = \lg n$$

For the lower limit, note that for each term of the function H, $-p_i \lg p_i \geq 0$ since probability is always nonnegative and $\lg p_i \leq 0$ for $0 < p_i \leq 1$.

Observe that because all probabilities add up to 1, $\sum_{i=1}^{n} p_i = 1$, one probability depends on others, $p_n = 1 - \sum_{i=1}^{n-1} p_i$, from which $\frac{\partial p_n}{\partial p_i} = -1$.

The function

$$F(p_1, \ldots, p_{n-1}) = -\sum_{i=1}^{n-1} p_i \lg p_i - \left(1 - \sum_{i=1}^{n-1} p_i\right) \lg \left(1 - \sum_{i=1}^{n-1} p_i\right)$$

has an extremum at a point p if all partial derivatives of F, $\frac{\partial F}{\partial p_i} = 0$. This extremum is maximum if for the determinant of the matrix composed of the second derivatives, $F_{i,j} = \frac{\partial^2 F}{\partial p_i \partial p_j}$,

$$\det_{n-1} = \begin{vmatrix} F_{1,1} & F_{1,2} & \cdots & F_{1,n-1} \\ \cdots & \cdots & \cdots & \cdots \\ F_{n-1,1} & F_{n-1,2} & \cdots & F_{n-1,n-1} \end{vmatrix}$$

for each $i = 1, \ldots, n-1$, we have $(-1)^i \det_i > 0$, which is determinant $\det_{i+1}$ obtained by including one more row and one more column to determinant $\det_i$ changes its sign.

First, let us find a partial derivative of F.

$$\frac{\partial F}{\partial p_i} = -(p_i \lg p_i)' - (p_n \lg p_n)'$$

$$= -(\lg p_i + p_i (\lg p_i)') - (p_n' \lg p_n + p_n (\lg p_n)')$$

$$= -\left(\lg p_i + p_i \frac{\lg e}{p_i}\right) - \left(-\lg p_n - p_n \frac{\lg e}{p_n}\right)$$

$$= -\lg p_i - \lg e + \lg p_n + \lg e$$

$$= \lg \frac{p_n}{p_i}$$

This derivative equals 0 only if the fraction $\frac{p_n}{p_i} = 1$ (i.e., if $p_n = p_i$). Since this is true for all p_is, each p_i must equal $\frac{1}{n}$.

Does the function F have minimum or maximum at the point $(\frac{1}{n}, \frac{1}{n}, \ldots, \frac{1}{n})$? First, let us find second derivatives.

$$F_{i,i} = \frac{\partial^2 F}{\partial p_i^2} = \left(\lg \frac{p_n}{p_i}\right)'_{p_i} = \frac{\lg e}{\frac{p_n}{p_i}} \frac{p_n' p_i - p_n}{p_i^2} = -\frac{\lg e (p_i + p_n)}{p_i p_n} = -\lg e \left(\frac{1}{p_i} + \frac{1}{p_n}\right)$$

and at the point $(\frac{1}{n}, \frac{1}{n})$, $F_{i,i} = -2n \lg e$. Also

$$F_{i,j} = \frac{\partial^2 F}{\partial p_i \partial p_j} = \left(\lg \frac{p_n}{p_i}\right)'_{p_j} = \frac{\lg e}{\frac{p_n}{p_i}} \frac{p_n' p_i}{p_i^2} = -\frac{\lg e}{p_n} = -n \lg e$$

hence, the corresponding determinant

$$
\det{}_{n-1} = \begin{vmatrix} -2n\lg e & -n\lg e & \cdots & -n\lg e \\ -n\lg e & -2n\lg e & \cdots & -n\lg e \\ \cdots & \cdots & \cdots & \cdots \\ -n\lg e & -n\lg e & \cdots & -2n\lg e \end{vmatrix}
$$

The determinant remains the same if a multiple of one row is added to another row. Let us subtract the last row from any other row.

$$
\det{}_{n-1} = \begin{vmatrix} -n\lg e & 0 & \cdots & n\lg e \\ 0 & -n\lg e & \cdots & n\lg e \\ \cdots & \cdots & \cdots & \cdots \\ -n\lg e & -n\lg e & \cdots & -2n\lg e \end{vmatrix}
$$

Now subtract each line from the last line

$$
\det{}_{n-1} = \begin{vmatrix} -n\lg e & 0 & \cdots & 0 \\ 0 & -n\lg e & \cdots & 0 \\ \cdots & \cdots & \cdots & \cdots \\ 0 & 0 & \cdots & -2n\lg e - (n\lg e)(n-2) \end{vmatrix}
$$

Since this is a determinant of a diagonal matrix, the determinant is equal to the product of the diagonal elements; that is,

$$
\det{}_{i-1} = (-n\lg e)^{i-2}(-2n\lg e - (n\lg e)(n-2))
$$
$$
= (-n\lg e)^{i-2}(-n^2\lg e) = n(-n\lg e)^{i-1}
$$

Therefore, the condition concerning alternating signs is true, and hence, the obtained extremum is the maximum of H.

1.4   Appendix: Tables of Functions $-\lg p$ and $-p\lg p$

$-\lg p$

p	.00	.01	.02	.03	.04	.05	.06	.07	.08	.09
.0		6.64386	5.64386	5.05889	4.64386	4.32193	4.05889	3.83650	3.64386	3.47393
.1	3.32193	3.18442	3.05889	2.94342	2.83650	2.73697	2.64386	2.55639	2.47393	2.39593
.2	2.32193	2.25154	2.18442	2.12029	2.05889	2.00000	1.94342	1.88897	1.83650	1.78588
.3	1.73697	1.68966	1.64386	1.59946	1.55639	1.51457	1.47393	1.43440	1.39593	1.35845
.4	1.32193	1.28630	1.25154	1.21759	1.18442	1.15200	1.12029	1.08927	1.05889	1.02915
.5	1.00000	.97143	.94342	.91594	.88897	.86250	.83650	.81097	.78588	.76121
.6	.73697	.71312	.68966	.66658	.64386	.62149	.59946	.57777	.55639	.53533
.7	.51457	.49411	.47393	.45403	.43440	.41504	.39593	.37707	.35845	.34008
.8	.32193	.30401	.28631	.26882	.25154	.23447	.21759	.20091	.18443	.16812
.9	.15200	.13606	.12030	.10470	.08927	.07400	.05889	.04394	.02915	.01450

$-p\lg p$

p	.00	.01	.02	.03	.04	.05	.06	.07	.08	.09
.0	.00000	.06644	.11288	.15177	.18575	.21610	.24353	.26856	.29151	.31265
.1	.33219	.35029	.36707	.38264	.39711	.41054	.42302	.43459	.44531	.45523

.2	.46439	.47282	.48057	.48767	.49413	.50000	.50529	.51002	.51422	.51790
.3	.52109	.52379	.52603	.52782	.52917	.53010	.53062	.53073	.53045	.52980
.4	.52877	.52738	.52565	.52356	.52115	.51840	.51534	.51196	.50827	.50428
.5	.50000	.49543	.49058	.48545	.48004	.47437	.46844	.46225	.45581	.44912
.6	.44218	.43500	.42759	.41994	.41207	.40397	.39565	.38710	.37835	.36938
.7	.36020	.35082	.34123	.33144	.32146	.31128	.30091	.29034	.27959	.26866
.8	.25754	.24625	.23477	.22312	.21129	.19930	.18713	.17479	.16229	.14963
.9	.13680	.12382	.11067	.09737	.08391	.07030	.05654	.04263	.02856	.01436

EXERCISES

1. What is the self-information of one of 2^m equally probable events for some m?

2. What should be the base of the logarithm in the definition of self-information, $I(x_i) = -\log_k p_i$ so that this equation could be regarded as defining bytes?

3. Give the amount of information of a license plate that uses three letters followed by three digits.

4. What is the amount of information of a *sequence* of all cards from a standard deck of cards? What is an average information associated with drawing a card from the deck? What does your answer depend on?

5. Show that for two probability distributions P and Q, $-\sum_u P(u) \lg P(u) \le -\sum_u P(u) \lg Q(u)$.

6. The Kraft inequality holds not only for binary codes but for codes that use any number of different letters r: $\sum_{i=1}^{n} r^{-l_i} \le 1$. Check whether a prefix code exists for the following three sets of lengths: a. $\{1, 1, 2, 2, 2, 2, 3, 3, 4, 4\}$; b. $\{1, 2, 2, 2, 2, 3, 3, 4, 4\}$; c. $\{1, 1, 2, 2, 3, 3, 4, 4, 4\}$. If possible, build codes using trees as in Figure 1.8. Note that each node of the tree now has three children.

7. Show that for a source alphabet of three letters, $S = \{x_1, x_2, x_3\}$, and the set of two-letter strings $S_2 = \{x_1x_1, x_1x_2, x_1x_3, x_2x_1, x_2x_2, x_2x_3, x_3x_1, x_3x_2, x_3x_3\}$, $H(S_2) = 2H(S)$ assuming that the messages are independent. Generalize your proof to show that $H(S_k) = kH(S)$.

8. For a source alphabet $S = \{a, b, c\}$ and probabilities $P = \{.1, .2, .7\}$ find the average Shannon length of codewords and then do the same for all possible pairs of these three letters.

BIBLIOGRAPHY

Abramson, Norman, *Information theory and coding*, New York: McGraw-Hill, 1963.

Ash, Robert, *Information theory*, New York: Interscience Publishers, 1967.

Brillouin, Leon, *Science and information theory*, New York: Academic Press, 1963.

Cover, Thomas M., and Thomas, Joy A., *Elements of information theory*, New York: Wiley, 1991.

Gallager, Robert G., *Information theory and reliable communication*, New York: Wiley, 1968.

Hamming, Richard W., *Coding and information theory*, Englewood Cliffs: Prentice Hall, 1986.

Hancock, John C., *An introduction to the principles of communication theory*, New York: McGraw-Hill, 1961.

Harman, Willis W., *Principles of the statistical theory of communication*, New York: McGraw-Hill, 1963.

Jones, D[ouglas] S., *Elementary information theory*, Oxford: Clarendon Press, 1979.

Kraft, Leon, *A device for quantizing, grouping and coding amplitude modulated pulses*, Master's Thesis, MIT, 1949.

McEliece, Robert J., *The theory of information and coding*, Reading, MA: Addison-Wesley, 1977.

McMillan, Brockway, Two inequalities implied by unique decipherability, *IRE Transactions on Information Theory* IT-2 (1956), 115–116.

Reza, Fazlollah M., *An introduction to information theory,* New York: McGraw-Hill, 1961.

Shannon, Claude E., A mathematical theory of communication, *Bell System Technical Journal* 27 (1948), 379–423, 623–656.

Chapter 2

Shannon-Fano Coding

The preceding chapter was largely theoretical, and it established a lower bound on the average length of codewords through the concept of entropy. It is important to note that this bound was found for a noiseless channel in which no information is lost or distorted during data transmission and for a memoryless source in which sending one letter has no influence on the probability of sending the next letter. Letters are thus sent independently.

In the proof of the theorem establishing bounds on data compression, the Shannon length was used. However, there was no method shown on what are the actual codewords. By Kraft's inequality, the code has a prefix property, but no algorithm was given to generate such codes systematically. In this and the next chapters, we analyze some of these codes, several of which are optimal and others of which are suboptimal or nearly optimal. Two such suboptimal codes are the Shannon code and the Shannon-Fano code, and the optimal codes are the Huffman code and arithmetic coding. The efficiency of different codes will be measured using the following formula:

$$\text{efficiency} = \frac{H(S)}{L_{avg}} \cdot 100\%$$

where $H(S)$ is the source entropy and L_{avg} is the average length of codewords generated by a particular coding algorithm.

2.1 Shannon Coding

In presenting one of two ways to prove his fundamental theorem for a noiseless channel, Shannon showed a method of constructing a uniquely decodable code. As in the previous chapter, we assume that $S = \{x_1, \ldots, x_n\}$ is a source alphabet and $P = \{p_1, \ldots, p_n\}$ is a set of probabilities associated with the set S. First, the probabilities $p_i = p(x_i)$ of all source letters x_i are put in a nonincreasing order, $p_1 \geq p_2 \geq \ldots \geq p_n$, and *incomplete cumulative probabilities* are defined, $P_i = p_1 + \ldots + p_{i-1}$, so that the cumulative probability P_i is the sum of the first $i - 1$ probabilities (p_i is not included). The codeword for letter x_i is obtained by taking the first $l_i = \lceil -\lg p_i \rceil$ digits from the binary expansion of P_i. Thus, the cumulative probability P_i provides the material for codewords, and the

Shannon length l_i derived from probability p_i of letter x_i determines how many digits belong to the codeword.

The Shannon coding has the prefix property. First, P_i is given in a binary expansion form so that

$$P_i = 0.b_1 b_2 b_3 b_4 \ldots = \frac{b_1}{2^1} + \frac{b_2}{2^2} + \frac{b_3}{2^3} + \ldots$$

where b_i is either 0 or 1. By definition of l_i,

$$\lg \frac{1}{p_i} \le l_i < \lg \frac{1}{p_i} + 1$$

which in conjunction with the definition of P_i renders

$$P_{i+1} - P_i = p_i \ge \frac{1}{2^{l_i}}$$

That is, each $P_j \ge P_{i+1} > P_i$ is greater than P_i by at least $1/2^{l_i}$. Also, because the p_is are given in a nonincreasing order, so $l_j \ge l_i$, therefore, the binary expansion of every $P_j > P_i$ must differ from the binary expansion of P_i in at least one of its first l_i positions. Hence, P_i is not a prefix of any P_j that succeeds.

Example 2.1

Consider the source $S = \{A, B, C, D, E\}$ with probabilities $P = \{.35, .17, .17, .16, .15\}$. The table in Figure 2.1 shows the codewords derived from these probabilities using Shannon's method. The table includes both the decimal values for P_is and their binary equivalents. The equivalents are obtained by repetitive multiplication. For example,

$.7 \cdot 2 = 1.4 \rightarrow 1$
$.4 \cdot 2 = 0.8 \rightarrow 0$
$.8 \cdot 2 = 1.6 \rightarrow 1$
$.6 \cdot 2 = 1.2 \rightarrow 1$
$.2 \cdot 2 = 0.4 \rightarrow 0$
$.4 \cdot 2 = 0.8 \rightarrow 0$
$\ldots$

That is, .7 decimal is equal to .1(0110) with the parenthesized four digits repeated indefinitely.

The average length of codewords generated with this method equals

$$L_{Sh} = .35 \cdot 2 + .17 \cdot 3 + .17 \cdot 3 + .16 \cdot 3 + .15 \cdot 3 = 2.65 \text{ bits/letter}$$

x_i	p_i	l_i		P_i	codeword
A	.35	2	.0	.0000000 …	00
B	.17	3	.35	.0101100 …	010
C	.17	3	.52	.1000010 …	100
D	.16	3	.69	.1011000 …	101
E	.15	3	.85	.1101100 …	110

Figure 2.1   Generating codewords with Shannon coding

and the source entropy equals (see the table in Section 1.4)

$$H(S) = .53010 + .43459 + .43459 + .42302 + .41054 = 2.23284 \text{ bits/letter}$$

Thus, the efficiency of Shannon coding for this particular source is $\frac{2.23284}{2.65} \cdot 100 = 84.26\%$, which is not particularly good.

The Shannon code is not optimal, which is indicated by the preceding example: The codewords for B and E can be shortened to two bits, and we would still have a prefix code.

2.2   Shannon-Fano Coding

Another method that generates a suboptimal code has been proposed by Robert Fano. The method can be considered a different way of producing the Shannon codes just discussed. A difference is that Shannon codewords can have an additional bit at the end, and there may be some differences on the remaining positions. Because of the similarity, the method is generally called Shannon-Fano coding. The algorithm is as follows:

order the source letters into a sequence s *according to the probability of occurrence;*
ShannonFano (*sequence* s)
    if s *has two letters*
        attach 0 *to the codeword of one letter and* 1 *to the codeword of another;*
    else if s *has more than one letter*
        divide s *into two subsequences* s_1 *and* s_2, *with the minimal difference between*
            probabilities of each subsequence;
        extend the codeword for each letter in s_1 *by attaching* 0, *and attaching* 1 *to*
            each codeword for letters in s_2;
        ShannonFano(s_1);
        ShannonFano(s_2);

Example 2.2

Let us apply the Fano method to the same source $S = \{A, B, C, D, E\}$ with corresponding probabilities $P = \{.35, .17, .17, .16, .15\}$ used in Example 2.1. First, the sequence $s = (A, B, C, D, E)$ is divided into subsequences $s_1 = (A, B)$, and $s_2 = (C, D, E)$ since the difference between $p(s_1) = p(A) + p(B) = .52$ and $p(s_2) = p(C) + p(D) + p(E) = .48$ is the smallest among all subsequences of s obtained by dividing s into two sequences. The next closest candidates are subsequences (A) and (B, C, D, E) with probabilities .35 and .75, but these subsequences are rejected because the difference $.75 - .35 > .52 - .48$. The codeword for each letter from s_1 starts with 0, and the codeword for s_2 starts with 1. Next, ShannonFano() is applied to the sequence s_1 because it has two letters; the codeword for letters in s_1 is extended by attaching 0 to form the codeword 00 for the first letter, A, and 1 to form the codeword 01 for the second letter, B. Next, ShannonFano() is called for the sequence s_2 that becomes divided into $s_{21} = (C)$ and $s_{22} = (D,E)$ with probabilities .17 and .31; the

x_i	p_i	codeword
A	.35	00
B	.17	01
C	.17	10
D	.16	110
E	.15	111

Figure 2.2   Execution of the Fano algorithm applied to five letters A, B, C, D, and E with probabilities .35, .17, .17, .16, and .15

codeword for C is formed from the codeword 1 for letters in s_2 by attaching 0 so that it becomes 10, and the temporary codeword for D and E is extended by attaching 1 to it. Since the sequence s_{22} has two letters, the next invocation of ShannonFano() forms the codeword 110 for D by adding 0 to the codeword 11 for s_{22} and the codeword 111 for E by attaching 1 to it. All these steps are summarized in Figure 2.2.

The average length of the codewords generated by the Fano method for the five letters A, B, C, D, and E with probabilities .35, .17, .17, .16, and .15 is

$$L_{Sh} = .35 \cdot 2 + .17 \cdot 2 + .17 \cdot 2 + .16 \cdot 3 + .15 \cdot 3 = 2.31$$

and the efficiency $\frac{2.23284}{2.31} \cdot 100 = 96.66\%$, which is a significant improvement over Shannon coding.

This example indicates that Shannon-Fano coding gives a very efficient code. Generally, it does not guarantee that an optimal code is generated. But the closer the probabilities are to inverses of powers of 2, the more efficient the Shannon-Fano algorithm is.

Note that the Shannon-Fano codewords 00, 01, 10, 110, 111 are similar to the Shannon codewords 00, 010, 100, 101, 110, but two codewords have additional bits and two codewords are slightly different. This indicates why Shannon can write that between his coding and Shannon-Fano coding there are only "minor differences, generally in the last digit."

EXERCISES

1. In the discussion of Shannon coding, it was required that all probabilities of source symbols are put in nonincreasing order. However, one more condition has to be imposed on these probabilities to generate unique codes. What is this condition?

2. What would happen in the Shannon coding if the probabilities were not put in nonincreasing order? Try generating Shannon code for the order .09, .12, .39, .21, .19.

3. Use the Shannon coding method to generate codewords for a source with probabilities a. $\left(\frac{1}{2}, \frac{1}{4}, \frac{1}{8}, \frac{1}{16}, \frac{1}{16}\right)$; b. (.4, .3, .2, .1).

4. Explain the significance of putting all probabilities in order before starting Fano method.

BIBLIOGRAPHY

Fano, Robert M., *Transmission of information,* Cambridge, MA: MIT Press, 1961.

Jelinek, Frederick, *Probabilistic information theory: Discrete and memoryless models,* New York: McGraw-Hill, 1968.

Shannon, Claude E., A mathematical theory of communication, *Bell System Technical Journal* 27 (1948), 379–423, 623–656.

Chapter 3

Huffman Coding

The first optimal code was developed by David Huffman. Before suggesting an algorithm for generating an optimal code, he pointed out that an optimal code has some characteristics which are summarized in the following theorem that uses a source alphabet $S = \{x_1, \ldots, x_n\}$, a set of associated probabilities $P = \{p_1, \ldots, p_n\}$ and codewords $\{c_1, \ldots, c_n\}$ with corresponding lengths $\{l_1, \ldots, l_n\}$.

Theorem 3.1   For a source S, there exists an optimal binary prefix code with the following properties:

  (a) If $p_j > p_i$, then $l_j \leq l_i$.
  (b) The codewords corresponding to the two least probable letters are of equal length.
  (c) The two longest codewords are identical except for the last digit.

Proof (a).   L If $p_j > p_i$ and $l_j > l_i$ then the code can be improved by interchanging the codewords for letters x_i and x_j. The difference between the new and old average lengths is

$$\underbrace{p_j l_i + p_i l_j}_{new} - \underbrace{(p_j l_j + p_i l_i)}_{old} = (p_j - p_i)(l_i - l_j) < 0$$

Therefore, the new code is better.

Proof (b).   If p_n and p_{n-1} are the smallest probabilities and $p_n < p_{n-1}$, then $l_n \geq l_{n-1}$ on account of (a). If $l_n > l_{n-1}$, then the last digit can be discarded from c_n to shorten c_n because no other codeword is a prefix of c_n.

Proof (c).   For the longest codeword c_n, there must be another codeword c_k differing from c_n only in the last position. If it does not, the last digit in c_n can be omitted and the resulting code would still be a prefix code. From (a), $c_k = c_{n-1}$.

By the preceding theorem, it is enough to find a code for all source letters except for the two least probable ones and then extend this code to include the two least probable source letters. To accomplish it, we first order the probabilities of occurrence of the source letters; also, for source $S = \{x_1, \ldots, x_n\}$, we define a source $S' = \{x'_1, \ldots, x'_{n-1}\}$ with probabilities $P' = \{p_1, \ldots, p_{n-2}, p_{n-1} + p_n\}$; that is,

$$p(x'_k) = \begin{cases} p(x_k) & \text{if } k \leq n-2 \\ p(x_{n-1}) + p(x_n) & \text{if } k = n-1 \end{cases}$$

Any prefix condition for S' can be changed to a prefix condition for S simply by adding 0 to the codeword c'_{n-1} for x'_{n-1} to generate c_{n-1} and adding 1 to the same c'_{n-1} to generate c_n.

Theorem 3.2

If the prefix code for S' is optimal, then the prefix code for S is also optimal.

Proof. Let lengths of codewords in S and S' be related by

$$l_k = \begin{cases} l'_k & \text{if } k \leq n-2 \\ l'_{n-1} + 1 & \text{if } k = n-1 \text{ or } n \end{cases}$$

Hence, the average lengths L_{avg} and L'_{avg} are related by

$$\begin{aligned} L_{avg} &= \sum_{i=1}^{n} p_i l_i \\ &= \sum_{i=1}^{n-2} p_i l'_i + (p_{n-1} + p_n)(l'_{n-1} + 1) \\ &= \sum_{i=1}^{n-2} p_i l'_i + (p_{n-1} + p_n)l'_{n-1} + (p_{n-1} + p_n) \\ &= L'_{avg} + (p_{n-1} + p_n) \end{aligned}$$

But the sum $p_{n-1} + p_n$ is constant since it is independent of the new code; therefore, L_{avg} can be minimized by minimizing L'_{avg} In this way, the problem of minimizing L_{avg} for n source letters is reduced to minimizing L'_{avg} for $n-1$ letters.

To find an optimal code, the procedure indicated in this theorem is recursively repeated until only two letters are left. The codewords of these letters are 0 and 1.

HuffmanAlgorithm()
>for *each letter create a tree with a single root node and order all trees according to the probability of letter occurrence;*
>while *more than one tree is left*
>>take *the two trees* t_1, t_2 *with the lowest probabilities* p_1, p_3 *and create a tree with probability in its root equal to* $p_1 + p_2$ *and with* t_1 *and* t_2 *as its subtrees;*
>>associate 0 *with each left branch and* 1 *with each right branch;*
>>create *a unique codeword for each letter by traversing the tree from the root to the leaf containing the probability corresponding to this letter and putting all encountered 0s and 1s together;*

The resulting tree has a probability of 1 in its root.

Huffman saw the structure resulting from application of his algorithm as a net of tributary rivers eventually flowing into a large river. He thought associating 1s and 0s with branches was analogous to "the placing of signs by a water-borne insect at each of these junctions as he journeys downstream" with right turn posts (marked with 1) and left turn posts (marked with 0), which would allow the insect to return back to the starting point.

It should be noted that the algorithm is not deterministic in the sense of producing a unique tree because, for trees with equal probabilities in the roots, the algorithm does not prescribe their positions with respect to each other either at the beginning or during execution. If t_1 with probability p_1 is in the sequence of trees and the new tree t_2 is created with $p_2 = p_1$, should t_2 be positioned to the left of t_1 or to the right? Also, if there are three trees t_1, t_2, and t_3 with the same lowest probability in the entire sequence, which two trees should be chosen to create a new tree? There are three possibilities for choosing two trees. As a result, different trees can be obtained depending on where the trees with equal probabilities are placed in the sequence with respect to each other. Interestingly, however, regardless of the shape of the tree, the average length of codeword remains the same.

Example 3.1

Figure 3.1 contains the same letters as Figure 2.2. Figure 3.1a shows step-by-step how a Huffman tree is generated; Figure 3.1 presents abbreviated (and more

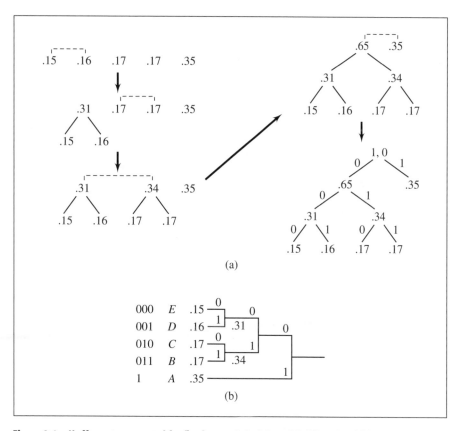

Figure 3.1   **Huffman tree created for five letters *A, B, C, D,* and *E* with probabilities .35, .17, .17, .16, and .15**

commonly used) version of the way tree 3.1a was created. The average length for the tree is

$$L_{Huff} = .35 \cdot 1 + .17 \cdot 3 + .17 \cdot 3 + .16 \cdot 3 + .15 \cdot 3 = 2.3$$

which is slightly better than the result given by Shannon-Fano coding in Example 2.2. It also means that there is only 3% difference between the average Huffman codeword length and the average codeword length of the ideal code, $H(S) = 2.23284$, since the efficiency of the Huffman code is $\frac{2.23284}{2.3} \cdot 100 = 97.08\%$.

As mentioned, each way of building a Huffman tree, starting from the same alphabet possibilities, should result in the same average length regardless of the shape of the tree. Figure 3.2 shows two Huffman trees for the four letters P, Q, R, and S with the probabilities .2, .2, .2, and .4. It can be seen that, depending on how the lowest probabilities are chosen, different codewords are assigned to these letters, with different lengths, at least for some of them. However, the average length remains the same and is equal to 2.0.

Using the Huffman tree, a table can be constructed which gives the equivalents for each letter in terms of 1s and 0s encountered along the path leading to each of the leaves of the tree. For our example, the tree from Figure 3.1a will be used, and the resulting table is:

A	1
B	011
C	010
D	001
E	000

The coding process transmits codewords corresponding to the letters to be sent. For example, instead of sending *ABAAD,* the sequence 101111001 is dispatched. To decode this message, the conversion table has to be known to the message receiver. Using this table, a Huffman tree can be constructed with the same paths as the tree used for coding, but its leaves would (for the sake of efficiency) store letters instead of their probabilities. In this way, upon reaching a leaf, the letter can be retrieved directly from it. Using this tree, each letter can be decoded uniquely. For example, if

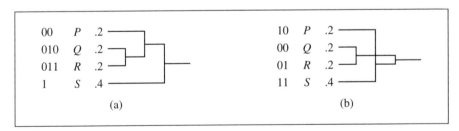

(a)   (b)

Figure 3.2   Two Huffman trees generated for letters P, Q, R, and S with probabilities .2, .2, .2, and .4

0011011 is received, then we try to reach a leaf of the tree using the path indicated by leading 1s and 0s. The first 0 takes us to the left, another 0 to the left again, and 1 to the right, whereby we end up in a leaf containing *D*. After reaching this leaf, decoding continues by starting from the root of the tree and trying to reach a leaf using remaining 0s and 1s. Since 001 has been processed, 1011 has to be decoded. Now, 1 takes us to the right and we reach the leaf *A*. We start again from the root, and the sequence 011 is decoded as *B;* the entire message is now decoded as *DAB.*

This example raises one problem: Both the encoder and decoder have to use the same coding (i.e., the same Huffman tree); otherwise, decoding will be unsuccessful. How can the encoder let the decoder know which particular code has been used? There are at least two possibilities.

1. Both the encoder and decoder agree beforehand on a particular Huffman tree, and then both use it for sending any message.

2. The encoder constructs the Huffman tree afresh every time a new message is sent and sends the conversion table along with the message. The decoder either uses the table to decode the message or reconstructs the corresponding Huffman tree and then performs translation.

The second strategy is more versatile, but its advantages are visible only when large files are coded and decoded. For our simple example, *ABAAD*, sending both the table of codewords and the coded message 101111001 would hardly be perceived as data compression. However, if a file contains a message of 10,000 letters *A* through *E,* then the savings are significant. Using the probabilities indicated earlier for these letters, we know that there are 3500 *A*s, 1700 *B*s, 1700 *C*s, 1600 *D*s, and 1500 *E*s. Hence, the number of bits needed to encode this file is

$$3500 \cdot 1 + 1700 \cdot 3 + 1700 \cdot 3 + 1600 \cdot 3 + 1500 \cdot 3 = 23{,}000 \text{ bits} = 2875 \text{ bytes}$$

which is approximately one-fourth of the 10,000 bytes required for sending the original file. Even if the conversion table is added to the file, this proportion is only minimally affected.

However, even with this approach, there may be some room for improvement. As indicated, an ideal compression algorithm should give the same average codeword length as the source entropy. The letters from Figure 3.1 have been assigned codewords whose average length is 2.3, about 3% worse than the ideal 2.23284. Sometimes, however, the difference is larger. Consider, for example, three letters *X*, *Y*, and *Z* with probabilities .1, .2, and .7. Figure 3.3a shows a Huffman tree for these letters and the codewords assigned to them. The average length, according to this tree, is

$$L_{Huff1} = 2 \cdot .1 + 2 \cdot .2 + 1 \cdot .7 = 1.3$$

and the best expected average $H(S) = 1.15678$. Therefore, there is a possibility to improve Huffman coding by about 11%. How is this improvement possible? As already stated, all Huffman trees render the same average length; therefore, no improvement can be expected if only letters *X*, *Y*, and *Z* are used to construct this tree. On the other

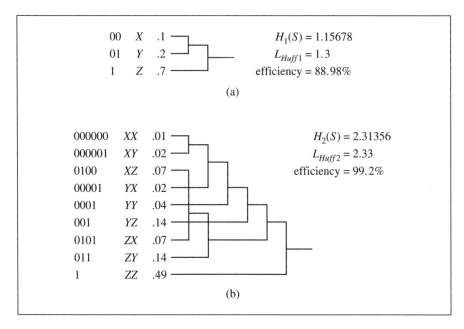

Figure 3.3   Improving the average length of the codeword by applying the Huffman algorithm to pairs of letters (b) instead of single letters (a)

hand, as Shannon's fundamental theorem 1.4 suggests, if all possible pairs of letters are used for building a Huffman tree, the data compression can be improved. Figure 3.3b illustrates this procedure. Out of three letters X, Y, and Z, nine pairs are created whose probabilities are computed by multiplying probabilities of both letters. For example, since the probability for both X and Y is .1, the probability of the pair XX equals .01 = .1 · .1. The average codeword length $L_{Huff2} = 2.33$ and the expected average $H(S) = 2.31356$ (twice the previous entropy), where the difference between these two averages is merely 1%. However, L_{Huff2} refers to pairs of letters, which means that in the coding of pairs of letters, the average number of bits per one letter equals $L_{Huff2}/2 = 1.165$. This represents a 10% improvement over $L_{Huff1} = 1.3$ at the cost of including a larger conversion table (nine entries instead of three) as part of the message to be sent. If the message is large and the number of letters used in the message is relatively small, then the increase in the size of the table is insignificant. However, for a large number of letters, the size of the table may be much too large to notice any improvement. For 26 English letters, the number of pairs is 676, which is relatively small. But if all printable characters would have to be distinguished in an English text—from a blank character, with ASCII code of 32, to the tilde, with ASCII code of 126, plus the carriage return character—then there are 96 characters and 9216 pairs of characters. Many of these pairs are not likely to occur at all (e.g., XQ or ZK). But even if 50% are found, the resulting table containing these pairs along with codewords associated with them may be too large to be useful.

Using pairs of letters is still a good idea, even if the number of letters is large. For example, a Huffman tree can be constructed for all letters and for all pairs of letters, which occur at least five times. The efficiency of variations of Huffman encoding can be measured by comparing the size of compressed files. Experiments were performed on an English text, a PL/1 program, and a digitized photographic image (Rubin, 1976) using the compression rate metrics defined in Section 1.2.2. When only single characters were used, compression rates were approximately 40%, 60%, and 50%, respectively. When single characters were used along with the 100 most frequent groups (not only two characters long), the compression rates were 49%, 73%, and 52%. When the 512 most frequent groups were used, the compression rates were around 55%, 71%, and 62%.

3.1   Huffman Coding with Low Memory Requirements

The size of the Huffman tree is proportional to the number of coded letters and, as we have just seen, this size can grow substantially if pairs, triples, or larger n-tuples are coded. Thus, a large tree has to be created, transmitted before the message itself, and maintained by the receiver. Also, the lengths of codewords grow with the number of letters. The longer the codewords, the less frequently they are used, and yet they should be kept in the tree at all times. However, this does not have to be the case. As suggested by C. S. Weaver and elaborated by Michael Hankamer, infrequently used letters are put together in the set called ELSE. Letters in this set are not assigned any codewords. When a letter from ELSE is to be encoded, the Huffman codeword corresponding to ELSE is sent followed by the letter itself, which would be, for example, the ASCII for this letter. Thus, if the Huffman codeword for ELSE is 011 and the character '@' is included in ELSE, then the codeword for '@' is 01101000000 since ASCII('@') = 64, which is 01000000 in binary. In the following procedure, it is assumed that the source letters are composed of 0s and 1s.

WeaverHankamerAlgorithm()
> *divide source letters $S = \{x_1, \ldots, x_n\}$, where each x_i is L bits long, into two sets,*
>
> $$S_1 = \{x: p(x) > 1/2^L\} \text{ and } S_2 = \{x: p(x) \leq 1/2^L\};$$
>
> $$p(\text{ELSE}) = \sum_{x \in S_2} p(x);$$
>
> *create Huffman code for the set $S_0 = S_1 \cup \{\text{ELSE}\};$*
> *the codeword for an element $x \in S_2$ is the Huffman codeword of ELSE concatenated with x;*

Example 3.2

Consider 128 seven-bit long ASCII symbols, two of them, x and y, occurring with probability $\frac{1}{4}$, and every other symbol among the remaining 126 symbols with probability $\frac{1}{252}$. The Huffman coding renders two codewords of length 2, two codewords of length 7 and remaining 124 of length 8, whereby

$$L_{Huff} = 2 \cdot \frac{1}{4} \cdot 2 + 2 \cdot \frac{1}{252} \cdot 7 + 124 \cdot \frac{1}{252} \cdot 8 = 4.992 \text{ bits/symbol}$$

At the same time, the entropy of the source equals

$$H(S) = -2 \cdot \frac{1}{4} \cdot \lg \frac{1}{4} - 126 \cdot \frac{1}{252} \cdot \lg \frac{1}{252} = 4.989 \text{ bits/symbol}$$

However, the number of bits in all the codewords generated by the Huffman algorithm is

$2 \cdot 2 + 2 \cdot 7 + 124 \cdot 8 = 1010$ bits

According to WeaverHankamerAlgorithm(), $S_1 = \{x, y\}$, $S_0 = \{x, y, \text{ELSE}\}$, and the Huffman codewords generated for source S_0 are 00 for x, 01 for y, and 1 for ELSE, that is only 5 bits versus 1010. Moreover,

$$L_{WH} = 2 \cdot \frac{1}{4} \cdot 2 + 126 \cdot \frac{1}{252} \cdot (1 + 7) = 5 \text{ bits/symbol}$$

which, as before, is slightly more than 4.992. Therefore, Hankamer's modification of Huffman coding is not optimal, although satisfactorily close to the optimum.

3.2   Adaptive Huffman Coding

The foregoing discussion has assumed that the probabilities of letters used in messages are known in advance. However, a natural question is: How do we know them? Our answer is: From experience. There are a number of approaches to gaining this experience.

One solution computes the number of occurrences of each symbol expected in messages in some fairly large sample of texts of, say, 10-million characters. For messages in natural languages such as English, such samples may include some literary works, newspaper articles, and a portion of an encyclopedia. After each character's probability has been determined, a conversion table can be constructed for use by both the sending and receiving ends of the data transfer. This eliminates the need to include such a table every time a file is transmitted. However, this method may not be useful for sending some specialized files, even if written in English. A computer science paper includes a much higher percentage of digits and parentheses (especially if it includes extensive illustrations in LISP or Java code) than a paper on John Milton's poetry. In such circumstances, it is more judicious to use the text to be sent to determine the needed frequencies, which also requires enclosing the table as overhead in the file being sent. A preliminary pass through the file is required before an actual conversion table can be constructed. However, the file to be preprocessed in this way may be very large, and the preprocessing slows down the entire transmission process. Second, the file may not be known in its entirety when it is being sent, and yet compression is necessary. For example, when a text is being typed and sent line by line, then there is no way to know the whole file at the time of sending. In such a situation, adaptive compression is a viable solution.

An adaptive Huffman coding was devised first by Newton Faller and Robert G. Gallager and then improved by Donald Knuth and by Jeffrey S. Vitter. An example of adaptive coding is a method to dynamically update two identical Huffman trees both by the sender and receiver. The Huffman codewords included currently in the trees are based upon the information about text being transmitted up to the present moment. Since the same tree is used on both sides of the transmission channel, there is no need to send any separate information about the tree itself, as was the case with static Huffman coding.

First, a subclass of Huffman trees is characterized independently of the algorithm that generates it. This characterization is done through the sibling property.

Definition 3.1

A binary tree whose nodes have frequency counter fields has a *sibling property* if each node has a sibling (except for the root) and the breadth-first right-to-left tree traversal generates a list of nodes with nonincreasing frequency counters.

This definition leads to the following theorem.

Theorem 3.3

(Faller-Gallager Theorem). A tree with the sibling property is a Huffman tree.

Proof. If the tree has the sibling property, then the last two nodes on the list in Definition 3.1 are sibling leaves. If one of them were not a leaf, then its child would have a smaller counter, thereby violating the ordering requirement. These two nodes have the smallest counters, and thus, they are removed from the sibling list and from the tree. The remaining tree still has the sibling property, and the leaves in this tree correspond to the list of trees after one iteration of HuffmanAlgorithm(). This procedure is repeated, and every time two sibling leaves with the smallest counters are removed from the tree, so that the tree has one fewer leaf after each iteration, the list of trees generated by HuffmanAlgorithm() is also reduced by one tree. After only the root is left, the 0 and 1 branch labels of the Huffman tree that resulted from this procedure are matched with the branch labels of the original tree with the siblings property to see that they are the same.

In adaptive Huffman coding, the Huffman tree includes a counter for each symbol, and the counter is updated every time a corresponding input symbol is being coded. Checking whether the sibling property is retained assures that the Huffman tree under construction is still a Huffman tree. If the sibling property is violated, the tree has to be restructured to restore this property. Here is how this is accomplished.

First, it is assumed that the algorithm maintains a doubly linked list, *nodes,* that contains the nodes of the tree ordered by breadth-first right-to-left tree traversal. A $block_i$ is a part of the list where each node has frequency i, and the first node in each block is called a *leader.* For example, Figure 3.4 shows the Huffman tree and also the list $nodes = (\mathbf{7}\,\mathbf{4}\,\mathbf{3}\,2\,\mathbf{2}\,2\,\mathbf{1}\,1\,1\,\mathbf{1}\,\mathbf{0})$ that has six blocks—$block_7$, $block_4$, $block_3$, $block_2$, $block_1$, and $block_0$—with leaders shown with counters in boldface.

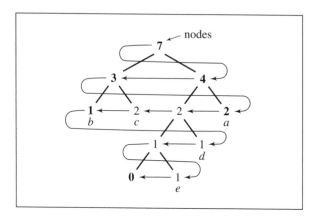

Figure 3.4   A Huffman tree with the list nodes connecting its notes in a breadth-first right-to-left manner

All unused symbols are kept in one node with frequency of 0, and each symbol encountered in the input has its own node in the tree. Initially, the tree has just one 0-node that includes all symbols. If an input symbol did not appear yet in the input, the 0-node is split in two, with the new 0-node containing all symbols except the newly encountered symbol and the node referring to this new symbol with counter set to 1; both nodes become children of the one parent whose counter is also set to 1. If an input symbol already has a node p in the tree, its counter is incremented. However, such an increment may endanger the sibling property, so this property has to be restored by exchanging the node p with the leader of the block to which p currently belongs, except when this leader is p's parent. This node is found by going in nodes from p toward the beginning of this list. If p belongs to $block_i$ before incrementing, it is swapped with the leader of this block, whereby it is included in $block_{i+1}$. Then the counter increment is done for the p's, possibly new, parent, which may also lead to tree transformation to restore the sibling property. This process is continued until the root is reached. In this way, the counters are updated along the *new* path from p to the root rather than along its old path. For each symbol, the codeword is issued which is obtained by scanning the Huffman tree from the root to the node corresponding with this symbol *before* any transformation in the tree takes place.

There are two different types of codeword transmitted during this process. If a symbol being coded has already appeared, then the normal coding procedure is applied: The Huffman tree is scanned from the root to the node holding this symbol to determine its codeword. If a symbol appears in the input for the first time, it is in the 0-node, but just sending the Huffman codeword of the 0-node would not suffice. Therefore, along with the codeword allowing to reach the 0-node, the codeword is sent which indicates the position of the encountered symbol. For the sake of simplicity, we assume that position n is coded as n 1s followed by a 0. A 0 is used to indicate when the 1s stop to separate them from the 1s belonging to the next codeword. For example, when the letter c is coded for the first time, its codeword, 001110, is a combination of the codeword for the 0-node, 00, and the codeword 1110 indicating that c can be found in the third position in the list of unused symbols associated with the 0-node. These two codewords (or rather, parts of one codeword) are marked in Figure 3.5 by underlining them separately. After a symbol is removed from the list in 0-node, its place is taken by the last symbol of this list. This also indicates that the encoder and receiver have to agree on the alphabet being used and its ordering. The algorithm is shown in this pseudocode.

FGK Dynamic Huffman Encoding(*symbol* s)
    p = *leaf that contains symbol* s;
    c = *the Huffman codeword for* s;
    if p *is the* 0-*node*
        c = c *concatenated with the number of* 1s *representing position of* s *in* 0-*node*
            and with 0;
        write the last symbol in the 0-*node over* s *in this node;*
        create a new node q *for symbol* s *and set its counter to* 1;
        p = *a new node to become the parent of both* 0-*node and node* q;
        counter(p) = 1;
        include the two new nodes to nodes;
    else *increment counter*(p);
    while p *is not the root*
        if p *violates the sibling property*
            if *the leader of the block$_i$ that still includes* p *is not parent*(p)
                swap p *with the leader;*
        p = *parent*(p);
        increment counter(p);
    return *codeword* c;

Example 3.3

A step-by-step example for encoding the string *aafcccbd* is shown in Figure 3.5.

1. Initially, the tree includes only the 0-node with all the source letters, (*a, b, c, d, e, f*). After the first input letter, *a*, only the codeword for the position occupied by *a* in the 0-node is output. Because it is the first position, one 1 is output followed by 0. The last letter in the 0-node is placed in the first position, and a separate node is created for the letter *a*. The node, with the frequency count set to 1, becomes a child of another new node that is also the parent of the 0-node.

2. After the second input letter, also an *a*, 1 is output which is the Huffman codeword for the leaf that includes *a*. The frequency count of *a* is incremented to 2, which violates the sibling property, but because the leader of the block is the parent of node p (i.e., node *a*), no swap takes place; only p is updated to point to its parent and then p's frequency count is incremented.

3. The third input letter, *f*, is a letter output for the first time. Thus, the Huffman codeword for the 0-node, 0, is generated first, followed by the number of 1s corresponding to the position occupied by *f* in the 0-node, followed by 0: 10. The letter

e is put in place of the letter *f* in the 0-node, a new leaf for *f* is created, and a new node is generated to become the parent of the 0-node and the leaf just created. The node p, which is the parent of leaf *f,* does not violate the sibling property, so p is updated, p = *parent*(p), thereby becoming the root which is incremented.

4. The fourth input letter is *c,* which appears for the first time in the input. The Huffman codeword for the 0-node is generated followed by three 1s and a 0 since *c* is the third letter in the 0-node. After that, *d* is put in place of *c* in the 0-node and *c* is put in a newly created leaf; p is updated twice allowing for incrementing counters of two nodes, left child of the root and the root itself.

5. The letter *c* is the next input letter; thus, first, the Huffman codeword for its leaf is given, 001; next, because the sibling property is violated, the node p (i.e., the leaf *c*) is swapped with the leader *f* of *block*$_1$ that still includes this leaf. Then, p = *parent*(p), and the new parent p of the *c* node is incremented, which leads to another violation of the sibling property and to an exchange of node p with the leader of *block*$_2$, namely, with the node *a*. Next, p = *parent*(p), the node p is incremented, but because it is the root, the process of updating the tree is finished.

6. The sixth input letter is *c,* which has a leaf in the tree; thus, first, the Huffman codeword, 11, of the leaf is generated and the counter of the node *c* is incremented. The node p, which is the node *c*, violates the sibling property, so p is swapped with the leader, node *a*, of *block*$_3$. Now, p = *parent*(p), p's counter is incremented, and because p is the root, tree transformation is concluded for this input letter. The remaining steps can be traced in Figure 3.5.

It is left to the reader to make appropriate modifications to this pseudocode to obtain a FGKDynamicHuffmanDecoding(*codeword* c) algorithm.

The FGK algorithm is concerned with restoring the sibling property in the Huffman tree as soon as it is violated. The algorithm accomplishes it easily by one node exchange. However, if node p violates this property, the algorithm does not pay any attention to the type of node with which p is swapped. It could be a leaf or an internal node, which was the consequence of the fact that the type of node is not taken into account when maintaining the order in the list nodes. But this may matter if our concern is not only maintaining the Huffman tree but also having this tree with as few levels as possible because the number of levels in the tree determines the length of generated codewords. For example, the very last tree in Figure 3.5 would still have the sibling property if the left child of the root, node *c*, were exchanged with the right child of the right child of the root, but a new tree would have one less level than it has now.

In an algorithm devised by Jeffrey S. Vitter, there is one requirement imposed on the elements of nodes: It is a nonincreasing list of nodes, but for nodes having the same counter, internal nodes precede leaves in the list (precedence is in the breadth-first right-to-left tree traversal order) so that they can be higher up in the tree. In other words, each block in *nodes* is composed of a nonleaf subblock followed by a leaf subblock. Thereby, Vitter not only optimizes the average codeword length $\sum l_i p_i$, but also the internal path length, $\sum l_i$, and the length of the longest codeword, l_{max}. In this way,

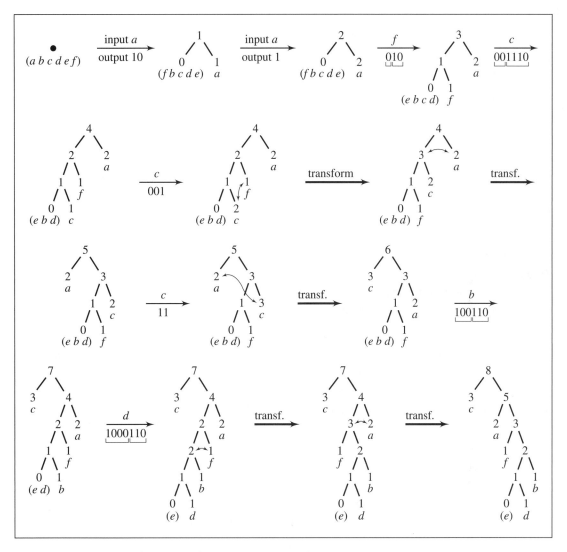

Figure 3.5   Transmitting the message *aafcccbd* **using FGKDynamicHuffmanEncoding(). Some codewords have two parts underlined: One part is the codeword for the 0-node; the other part is a position of the symbol being transmitted**

the nonleaf nodes have a tendency to be located on a level closer to the root than leaves with the same frequencies. Therefore, the codewords for letters corresponding to leaves accessible from these nonleaf nodes are shorter than when the nonleaves are lower down in the tree.

The key operation to accomplish this goal is sliding the entire subblock if necessary. There are two types of sliding operations. If a leaf follows a nonleaf subblock and the sibling property has to be restored, then the subblock of nonleaves is slid to the left by one position, the leaf is placed in the open position, and the procedure continues from the new parent of the leaf (Figure 3.6a). On the other hand, if a nonleaf follows

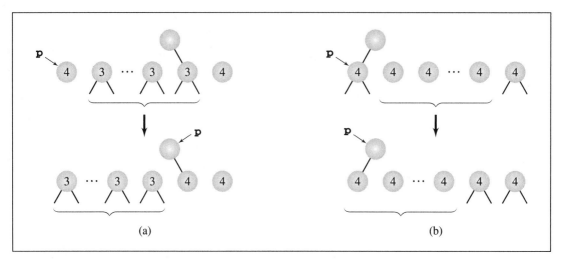

(a)   (b)

Figure 3.6   (a) A leaf follows a subblock of nonleaves with a larger count so that the block is slid to the left and the nonleaf is put in front of the preceding subblock. (b) A nonleaf follows a subblock of leaves with the same counter; therefore, the block is slid to the left to make room for the nonleaf

a leaf subblock with the same counters, then the block is slid to the left by one position, the nonleaf is placed in the open slot, and the procedure continues from the old parent of the nonleaf (Figure 3.6b). Moreover, if a leaf is being accessed, except for the 0-node, the leaf is put in front of its subblock; afterwards, counters are incremented and, when the sibling property is violated, sliding operations take place until the root of the tree is reached. The procedure is summarized in the following pseudocode.

VitterEncoding(*symbol* s)
    p = *leaf corresponding to* s;
    c = *the Huffman codeword for* s;
    if p *is the* 0-*node*
        c = c *concatenated with the number of* 1s *representing position of* s *in* 0-*node*
            and with 0;
        p = *a new node with the* 0-*node as its left child and*
            a new node corresponding to s *as its right child;*
        counter(p) = 0;
        counter(p's *right child*) = 1;
    else *exchange* p *with the leader of its subblock;*
    while p *is not the root*
        increment counter(p);
        SlideAndIncrement(p);
        if SlideAndIncrement(p) *did not update* p
            p = *parent*(p);
    increment counter(p);   // p is the root;
    return c;

SlideAndIncrement(*node* p)
> b = *subblock preceding* p;
> if p *is a leaf and* b *is nonleafSubblock(counter*(p) -1) *and* p's *parent is not in* b
> > // p's parent could be in b if p were a sibling of the 0-node;
> > *or* p *is an internal node and* b *is leafSubblock(counter*(p))
> > > *slide* b *to the left by one node position;*
> > > *put* p *in the opened slot;*
> > > if p *is a leaf*
> > > > p = *parent*(p);
> > > else p = *previous parent*(p);

Example 3.4

Figure 3.7 illustrates this algorithm by applying it to the same stream of source symbols as in Figure 3.5.

1. Initially, the tree includes only the 0-node with all the source letters, (*a, b, c, d, e, f*). After the first input letter, *a*, the codeword 10 corresponding to the position occupied by *a* in the 0-node is created. A new node p with counter 0 is created, and this node becomes the parent of the 0-node and the leaf *a* with counter 1. Because p is the root, its counter is incremented and the codeword 10 is returned.

2. When processing the second input letter, *a*, p becomes the leaf *a* whose counter is incremented in the while loop. SlideAndIncrement() does not update p because *leafSubblock*₁ includes its parent. Thus, p = *parent*(p), whereby it becomes the root, whose counter is 1. It is incremented after exiting the loop, and then the codeword 1 is output.

3. The third input letter, *f*, is a letter output for the first time. Thus, a new node p is created that becomes the parent of the 0-node and a new node to house the letter *f*; p's counter is set to 0 and is immediately incremented to 1 inside the loop. Because the sibling property is not violated, SlideAndIncrement() makes no updates; thus, p is updated after return from SlideAndIncrement() to its parent, whereby the loop is exited, the root's counter is incremented to 3 outside the loop, and then the codeword 010 is output.

4. The fourth input letter is *c,* which appears for the first time in the input. At first, p is the parent of the node *c*; since it is not the root, the while loop is entered, where p's counter is incremented to 1, after which SlideAndIncrement() is invoked. Because p is a nonleaf following a one-node *leafSubblock*₁ = {leaf *f*}, the subblock is slid to the left, p is put in place of the leaf *f*, and p = *previous parent*(p) (the previous parent also happens to be the new parent). Upon return from SlideAndIncrement(),p's counter is incremented to 2, and then SlideAndIncrement() is called again to see the same situation as before, namely, p is a nonleaf following a leaf subblock with the same counters; therefore, the subblock is slid and p is put in the position occupied by the leader of the subblock, the node *a*. Now, p = *previous parent*(p), and because p is the root, the while loop is exited after return from SlideAndIncrement(), and p's counter is incremented to 4.

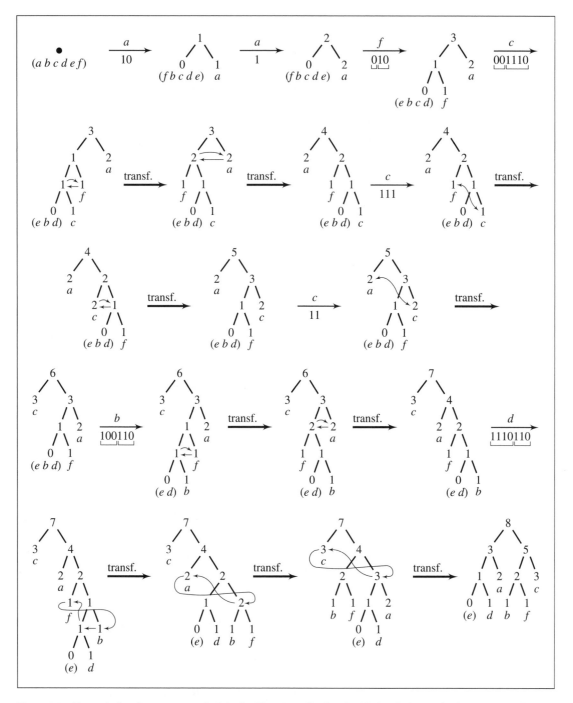

Figure 3.7 Transmitting the message *aafcccbd* using VitterEncoding(). A double-headed arrow indicates exchanging nodes; a single-headed arrow denotes the sliding operation

5. The letter c is the next input letter; because the node c is a leaf, it is exchanged with the leader of its subblock, the node f, and then incremented, after which Slide-AndIncrement() is called. The node p (i.e., leaf c) follows a subblock of nonleaves with lower count. Thus, the subblock is slid, and p is put in place of the leader of the subblock. Afterwards, p is updated, p $= parent$(p), is incremented to 3, updated again, p $= parent$(p), and because it is the root, the loop is exited, which is followed by incrementing the counter of the root.

6–7. Input letters c and b lead to tree transformations similar to the ones just discussed.

8. The eighth input letter is d, which appears for the first time in the input. Thus, two new nodes are created; p becomes the parent of the leaf d, and the while loop is entered; increment of p's counter is followed by the call to SlideAndIncrement(). The nonleaf p follows a two-node leaf subblock which is slid by one position, and then p is put in the place occupied before by the leaf f. Now, p $= previous$ $parent$(p), and after exiting SlideAndIncrement(), p's counter is incremented to 2, and SlideAndIncrement() is called again. Because p follows a leaf subblock, the subblock is moved and then p is placed in the position occupied before by the leader of the subblock, leaf a. Now, p is updated to become $previous$ $parent$(p) and updated after returning from SlideAndIncrement(). For the third time in this step, a nonleaf is following a leaf subblock, which is rectified by sliding the subblock and putting p in place of the leaf c. After this, p $= previous$ $parent$(p) and SlideAndIncrement() is finished. The node p is not the root; thus, its counter is incremented inside the loop. Another call to SlideAndIncrement() brings no changes in the tree (the condition in the if statement is false) so that after return from this procedure, p is updated to $parent$(p), which causes exit from the while loop since p is the root. Before exiting the procedure VitterEncoding(), the root's counter is updated and the codeword is returned.

If we compare the output produced in the two preceding examples, we will not see any significant difference, but in two cases, the codewords are different, although they are of the same length in all cases. The reason is that the first five sliding operations involved leaves and nonleaves located at the same level so that the subsequent leaf accesses did not see the benefit of the operations in terms of generating shorter codewords. However, internal path length $\sum l_i = 20$ for the tree in Figure 3.6 and 16 for the tree in Figure 3.7. In particular, if the next input letter were d or any letter from the 0-node, then FGKDynamicHuffmanEncoding() would output a codeword of length five, and VitterEncoding() would generate a codeword of length three. Also for letter b, VitterEncoding() would produce a shorter codeword (3 vs. 4); for letters f and a, both algorithms would give codewords of the same length, only for c FGKDynamicHuffmanEncoding() would have an upper hand. Therefore, as expected, by flattening the tree, VitterEncoding() allows for generating shorter codewords than FGKDynamicHuffmanEncoding().

There is still some room for improvement of the dynamic Huffman coding. In the original Gallager approach, a Huffman tree was created at the beginning by using frequency 0 for each symbol to be used by the source. If any of the symbols were not used, then the part of the tree pertaining to the symbol was redundant. In the FGK and Vitter algorithms, it was also assumed that the set of symbols used in encoding and decoding is known before the transmission begins, but this set of symbols was stored in the 0-node to which the Huffman tree was initialized. If any of the symbols were not actually used by the source, they remained in the 0-node so that the leaves of the Huffman tree included only the symbols actually sent by the source. This approach, however, may be made a bit more flexible.

It is possible to design a Huffman coding that does not require any initial knowledge of the set of symbols used by the encoder (Cormack and Horspool, 1984). The Huffman tree is initialized to a special escape character. If a new symbol is to be sent, it is preceded by the escape character (or its current codeword in the tree) and followed by the symbol itself. The receiver can now know this symbol so that if its codeword arrives later, it can be properly decoded. The symbol is inserted in the tree by making the leaf L with the lowest frequency a nonleaf so that L has two children, one pertaining to the symbol previously in L and one to the new symbol.

Adaptive Huffman coding is superior to simple Huffman coding in two respects: It requires only one pass through the input, and it adds little or no overhead to the output. But both versions are relatively fast and importantly, they can be applied to any kind of files, not only to text files. In particular, they can compress object or executable files by using bytes as symbols to be coded. The problem with executable files, however, is that they generally use a larger character set than the source code, and distribution of these characters is more uniform than in text files. Therefore, the Huffman tree is large, codewords are of similar length, and the output file is not much smaller than the original (it is compressed merely by 10–20%).

EXERCISES

1. The Shannon length renders Shannon code nonoptimal. Does this mean that an optimal code has to use codewords whose lengths are not greater than Shannon lengths? Consider Huffman coding of four letters sent with probabilities $\frac{1}{3}, \frac{1}{3}, \frac{1}{4}, \frac{1}{12}$.

2. Find the entropy $H(S)$ for the source $S = \{X, Y, Z\}$ with corresponding probabilities $P = \{.05, .05, .9\}$ and compare it to L_{Huff} computed for single letters and pairs of letters, as in Figure 3.3. Does L_{Huff} approximate $H(S)$ satisfactorily? How can one remedy the problem?

3. What condition guarantees that all codewords generated by the Huffman algorithm are of the same length?

4. Huffman coding can be extended to nonbinary codes. For example, for a ternary code, the source sending only three symbols uses the codewords 0, 1, and 2 to represent them regardless of their probabilities. However, if more symbols are used

by the source, at least some of the codewords have to be longer than one letter. Consider the source of eight symbols sent with probabilities .22, .2, .18, .15, .1, .08, .05, .02 and coded with four digits. This time, at each stage, nodes with the four smallest probabilities are combined to form a new node in the Huffman tree. But is this always true? How can one rectify the problem if in the last step there are fewer than four probabilities left? Generalize your observation.

5. For the source of 128 seven-bit symbols, four having probability $\frac{1}{16}$, twelve $\frac{1}{48}$, forty eight $\frac{1}{192}$, and the remaining sixty four $\frac{1}{256}$, find the average codeword length and number of bits used by all codewords using the Huffman static algorithm and Hankamer's modification of Huffman coding.

6. In what situations does Hankamer's modification of Huffman's algorithm give best results?

7. Do all Huffman trees have the sibling property?

8. The HuffmanAlgorithm() builds the tree bottom-up by starting with a sequence of trees and collapsing them together gradually to a smaller number of trees and eventually to one. However, this tree can be built top-down, starting from the highest frequency. Write an algorithm to accomplish this. Note that initially, only probabilities to be placed in the leaves are known. The highest frequency is known, if lower probabilities have been determined, and they are known if still lower probabilities have been computed and so on. Therefore, creating nonterminal nodes has to be deferred until probabilities to be stored in them are found. Hence, consider using recursion.

9. Without much elaboration, Gallager proposes that adaptive Huffman coding multiplies each counter in the tree by a positive number $\alpha < 1$ after each nth input letter has been processed. What do you think is the rationale?

10. VitterEncoding() uses sliding operations, which appear to be quite inefficient. Can sliding be replaced by swapping? For example, the parent of the 0-node in the fourth from the last tree in Figure 3.7 could be swapped with the leaf f instead of sliding the $leaf Subblock_1 = \{leaf\ f, leaf\ b\}$.

BIBLIOGRAPHY

Cormack, Gordon V., and Horspool, R. Nigel, Algorithms for adaptive Huffman codes, *Information Processing Letters* 18 (1984), 159-165.

Drozdek, Adam, *Data structures and algorithms in C++*. Pacific Grove, CA: Brooks/Cole, 2000, Ch. 11.

Faller, Newton, An adaptive system for data compression, *Conference Record of the Seventh IEEE Asilomar Conference on Circuits, Systems, and Computers*, San Francisco: IEEE Press, 1974, 593-597.

Gallager, Robert G., Variations on a theme of Huffman, *IEEE Transactions on Information Theory* IT-24 (1978), 668-674.

Hankamer, Michael, A modified Huffman procedure with reduced memory requirement, *IEEE Transactions on Communication* COM-27 (1979), 930-932.

Huffman, David A., A method for the construction of minimum-redundancy codes, *Proceedings of the Institute of Radio Engineers* 40 (1952), 1098-1101.

Knuth, Donald E., Dynamic Huffman coding, *Journal of Algorithms* 6 (1985), 163-180.

Lelever, Debra A., and Hirschberg, Daniel S., Data compression, *ACM Computing Surveys* 19 (1987), 261-296.

Rubin, Frank, Experiments with text file compression, *Communications of the ACM* 19 (1976), 617-623.

Vitter, Jeffrey S., Design and analysis of dynamic Huffman coding, *Journal of the ACM* 34 (1987), 825-845.

Vitter, Jeffrey S., Algorithm 673: Dynamic Huffman coding, *ACM Transactions on Mathematical Software* 15 (1989), 158-167.

Chapter 4

Arithmetic Coding

In the preceding chapter, we saw how Huffman coding can be modified to achieve a better compression rate. One way is to modify the alphabet by considering a source composed of strings of symbols of the original source. This is the way of improving the efficiency suggested by Shannon's fundamental theorem 1.4. But it has been proven that there is nothing to be gained by extending the alphabet; if, as in the Huffman coding, an improvement of the compression rate is accomplished by extending the alphabet, then it is also possible to devise a method that accomplishes the same efficiency without resorting to the alphabet modification (Rissanen and Langdon, 1981). One such method is arithmetic coding, which originates in the Shannon method discussed in Chapter 2 (for detailed description in developing arithmetic coding, see Langdon, 1984).

Let us assume that all messages are concatenations of source letters from an alphabet $S = \{x_1, \ldots, x_n\}$, where each letter x_i has an associated probability of occurrence p_i from the set of probabilities $P = \{p_1, \ldots, p_n\}$. In arithmetic coding, a message is encoded as a number from the interval $[0,1) = \{y: 0 \le y < 1\}$. The number is found by expanding it according to the probability of the currently processed letter of the message being encoded. This is done by using a set of interval ranges determined by the probabilities in P

$$IR = \{[0, p_1), [p_1, p_1 + p_2), [p_1 + p_2, p_1 + p_2 + p_3), \ldots,$$
$$[p_1 + \ldots + p_{n-1}, p_1 + \ldots + p_n)\}$$

or in terms of cumulative probability $P_i = \sum_{j=1}^{i} p_j$,

$$IR = \{[0, P_1), [P_1, P_2), [P_2, P_3), \ldots, [P_{n-1}, 1)\}$$

These are subintervals of the interval $[0, 1)$, but in the course of arithmetic coding, they also determine the proportional division of any other interval $[L, R)$ contained in $[0, 1)$ into subintervals:

$$IR_{[L,R]} = \{[L, L + (R - L)P_1), [L + (R - L)P_1, L + (R - L)P_2), [L + (R - L)P_2,$$
$$L + (R - L)P_3), \ldots, [L + (R - L)P_{n-1}, L + (R - L))\}$$

With these definitions, we have the following algorithm for finding the floating-point number that encodes a particular message:

ArithmeticEncoding(message)
    currentInterval = [0,1);
    while *the end of* message *is not reached*
        read letter x_i *from the* message;
        divide currentInterval *into subintervals* $IR_{currentInterval}$;
        currentInterval = *subinterval*$_i$ *in* $IR_{currentInterval}$;
    output bits uniquely identifying currentInterval;

Example 4.1

With $S = \{A, B, C, \#\}$ and $P = \{.4, .3, .1, .2\}$, we encode the message *ABBC#*. *A* is the first letter of the message, and because it is also the first letter in the set *S*, the first subinterval, [0, .4), is chosen from currentInterval [0, 1). The second letter, *B*, is also second in *S;* thus, the second subinterval,

$$[0 + (.4 - 0) \cdot .4, 0 + (.4 - 0) \cdot (.4 + .3)) = [.16, .28)$$

of currentInterval [0, .4) is elected. The third letter of the message, *B*, also causes the second subinterval of the currentInterval to be chosen, which is

$$[.16 + (.28 - .16) \cdot .4, .16 + (.28 - .16) \cdot (.4 + .3)) = [.208\ .244)$$

After processing the letter *C*, currentInterval is equal to

$$[.208 + (.244 - .208) \cdot (.4 + .3), .208 + (.244 - .208) \cdot (.4 + .3 + .1)) = [.2332, .2368)$$

and after the fifth message symbol, #, the subinterval is

$$[.2332 + (.2368 - .2332) \cdot (.4 + .3 + .1), .2332 + (.2368 - .2332) \cdot (.4 + .3 + .1 + .2))$$
$$= [.23608, .2368)$$

This concludes the process of subdividing currentInterval into subintervals. Now a codeword is output that uniquely identifies currentInterval. It can be any number from this interval. Usually, it is the left boundary—.23608 in our example—or the arithmetic mean: $(.23608 + .2368)/2 = .23644$. The steps are summarized in Figure 4.1. To see exactly subdivisions, Figure 4.1b shows current intervals in expanded form. The steps are also shown in the table in Figure 4.2. Note that currentInterval's length is always equal to the product of probabilities of the already encoded letters, which is simply the probability of the already encoded submessage.

Decoding consists of determining the subinterval of currentInterval, which includes the codeword, and outputting the letter corresponding to this subinterval. After each output, currentInterval must be rescaled exactly as in the coding algorithm. The decoding algorithm is summarized as follows:

ArithmeticDecoding(codeword)
    currentInterval = [0,1);
    while (1)
        divide currentInterval *into subintervals* $IR_{currentInterval}$;
        determine the subinterval$_i$ *of* currentInterval *to which* codeword *belongs*;
        output letter x_i *corresponding to this subinterval*;
        if x_i *is the symbol '#'*
            return;
        currentInterval = *subinterval*$_i$ *in* $IR_{currentInterval}$;

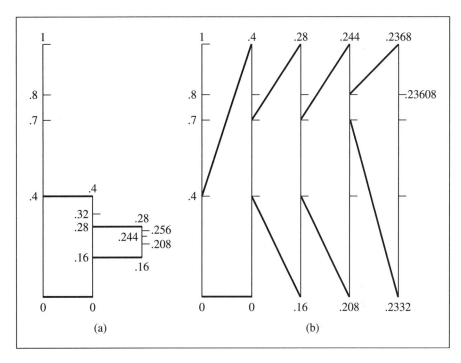

Figure 4.1   Limiting a range during arithmetic coding of the message *ABBC#* for the source
$S = \{A, B, C, \#\}$ **and probabilities** $P = \{.4, .3, .1, .2\}$

current-Interval	length	input letter	subintervals			
[0, 1)	1	A	[0, .4)	[.4, .7)	[.7, .8)	[.8, 1)
[0, .4)	$.4 = p_1$	B	[0, .16)	[.16, .28)	[.28, .32)	[.32, .4)
[.16, .28)	$.12 = p_1 p_2$	B	[.16, .208)	[.208, .244)	[.244, .256)	[.256, .28)
[.208, .244)	$.036 = p_1 p_2 p_2$	C	[.208, .2224)	[.2224, .2332)	[.2332, .2368)	[.2368, .242)
[.2332, .2368)	$.0036 = p_1 p_2 p_2 p_3$	#	[.2332, .23464)	[.23464, .23572)	[.23572, .23608)	[.23608, .2368)
[.23608, .2368)	$.00072 = p_1 p_2 p_2 p_3 p_4$					

Figure 4.2   Summary of the divisions of currentInterval during arithmetic coding of the message *ABBC#*

Example 4.2   Using the source S and probabilities P from Example 4.1, we decode the codeword .23608. First, the number .23608 causes the first subinterval, [0, .4), of the initial interval [0, 1) to be chosen; because it is the first subinterval, the letter A is output. Then, currentInterval is set to [0, .4), and in the second iteration of the loop, it is determined that the codeword .23608 belongs to the second subinterval of currentInterval [0, .4), which corresponds to the second letter of the source S, namely, the letter B. All the steps are summarized in Figure 4.3.

current-Interval	subintervals				ouput letter
[0, 1)	[0, .4)	[.4, .7)	[.7, .8)	[.8, 1)	A
[0, .4)	[0, .16)	[.16, .28)	[.28, .32)	[.32, .4)	B
[.16, .28)	[.16, .208)	[.208, .244)	[.244, .256)	[.256, .28)	B
[.208, .244)	[.208, .2224)	[.2224, .2332)	[.2332, .2368)	[.2368, .242)	C
[.2332, .2368)	[.2332, .23464)	[.23464, .23572)	[.23572, .23608)	[.23608, .2368)	#

Figure 4.3   Decoding the codeword .23608

4.1   Implementation of Arithmetic Coding

ArithmeticEncoding() and ArithmeticDecoding() are algorithms that summarize the logic of arithmetic coding, but they cannot be directly implemented as stated. First, the end of message has to be clearly marked since it may not be clear what stream of letters the codeword represents. The simplest example is the codeword .0, which can be produced by input A, AA, and so on. Therefore, the symbol '#' is used in our examples as the end-of-message marker.

A more serious problem is posed by the fact that the codeword is output after the entire message has been processed. It does not take long messages, however, to surpass the precision arithmetic of any computer. The problem is solved by outputting a digit after the decimal point when it is the same digit for lower and upper bounds of currentInterval and then doubling the length of the interval. However, a computer uses binary arithmetic; thus, the codeword corresponding to the message $ABBC\#$ in Example 4.1 is not really the decimal number .23608, but its binary equivalent 0011110001101. . . . This may suggest that when dealing with binary numbers, the while loop in ArithmeticEncoding() requires more passes than illustrated in Example 4.1.

The solution of the problem is illustrated in Figure 4.4. The method consists of systematically doubling currentInterval if its length is less than .5. There are three cases.

1. If currentInterval $= [.0b_1b_2 \ldots, .0b_1'b_2' \ldots)$, whereby it is contained in the first half of the interval [0, 1), then both of its bounds are less than $.5 = .1_2$ (a number in the binary system is indicated by using the subscript 2); that is, they both have 0 after floating point. This bit 0 is then shifted out and output as part of the codeword. Shifting to the left is the same as doubling; therefore, the size of the interval is doubled (Figure 4.4a).

2. A similar result is obtained if both bounds are greater than $.1_2$, which means that both have the bit 1 after the floating point. The bit is also shifted out, whereby the interval's size is doubled (Figure 4.4b).

3. A problem occurs when $.1_2$ is within currentInterval. The first bits following the radix point are different in both bounds. The size of the interval is doubled only if the lower bound $\geq .25$ and the upper bound $< .75$; that is, the interval is con-

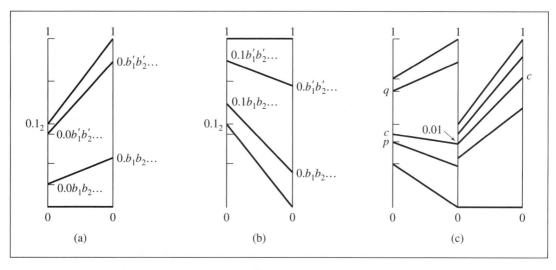

Figure 4.4   Scaling currentInterval when it is included in the interval (a) [0, .5), (b) [.5, 1), and (c) [.25, .75)

tained in the second and third quarters of the interval $[0, 1)$. The decision concerning the bit to be output is suspended, and only the fact of performing the operation of doubling the interval size is recorded. Now we have three possibilities.

a. If for currentInterval $= [p, q)$, as in Figure 4.4c, the codeword c being generated falls beneath the midpoint, then 0 is the bit to be added to the codeword. After that, if a subinterval of $[p, q)$ that contains c is expanded and c falls above the midpoint, then the next bit to be added to c should be 1.

b. On the other hand, if c is above the midpoint, then the bit to be output should be 1, and if after expanding a subinterval of $[p, q)$ that includes c, c falls below the midpoint, then the next bit to be added to c should be 0.

c. If after expansion the new currentInterval is still contained in the second and third quarters of $[0, 1)$, the decision is again suspended; after the process reaches the point that currentInterval is below the midpoint, 0 is output followed by as many 1s as the number of times currentInterval has been between .25 and .75. If currentInterval is contained above the midpoint, 1 is output followed by a number of 0s determined by how many times the interval was included in the two middle quarters.

This procedure is summarized in OutputBits()

```
OutputBits()
    while (1)
        if currentInterval ⊂ [0, .5)
            output 0 and bitCount 1s;
            bitCount = 0;
```

else if currentInterval $\subset$ [.5, 1)
  output 1 *and* bitCount 0*s*;
  bitCount = 0;
  subtract .5 from left and right bounds of currentInterval;
else if currentInterval $\subset$ [.25, .75)
  bitCount++;
  subtract .25 from left and right bounds of currentInterval;
else break;
double left and right bounds of currentInterval;

To finish encoding a message, two bits are output along with any number of underflow bits accumulated along the way. The two bits are either 01 or 10. If the lower bound of currentInterval $< .25 = .01_2$—that is, $.00 \ldots \leq$ lower bound $< .01_2$—then 0 is output to represent this fact and then 1 to choose a codeword number greater than the lower bound. At that point, the upper bound of currentInterval $> .5 = .1_2$; therefore, the chosen codeword is also smaller than the upper bound. On the other hand, if the lower bound $\geq .25 = .01_2$, then the upper bound $> .75 = .11_2$, and a number is chosen to be between the upper and lower bounds; that is, a number v, such that $.01_2 \leq v < .11_2$ and $v = .10_2$ meets this condition. This is summarized in the following procedure:

FinishArithmeticEncoding()
  bitCount++;
  if *lower bound of* currentInterval $< .25$
    output 0 *and* bitCount 1*s*;
  else *output* 1 *and* bitCount 0*s*;

With these two procedures, ArithmeticEncoding() can be modified in the following way:

ArithmeticEncoding(message)
  currentInterval = [0, 1);
  bitCount = 0;
  while *the end of* message *is not reached*
    read letter x_i *from the* message;
    divide currentInterval *into subintervals* $IR_{\text{currentInterval}}$;
    currentInterval = *subinterval$_i$ in* $IR_{\text{currentInterval}}$;
    OutputBits();
  FinishArithmeticEncoding();

Example 4.3   Let us use the same data as in Example 4.1—that is, $S = \{A, B, C, \#\}$ and $P = \{.4, .3, .1, .2\}$—to encode *ABBC#*.

1. Initially, currentInterval = [0, 1); the first letter of the input, A, causes the first subinterval, [0, .4), to be chosen, after which OutputBits() is invoked.

2. currentInterval $\subset$ [0, .5); therefore, the bit 0 is output and currentInterval is doubled in size.

3. currentInterval $=$ [0, .8), which causes breaking out of the while loop of Output-Bits() and exiting this procedure. The second letter of the input, B, leads to choosing the second subinterval of currentInterval, [.32, .56), after which OutputBits() is called for the second time.

4. currentInterval $\subset$ [.25, .75); thus, bitCount becomes 1 and no bit is output. Then currentInterval is scaled up by first subtracting .25 $= .01_2$ from both its bounds and then doubling them (see Figure 4.5a).

5. currentInterval's value causes exit from OutputBits(). The third input letter, B, causes the second subinterval to be elected, which is followed by the third call to OutputBits().

6. currentInterval $=$ [.332, .476) $\subset$ [0, .5); thus, 0 is output and one 1, and then currentInterval is doubled.

7. currentInterval $\subset$ [.5, 1), so first .5 $= .1_2$ is subtracted from both bounds of currentInterval (cf. Figure 4.5b), and then they are doubled.

8. The new value of currentInterval, [.328, .904), leads to an exit from OutputBits().

The remaining steps are shown in Figures 4.6 and 4.7. The codeword produced by the encoding procedure is $0.001111000111_2 = .236083984375$, which is the number contained in the interval [.23608, .2368) obtained in Example 4.1.

The decoding procedure follows in the footsteps of the encoding algorithm in expanding currentInterval to output the letter corresponding to this interval. The

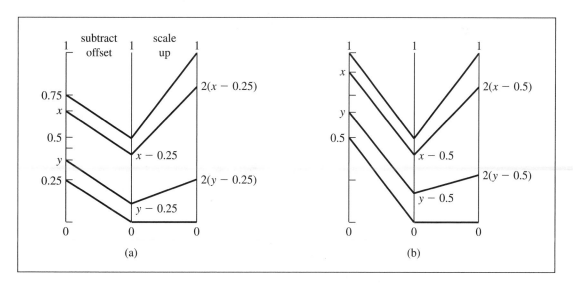

Figure 4.5   Details of scaling currentInterval when it is included in the interval (a) [0, .5) and (b) [.5, 1)

current-Interval	input letter	output bit	subintervals			
[0, 1)	A		[0, .4)	[.4, .7)	[.7, .8)	[.8, 1)
[0, .4)		0				
[0, .8)	B		[0, .32)	[.32, .56)	[.56, .64)	[.64, .8)
[.32, .56)		—				
[.14, .62)	B		[.14, .332)	[.332, .476)	[.476, .524)	[.524, .62)
[.332, .476)		01				
[.664, .952)		1				
[.328, .904)	C		[.328, .5584)	[.5584, .7312)	[.7312, .7888)	[.7888, .904)
[.7312, .7888)		1				
[.4624, .5776)		—				
[.4248, .6552)		—				
[.3496, .8104)	#		[.3496, .53392)	[.53392, .67216)	[.67216, .71824)	[.71824, .8104)
[.71824, .8104)		100				
[.43648, .6208)		—				
[.37296, .7416)		—				
[.24592, .9832)		0111				

Figure 4.6   Applying modified arithmetic coding to the message *ABBC#*

procedure uses the codeword as an input but limits its attention to some binary digits following the floating point. These digits are included in the bitBuffer, which is constantly updated by shifting in and shifting out bits belonging to the expansion of the codeword and possibly by subtracting .5 or .25 from the content of bitBuffer to account for scaling the currentInterval. The algorithm follows:

OutputLetter()
    divide currentInterval *into subintervals* $IR_{\text{currentInterval}}$;
    currentInterval = *the subinterval$_i$ of* currentInterval *to which* bitBuffer *belongs*;
    output letter x_i corresponding to currentInterval;
    while (1)
        if currentInterval $\subset$ [0, .5)
            ; // no action;
        else if currentInterval $\subset$ [.5, 1)
            subtract 0.5 *from* bitBuffer *and from left and right bounds of*
                currentInterval;
        else if currentInterval $\subset$ [.25, .75)
            subtract 0.25 *from* bitBuffer *and from left and right bounds of*
                currentInterval;
        else break;
        double left and right bounds of currentInterval;
        shift out one bit from bitBuffer *and shift in one bit to* bitBuffer;

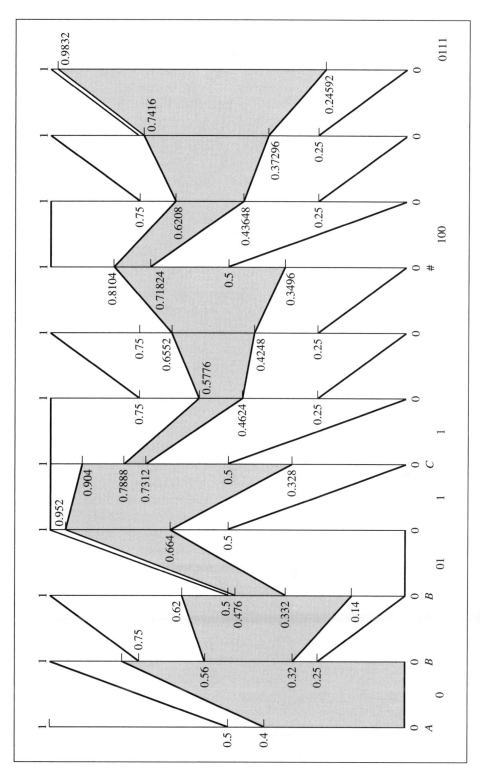

Figure 4.7　Diagram corresponding to the table in Figure 4.6

How large should bitBuffer be? The number in bitBuffer should be smaller than the size sz of the smallest subinterval of currentInterval to represent such an interval. At the time of choosing a subinterval, the minimum size of currentInterval is a number $> .25$ when currentInterval encompasses the interval $[.25, .5)$ or $[0.5, 0.75)$. Therefore, the minimum size k of bitBuffer is determined by $\frac{1}{2^k} \le 0.25sz$.

Example 4.4

We will use the codeword 001111000111 produced in Example 4.3 to decode a message. The size k of bitBuffer is found from $\frac{1}{2^k} \le .25 \cdot .1$ so that $k = 6$. Because the codeword is 001111000111, bitBuffer is initialized to the first six bits of the input, 001111. The operations are shown in a manner corresponding to the rows of the table in Figure 4.8.

1. The initial value of currentInterval is $[0, 1)$; because bitBuffer represents the number $.001111_2 = .234375$ and the number is included in the first subinterval of currentInterval, that is, subinterval $[0, .4)$, then this subinterval is chosen and the letter A that corresponds to the first subinterval is output.

2. $[0, .4)$ becomes currentInterval; because currentInterval is included in the interval $[0, .5)$, it is scaled up by multiplying its both bounds by 2, whereby it becomes $[0, .8)$; one bit is also shifted out from and one shifted in to bitBuffer.

3. currentInterval $= [0, .8)$, and because bitBuffer is holding a bit pattern representing the number $.45875$, the second subinterval of currentInterval is chosen, $[.32,$

current-Interval	bitBuffer input bits	bitBuffer in decimal		chosen subinterval	output letter
$[0, 1)$	001111 | 000111	.234375		$[0, .4)$	A
$[0, .4)$	001111 | 000111	.234375			
$[0, .8)$	011110 | 00111	.45875		$[.32, .56)$	B
$[.32, .56)$	011110 | 00111	.45875			
$[.14, .62)$	011100 | 0111	.4375	$(-.25)$	$[.332, .476)$	B
$[.332, .476)$	011100 | 0111	.4375			
$[.664, .952)$	111000 | 111	.8750			
$[.328, .904)$	110001 | 11	.765625	$(-.5)$	$[.7312, .7888)$	C
$[.7312, .7888)$	110001 | 11	.765625			
$[.4624, .5776)$	100011 | 1	.546875	$(-.5)$		
$[.4248, .6552)$	100111 |	.609475	$(-.25)$		
$[.3496, .8104)$	101110 |	.71875	$(-.25)$	$[.71824, .8104)$	$\#$
$[.71824, .8104)$	011100 |	.21875	$(-.5)$		
$[.43648, .6208)$	011000 |	.375	$(-.25)$		
$[.37296, .7416)$	010000 |	.25	$(-.25)$		
$[.24592, .9832)$					

Figure 4.8   Applying OutputLetter() to decode the codeword 001111000111

.56), and the letter B corresponding to this subinterval is output; currentInterval is assigned a new value.

4. currentInterval $= [.32, .56) \subset [.25, .5)$; it is scaled up by first subtracting $.25 = .01_2$ from both its bounds and then doubling them (Figure 4.5a); .25 is also subtracted from bitBuffer; this is marked by putting $(-.25)$ next to the decimal value of bitBuffer in the next line of the table in Figure 4.8.

5. currentInterval $= [.14, .62)$ and bitBuffer is shifted so that it now represents .4375, whereby the second subinterval of currentInterval is chosen, $[.332, .476)$, and the letter corresponding to it is output, namely, B.

6. currentInterval $= [.322, .476)$ is doubled and so is bitBuffer.

7. currentInterval $= [.664, .952) \subset [.5, 1)$, so first, $.5 = .1_2$ is subtracted from both bounds of currentInterval (cf. Figure 4.5b) and from bitBuffer, which is marked by having $(-.5)$ on the next line, and then both currentInterval and bitBuffer are doubled.

The remaining operations are shown in Figure 4.8.

4.1.1 Integer Implementation

In the preceding section, we used a floating-point implementation of arithmetic coding, which involved a time-consuming floating-point multiplication. However, in Example 4.4, bitBuffer was shown as an integer, which indicates the direction of improving the speed of implementation, namely, by using only integers. With integers, multiplication by 2 can be replaced by shifting, which significantly speeds up execution of the algorithm.

In the preceding sections, the range $[0, 1)$ was used, which required using floating-point arithmetic if we wanted to divide it into subranges. Instead, an integer range can be used, $[0, M)$. Also, instead of using probabilities $P = \{p_1, \ldots, p_n\}$, frequency counts can be used, $F = \{f_1, \ldots, f_n\}$, which are integers. With frequencies, the cumulative probabilities $P_i = \sum_{j=1}^{i} p_j$ are replaced by the cumulative frequencies $F_i = \sum_{j=z}^{i} f_j$. In this way, a cumulative probability P_i can be estimated by

$$P_i = \frac{F_i}{F_n}$$

Now integer interval ranges, IIR, are used in place of interval ranges, IR, as in

$$IIR = \{[0, F_1), [F_1, F_2), [F_2, F_3), \ldots, [F_{n-1}, M)\}$$

and a subrange i of an interval $[L, R)$ is determined by

$$\left[L + \frac{(R - L + 1)F_{i-1}}{F_n}, L + \frac{(R - L + 1)F_i}{F_n} - 1 \right]$$

where division is integer division; that is, the result is rounded down to the nearest integer. Note that by subtracting 1 from the upper bound, each interval can now be closed on both sides. This, however, raises a subtle problem. If for the sake of scaling them up two adjacent intervals are doubled, there would be a gap between them; that is, after intervals $[p, q - 1]$ and $[q, r]$ are doubled so that they become $[2p, 2(q - 1)]$ and $[2q, 2r]$, the number $2q - 1$ does not belong to any of the two subintervals. To avoid the problem, $2q - 1$ becomes the upper bound of the first subinterval. This is simply done by adding 1 to the upper bound after doubling the two bounds of $[p, q - 1]$.

The most significant change in the integer implementation is in OutputBits(), which now becomes as follows:

```
OutputBits() // integer version;
    while (1)
        if currentInterval ⊂ [0, M/2]
            output 0 and bitCount 1s;
            bitCount = 0;
        else if currentInterval ⊂ [M/2, M]
            output 1 and bitCount 0s;
            bitCount = 0;
            subtract M/2 from left and right bounds of currentInterval;
        else if currentInterval ⊂ [M/4, 3M/4]
            bitCount++;
            subtract M/4 from left and right bounds of currentInterval;
        else break;
        double left and right bounds of currentInterval;
        add 1 to right bound of currentInterval;
```

There remains a problem of determining the value of M—that is, the size of interval. M should be large enough to allow for representation of the smallest subinterval of currentInterval so that the endpoints of this smallest subinterval do not become equal. After scaling operations are finished, currentInterval $> M/4$ when currentInterval encompasses the interval $[M/4, M/2 - 1]$ or $[M/2, 3M/4 - 1]$. Therefore, it is required that $F_n \leq \frac{M}{4}$. If the number M is to be a power of 2, the latter condition turns into finding a k such that $F_n \leq \frac{2^k}{4}$ or $k \geq \lg 4F_n$.

Example 4.5   For source $S = \{A, B, C, \#\}$ and $P = \{.4, .3, .1, .2\}$, $F = \{4, 3, 1, 2\}$, $F_n = 10$, and $k = \lceil \lg (4 \cdot 10) \rceil = 6$ so that currentInterval is initialized to $[0, 64)$ or $[0, 63]$. To encode $ABBC\#$, the following steps are executed.

1. The first input letter, A, causes the first subinterval, $[0, 24]$, to be chosen, and OutputBits() is invoked.

2. currentInterval $\subset [0, 32]$; therefore, the bit 0 is output, currentInterval is doubled in size, and its upper bound is incremented by 1.

3. currentInterval = [0, 49], and thus, OutputBits() is exited. The second input letter, B, leads to choosing the second subinterval of currentInterval, [20, 34], after which OutputBits() is called again.

4. currentInterval ⊂ [16, 48], and thus, bitCount becomes 1 and no bit is output; then currentInterval is scaled up by first subtracting 16 from both its bounds, doubling them, and adding 1 to upper bound.

The remaining steps are shown in Figure 4.9. Note that the generated codeword, 001110101110, is different from the codeword generated in Example 4.3. This is due to decreased arithmetic precision by using only integer operations.

To decode a codeword, we have to adjust the procedure OutputLetter(), which is done in similar fashion as modifying OutputBits(). Because we are now using integers only, OutputLetter() will use $M/4$, $M/2$, and $3M/4$ in place of .25, .5, and .75. Also, after doubling an interval, its upper bound is decreased by 1.

Example 4.6

Decoding the codeword 001110101110 generated in the previous example for the same source S, frequencies F, and range size $M = 64$ follows the steps summarized in Figure 4.10. A number in parentheses after a decimal value of bitBuffer indicates by how much bitBuffer was decremented as a part of scaling process (cf. Example 4.4).

current-Interval	input letter	output bit	subintervals			
[0, 63]	A		[0, 24]	[25, 43]	[44, 50]	[51, 63]
[0, 24]		0				
[0, 49]	B		[0, 19]	[20, 34]	[35, 39]	[40, 49]
[20, 34]		—				
[8, 37]	B		[8, 19]	[20, 28]	[29, 31]	[32, 37]
[20, 28]		01				
[40, 57]		1				
[16, 51]	C		[16, 29]	[30, 40]	[41, 43]	[44, 51]
[41, 43]		1				
[18, 23]		0				
[36, 47]		1				
[8, 31]		0				
[16, 63]	#		[16, 34]	[35, 48]	[49, 53]	[54, 63]
[54, 63]		1				
[44, 63]		1				
[24, 63]		10				

Figure 4.9   Encoding *ABBC#* using integer arithmetic

current-Interval	bitBuffer output bits	bitBuffer in decimal		chosen subinterval	output letter
[0, 63]	001110 │ 101110	14		[0, 24]	A
[0, 24]	001110 │ 101110	14			
[0, 49]	011101 │ 01110	29		[20, 34]	B
[20, 34]	011101 │ 01110	29			
[8, 37]	011010 │ 1110	26	(−16)	[20, 28]	B
[20, 28]	011010 │ 1110	26			
[40, 57]	110101 │ 110	53			
[16, 51]	101011 │ 10	43	(−32)	[41, 43]	C
[41, 43]	101011 │ 10	43			
[18, 23]	010111 │ 0	23			
[36, 47]	101110 │	46			
[8, 31]	011100 │	28	(−32)		
[16, 63]	111000 │	56		[56, 63]	#
[56, 63]	111000 │	56	(−32)		
[48, 63]	110000 │	48	(−32)		
[32, 63]	100000 │	32	(−32)		
[0, 32]	000000 │	0	(−32)		

Figure 4.10   Decoding 001110101110 using integer arithmetic

EXERCISES

1. It was indicated in the discussion of the encoding procedure that the codeword representing an interval $[x, y)$ can be the number x. In Example 4.3, the codeword is binary .001111000111 or decimal .236083984375, which is not the lower bound of the the interval $[.23608, .2368)$ it represents. Can the algorithm be modified so that the lower bound is chosen?

2. Would OutputBits() work properly if the condition else if currentInterval ⊂ $[.25, .75)$ were removed? Try it for the data in Example 4.3.

3. Repeat the process from Example 4.4, but use bitBuffer of length 4, not 6. What problem can you observe?

4. What impact on the length of a codeword does an incorrect determination of probabilities have? Apply ArithmeticEncoding() as in Example 4.3 to the source $S = \{A, \#\}$, $P = \{.9, .1\}$, and the message $AAAA\#$ and then to the same source and message, but to $P = \{.1, .9\}$.

5. Does arithmetic coding produce a prefix code?

6. How resistant is arithmetic coding to errors in codewords?

7. In adaptive arithmetic coding, the frequencies change in the course of processing input letters. What else changes and how does it affect the efficiency of coding?

BIBLIOGRAPHY

Howard, Paul G., and Vitter, Jeffrey S., Practical implementations of arithmetic coding, in Storer, James A. (ed.), *Image and text compression*, Boston: Kluwer, 1992, 85–112.

Langdon, Glen G., An introduction to arithmetic coding, *IBM Journal Research and Development* 28 (1984), 135–149.

Rissanen, Jorma, and Langdon, Glen G., Universal modeling and coding, *IEEE Transactions on Information Theory* IT-27 (1981), 12–23.

Witten, Ian H., Neal, Radfrod M., and Cleary, John G., Arithmetic coding for data compression, *Communications of the ACM* 30 (1987), 520–540.

Chapter 5

Dictionary Techniques

Dictionary techniques utilize groups of symbols, words, and phrases with the corresponding abbreviations; the abbreviations are used during data transmission and the receiver translates them back to the original form using the same dictionary as the sender. The dictionaries can be static or dynamic. A *static dictionary* remains the same during the course of encoding the data. This can be as simple as utilizing commonly used acronyms (CEO, UN, ASCII), abbreviations (dr., Penna., ca.), or coined abbreviations (M—male, 192—acidfree paper, #$—load instruction). More systematically, an explicit dictionary is created that lists frequently used symbol patterns and their codewords. One such dictionary is not applied with equal efficiency in all situations. First, a dictionary should be language specific. One technique uses *n*-grams—that is, frequently used patterns of *n* consecutive symbols. If three-grams (trigrams) are used, then in an English text such trigrams as *the, que, ome,* or *neu* can be found much more often than *sch, hin,* or *wer,* but in a German text it would be the other way around. Second, dictionaries should be domain specific. If commonly used words are to be encoded in few bits, then in a dictionary pertaining to gardening texts and databases such words as *rake, soil, foliage,* or *parsley* would be found more often than the words *hardbound, Press, index,* or *pages,* which in turn would have a very high frequency of occurrence in the library setting.

After a dictionary is established, there still remains a problem of using it most efficiently. For example, for the dictionary {*ability, ility, pec, re, res, spect, tab*}, the word *respectability* can be broken down in two ways: *res, pec, tab, ility* and *re, spect, ability.* The first division requires four codewords, whereas the second requires only three. The algorithm that parses the word or words determines which one of the two choices is made, and of course, for a large dictionary, there may be more than two possible parsings of the same word or phrase. By far the most frequently used technique is a *greedy algorithm* that finds the longest match in the dictionary. For our example, the match *res* is longer than *re;* therefore, the word *responsibility* will be divided into four components with the greedy strategy. Although the greedy strategy is not optimal, it is easy to implement, and in the long run, the difference between its efficiency and that of an optimal algorithm is not very large (Schuegraf and Heaps, 1974).

Another set of techniques uses a *dynamic dictionary* that is built and modified dynamically during the course of encoding and decoding and that is composed of common patterns found in input. Then, a pattern is encoded by its index, offset, or address in the dictionary. It should be obvious that the speed of a particular coding technique depends on the size of the dictionary (i.e., the number of common patterns) and on the searching technique used to locate a particular pattern in the dictionary. Most of today's dynamic dictionary techniques are based on theoretical analyses conducted by Jacob Ziv and Abraham Lempel.

5.1   The LZ77 Technique

In this method, a buffer of symbols is maintained. The buffer is divided into two parts. The first part, called a *dictionary buffer*, is a buffer of l_1 positions, which holds the l_1 most recently encoded symbols from the input; the second part, called a *lookahead buffer*, is an l_2-position buffer containing the l_2 symbols about to be encoded. To initiate the process, the dictionary buffer is filled with l_1 copies of the first symbol of the input. In each iteration, the dictionary buffer is searched for a substring matching a prefix of a string located in the lookahead buffer. If such a match is found, a codeword is transmitted, which is a triple *<p, l, s>* composed of the position p in which the match was found, the length l of the match, and the first mismatching symbol s following the prefix. Then, the entire content of the buffer (dictionary buffer and lookahead buffer) is shifted to the left by the length l of match plus one; some symbols are shifted out, and some new symbols from the input are shifted in.

Example 5.1

Consider the case when $l_1 = l_2 = 4$ and input is a string *aababacbaacbaadaaa*. . . . Positions in the buffer are indexed with $0, \ldots, 7$.

1. The initial situation is shown at the top of Figure 5.1.

2. The first symbol of the input is *a*, and the positions 0 through 3 are filled up with *a*s. In the remaining positions, the first four symbols of the input are placed, *aaba*. The longest prefix matching any substring which begins in any position between 0 and 3 is *aa*. Therefore, the triple *<2, 2, b>* is generated, or simply 22*b*: The match starts in position 2, the match is two symbols long, and the symbol following the prefix is *b*. In Figure 5.1, the match in the dictionary buffer is underlined with a

input	buffer	output
aababacbaacbaadaaa . . .	*aaaa*	*a*
aababacbaacbaadaaa . . .	*aaaaaaba*	22*b*
abacbaacbaadaaa . . .	*aaababac*	23*c*
baacbaadaaa . . .	*abacbaac*	12*a*
cbaadaaa . . .	*cbaacbaa*	03*a*
daaa . . .	*cbaadaaa*	30*d*
aaa . . .	. . .	

Figure 5.1   Encoding the string *aababacbaacbaadaaa* . . . with the LZ77 method

dashed line, and the prefix equal to the match is underlined with a solid line. Next, a left shift occurs, three *a*'s are shifted out, and string *bac* is shifted in.

3. The longest match for a prefix also starts in position 2 and is three symbols long, *aba*, with *c* following the prefix. The issued triple is 23*c*. Note that the prefix *aba* and the match overlap; that is, the match can cross the boundary between the two parts of the buffer. Afterwards, *aaab* is shifted out and *baac* is shifted in.

4. The triple 12*a* is output and the content of the buffer is updated accordingly.

5. The longest match of a prefix is four symbols long, but because the third element of each triple should be a letter following the prefix, the match is considered three symbols long, and the last letter of the match, *a*, becomes the third element of the triple 03*a*.

6. The prefix *d* does not have any match in the dictionary buffer; therefore, the length *l* of the match in the generated triple is 0. Note that the starting position is 3, which is unimportant. It could be any number.

Numbers l_1 and l_2 are so chosen in this example that only two bits are needed for each. Because each symbol requires one byte (i.e., eight bits), one triple can be stored in twelve bits. Therefore, l_1 and l_2 should be powers of 2, so that no binary sequence of a particular length remains unused. If l_1 were 5, then three bits would be needed to code all possible positions 0 through 4, and three three-bit combinations corresponding to 5, 6, and 7 would not be used. It should also be added that in real applications the numbers l_1 and l_2 are significantly larger, in particular the number l_1.

To decode a stream of triples, the decoder must first initialize the dictionary buffer with the first received symbol. In each iteration, for each triple <*p, l, s*>, starting from the position *p*, it copies *l* symbols to the lookahead buffer and adds the symbol *s* at the end of the copied string. The copied substring along with the symbol *s* is also the output (i.e., the decoded symbols). Note that no special care needs to be taken for the case when the triple should be decoded only as the symbol *s*.

Example 5.2

Consider the sequence of triples output by the encoder in Example 5.1: *a*22*b*23*c*12*a*03*a*30*d* ...

1. The first symbol, *a*, is used to fill the dictionary buffer.

2. After receiving the triple 22*b*, the decoder copies two symbols starting from position 2 (i.e., *aa*) to the lookahead buffer and attaches *b* after it is finished copying. The string *aab* is also output as part of the message being decoded. Then, the buffer is shifted by $l + 1 = 3$ positions to the left to make room for up to four symbols in the lookahead buffer.

3. To decode the triple 23*c*, three symbols are copied starting from the position 2. Note that there is an overlap here between the string copied from the dictionary buffer and the string generated in the lookahead buffer. The third symbol of the buffer, *a*, is copied to the beginning of the lookahead buffer from which it is again copied to its third position. The remaining steps can be traced in Figure 5.2.

input	output	buffer	buffer after shifting
a		*aaaa*	
22b	*aab*	*aaaaaab*	*aaab*
23c	*abac*	*aaababac*	*abac*
12a	*baa*	*abacbaa*	*cbaa*
03a	*cbaa*	*cbaacbaa*	*cbaa*
30d	*d*	*cbaad*	*baad*

Figure 5.2   Decoding a stream of triples using the LZ77 algorithm

5.1.1   The LZSS Technique

One improvement that can be introduced is shortening the output of the encoder (Storer and Szymanski 1982; Bell 1986). By using a flag bit, the LZSS encoder indicates whether what follows the bit is the codeword for a symbol or an indicator of the position in the buffer and the length of an encoded string. Therefore, the output is either a pair $<1, s>$ or a triple $<0, p, l>$. Because 0 in the triple is a bit, the triples in LZSS are shorter than in LZ77 (assuming that the dictionary buffer and lookahead buffer are of the same length in both techniques). To determine whether to output a pair or a triple, the size of the pair $<p, l>$ is tested, and if this pair requires more space than the string they are encoding, the first letter in the lookahead buffer is output. Here is the algorithm.

LZSSencoding()
> while *not finished*
>> *determine the pair* $<p, l>$ *corresponding to the longest* match *in the lookahead buffer*;
>> if *sizeof*$(<p, l>) \geq$ *sizeof*(match)
>>> *output* $<1,$ *the first letter in the lookahead buffer*$>$;
>>> *shift the content of the entire buffer by one position*;
>> else *output* $<0, p, l>$;
>>> *shift the content of the entire buffer by l positions*;

Example 5.3

In Example 5.1, the maximum value for position p and length l is the number 3, which requires two bits; therefore, *sizeof*$(<p, l>) = 4$. If we assume that one letter occupies eight bits, then the only situation when *sizeof*$(<p, l>) <$ *sizeof*(match) is when the match is of size zero—that is, when the first symbol in the lookahead buffer has no match in the dictionary buffer. To make this example a bit more interesting, we assume—only in this example—that each input symbol is three bits long (thus, the dictionary source can contain up to eight symbols).

1. The dictionary buffer is initialized with the first input letter *a*.

2. The longest match is two symbols long (i.e., six bits) and $6 > 4 =$ *sizeof*$(<p, l>)$; therefore, the triple $<0, 2, 2>$, or 022 for short, is output and the buffer is shifted by two positions.

input	buffer	output
aababacbaacbaadaaa . . .	*aaaa*	*a*
aababacbaacbaadaaa . . .	*aaaaaaba*	022
babacbaacbaadaaa . . .	*aaaababa*	1*b*
abacbaacbaadaaa . . .	*aaababac*	023
cbaacbaadaaa . . .	*babacbaa*	1*c*
baacbaadaaa . . .	*abacbaac*	012
acbaadaaa . . .	*acbaacba*	004
adaaa . . .	*acbaadaa*	1*a*
daaa . . .	*cbaadaaa*	1*d*
aaa . . .	. . .	

Figure 5.3   Encoding the string *aababacbaacbaadaaa* . . . with the LZSS method

3. The letter *b* starting the lookahead buffer has no match in the dictionary buffer, and because *sizeof*(*b*) > *sizeof*(<0, 0>), the pair 1*b* is output and the buffer's content is moved by one position.

4. An overlapping match is found, and the triple 023 is output, which is followed by a shift.

The rest of steps can be seen in Figure 5.3. Note that in the next to the last line the letter *a* has a match in the dictionary buffer, but the size of the one-symbol long string is shorter than the size of the triple 031 needed to encode it. Therefore, the literal *a* is output preceded by a flag bit 1.

Note that although the maximum value for length *l* is 4, it can be coded with two bits only since the only possible values for *l* in this example are 2, 3, and 4, which can be coded as 0, 1, and 2, respectively. In this way, the number of bits used in encoding a part of the message equals 36 bits: $4 \cdot 5 = 20$ bits to encode four triples and $4 \cdot 4 = 16$ bits to encode four pairs. In Example 5.1, the same part of the message required five triples; that is, $5 \cdot 7 = 35$ bits (again assuming that symbols are three bits long), which is similar to the output of LZSS. However, in real situations, when symbols are eight bits long and the buffer is significantly larger so that the pair <*p, l*> is also larger, LZSS can be expected to have a better compression ratio.

A significant effort in LZ77 encoding is put in shifting the content of the buffer after encoding its subsequence. This, however, can be avoided if a circular buffer is used instead. In this way, the symbols in the buffer do not need to be shifted; only positions of the dictionary and lookahead buffers have to be modified.

5.2   The LZ78 Technique

The dictionary used in LZ77 and LZSS is constantly in flux: It is a dictionary buffer whose content depends on the part of the message currently encoded. Therefore, if the message contains patterns that have already appeared and were shifted out from the dictionary buffer, the encoder has to output more triples than in the situation when these patterns are available. To avoid this limitation, the LZ78 method maintains a dictionary that has the ability to keep entries permanently and is extended during the course of the encoding process.

LZ78 also differs from LZ77 in using pairs rather than triples. A pair $<p, s>$ indicates the position in the dictionary of the pattern being encoded, and s is a symbol following the pattern in the input. Note that the length of the pattern is not transmitted because the decoder expands the dictionary similarly to the encoder's; thus, it can find the length in its dictionary. For example, if a currently encoded part of a message is *abcdef*, then the generated pair $<15, f>$, or simply $15f$, means that the dictionary has a pattern *abcde* in position 15 and that the pattern *abcdef* appears nowhere in the dictionary so far. However, after processing it, the new pattern is added to the dictionary. There is also a special case, when the pair has 0 as its first element, $<0, s>$, which indicates that the symbol s is not in the dictionary and so it must be added there.

Example 5.4   Let us encode the message *aababacbaacbaadaaa*. . . . Steps undertaken during this process are summarized in Figure 5.4.

1. Initially, the dictionary is empty. The first letter, *a*, is not in the dictionary. Thus, the pair $0a$ is output and the string *a* is entered in the first position of the dictionary.

2. The encoder continues to find a match for the string *a* in the dictionary. It finds it and thus continues by attempting to find an entry for *ab*. Because it fails, the encoder outputs the pair $1b$ to indicate that a new symbol *b* is preceded in the input by a string to be found in the dictionary in position 1. Then, the string *ab* is placed in position 2 of the dictionary.

3. The remaining part of the input is now *abacbaacbaadaaa* . . . ; the encoder tries to find in the dictionary the longest match for the prefix of the current input. It finds a match for *a*, then for *ab*, but fails to find one for *aba*. Thus, it outputs the pair $2a$ to tell the decoder that the encoded part of the message is a string in

coder		dictionary	
input	output	index	entry
a	$0a$	1	*a*
ab	$1b$	2	*ab*
aba	$2a$	3	*aba*
c	$0c$	4	*c*
b	$0b$	5	*b*
aa	$1a$	6	*aa*
cb	$4b$	7	*cb*
aad	$6d$	8	*aad*
aaa	$6a$	9	*aaa*

Figure 5.4   Encoding the string *aababacbaacbaadaaa* . . . with the LZ78 method

position 2 of the dictionary followed by the letter *a*. Afterwards, the dictionary is extended by adding the string *aba*. The remaining steps are indicated in Figure 5.4.

The decoder is even simpler than the encoder. It takes pairs <*p, s*> as its input, concatenates the string from position *p* in the dictionary with the symbol *s*, outputs the concatenation as the decoded part of the message, but also enters it in the dictionary. In doing so, the decoder mimics the action of the encoder; that is, it expands the dictionary in exactly the same fashion as the encoder.

Example 5.5   Let us decode the stream of pairs 0*a*1*b*2*a*0*c* . . . .

1. After receiving the first pair, 0*a*, the letter *a* is output and a new entry is added to the dictionary, namely, *a*.

2. The second pair, 1*b*, causes the decoder to concatenate the string in position 1 of the dictionary, *a*, with the letter *b* and output *ab* both as part of the message being decoded and as a new dictionary entry.

3. After receiving the third pair, 2*a*, the decoder concatenates *ab* from position 2 with *a* and both outputs *aba* and expands the dictionary by adding to it this string. The remaining steps can be found in Figure 5.5.

5.2.1   The LZW Technique

The LZW algorithm is a commonly applied version of LZ78 that makes one significant modification: It reduces the output of the encoder from pairs to single numbers by not requiring a symbol, which is the second element of each pair in LZ78, to be transmitted. To accomplish it, the dictionary is initialized to all the symbols in the source input so that, if a symbol appears for the first time in the message, it already has an entry in the dictionary (Welch, 1984; Miller and Wegman, 1985).

LZW tries to output codewords for strings that are already in the dictionary. If it finds a string that is not in the dictionary, it adds this string there and outputs the

decoder		dictionary	
input	output	index	entry
0*a*	*a*	1	*a*
1*b*	*ab*	2	*ab*
2*a*	*aba*	3	*aba*
0*c*	*c*	4	*c*
0*b*	*b*	5	*b*
1*a*	*aa*	6	*aa*
4*b*	*cb*	7	*cb*
6*d*	*aad*	8	*aad*
6*a*	*aaa*	9	*aaa*

Figure 5.5   Decoding a stream of pairs using the LZ78 method

codeword for the known substring of this string. This simple algorithm for encoding can be presented in a more detailed form as follows:

LZWencoding()
>   *enter all letters to the dictionary;*
>   *initialize string* s *to the first letter from input;*
>   while *any input left*
>   *read symbol* c;
>   if s + c *is in the dictionary*
>   s = s + c;
>   else *output codeword*(s);
>   *enter* s + c *to the dictionary;*
>   s = c;
>   *output codeword*(s);

The string s is always at least one symbol long. After reading a new symbol, the concatenation of string s and symbol c is checked in the dictionary. A new symbol is read if the concatenation s+c is in the dictionary; if it is not, the codeword for s is output, the concatenation s+c is stored in the dictionary, and s is initialized to c.

Example 5.6

Figure 5.6 shows a trace of the execution of this procedure applied to the input *aababacbaacbaadaaa . . . .*

1. The dictionary is initialized with the four source letters, *a, b, c, d.*

2. The first input letter is *a*, the second is also *a*, but the dictionary does not have an entry for the string *aa.* Therefore, *aa* is added to the dictionary in position 5, the

encoder		dictionary	
input	output	index	entry
		1	*a*
		2	*b*
		3	*c*
		4	*d*
aa	1	5	*aa*
ab	1	6	*ab*
ba	2	7	*ba*
aba	6	8	*aba*
ac	1	9	*ac*
cb	3	10	*cb*
baa	7	11	*baa*
acb	9	12	*acb*
baad	11	13	*baad*
da	4	14	*da*
aaa	5	15	*aaa*

Figure 5.6   Encoding the string *aababacbaacbaadaaa* . . . with the LZW method

codeword 1 (the index of *a* in the dictionary) is output that corresponds to the prefix *a* of the string *aa*, and this prefix is removed from the encoder; however, the second *a* is retained.

3. The third input letter is *b,* which is concatenated with the retained *a* to produce the string *ab*. The string is not in the dictionary, so it is included in it. For the prefix *a* of the string *ab,* the codeword 1 is output. The prefix is removed from the string, and only its last letter, *b*, is retained.

4. The fourth letter of the input is *a,* which gives string *ba* after attaching it to *b*. The string is not in the dictionary, but its prefix, *b*, is there, so the codeword 2 corresponding to this substring is output. The prefix is removed and only *a* is retained.

5. The next letter is *b*, which gives a string *ab* when concatenated with *a* from the previous iteration. Because *ab* has an entry in the dictionary, another letter, *a*, is taken from the input and concatenated with *ab* to generate the string *aba*. The string has no entry in the dictionary; therefore, one is created, and the codeword 6 for *ab* is output. The remaining steps are shown in Figure 5.6. Note that in the encoder input column, each string begins with a letter that is the last letter of the string from the previous line.

For decoding, the same dictionary is being created by updating it for every incoming codeword except the first. For each codeword, a corresponding string is found in the dictionary and then the string is output. The decoder remembers this string and reads another codeword. This codeword was produced by the encoder because the previous string concatenated with the first letter of the current string (not to mention the remaining letters) did not have any entry in the dictionary, so the encoder created this entry. The decoder does the same by including the previous string concatenated with the first letter of the current string to the dictionary; it also outputs the current string. For each codeword except the first, the decoder expands the dictionary in the same way the encoder did. The decoding procedure can be summarized as follows:

LZWdecoding()
    enter all the source letters to the dictionary;
    read priorCodeword *and output one symbol corresponding to it*;
    while *codewords are still left*
        read codeword;
        priorString = *string*(priorCodeword);
        if codeword *is in the dictionary*
            enter in dictionary priorString + *firstSymbol*(*string*(codeword));
            output string(codeword);
        `else` // special case: `cscsc`, where string `s` can be null and
            // pattern `cs` is already in the dictionary;
            enter in dictionary priorString + *firstSymbol*(priorString);
            output priorString + *firstSymbol*(priorString);
        priorCodeword = codeword;

This relatively simple algorithm has to consider a special case, which will be discussed shortly. In the example that follows, the situation captured by the special case is not included.

Example 5.7

We shall decode the stream of codewords generated by the encoder in Example 5.6.

1. All the source letters are first entered to the dictionary. Then, the first codeword, 1, is read in, which amounts to outputting *a* and initializing priorString.

2. The second codeword, another 1, is also decoded as *a*, but now the previous string *a* is concatenated with the first letter of the current string, *a*, and the result, *aa*, is entered in the dictionary.

3. The third codeword, 2, is decoded as *b*, and the letter *b* is attached to the previous string, which is now *a*, to form a new dictionary entry, *ab*.

4. The next codeword is 6. After receiving it, the decoder outputs *ab* and then amplifies the dictionary with *ba,* which is the concatenation of priorString *b* and the first letter of the current string *a*.

5. The fifth codeword is 1, which stands for *a* and is attached to the end of the previous string *ab*. The result *aba* is added to the dictionary. The remaining steps are shown in Figure 5.7.

A special case occurs when a codeword being processed has no corresponding entry in the dictionary. This situation arises when the original message contains substring cscsc, where c is a single symbol, s is a string of any length, including 0, and cs is already in the dictionary. In this case, the decoder receives a codeword for csc,

decoder		dictionary	
input	output	index	entry
		1	*a*
		2	*b*
		3	*c*
		4	*d*
1	*a*		
1	*a*	5	*aa*
2	*b*	6	*ab*
6	*ab*	7	*ba*
1	*a*	8	*aba*
3	*c*	9	*ac*
7	*ba*	10	*cb*
9	*ac*	11	*baa*
11	*baa*	12	*acb*
4	*d*	13	*baad*
5	*aa*	14	*da*

Figure 5.7   Decoding a stream of numbers using the LZW method

but csc has no entry in the decoder's dictionary. If that happens, the decoder knows that the previously decoded string was cs and the current string csc has no dictionary entry. Therefore, it outputs the previous string cs concatenated with its first letter c, which results in the desired output string csc.

Example 5.8

Consider the message *abababacccdccdccdca*. A special case occurs here three times, which is marked by parenthesizing each of its occurrences: *ab(ababa)(ccc)d(ccdccdc)a*. The encoder generates the sequence of codewords: 1 2 5 7 3 9 4 10 12. After decoding 1, 2, and 5, the situation is as in the first seven rows of the dictionary in Figure 5.8. The last dictionary entry that the decoder generated is the entry 6, and now the codeword 7 arrives, which refers to a nonexisting entry. That is where the special case is invoked. First, the decoder creates this entry in the dictionary (i.e., it places *aba* in position 7), which is the previous string *ab* concatenated with its first letter *a*, and then retrieves this string to output it. In this case, the general special case cscsc is the string *ababa*, where the substring s of this pattern is composed of only one symbol, *b*. There are two more occurrences of this special case: *ccc*, for which the substring s of the general template cscsc is null, and its substring cs, or simply c, was put in the dictionary during initialization; and then *ccdccdc*, where the string s from the general pattern cscsc is equal to *cd*.

A crucial factor in the efficiency of any method analyzed in this chapter is the organization of the dictionary. Clearly, for more realistic examples, hundreds or thousands of entries can be expected in the dictionary so that an efficient searching method has to be applied. The many different variants of LZ78 and LZW are differentiated by using different data structures for implementing the dictionary. The most popular choices are hash tables, binary trees, and tries (Bell, Cleary, and Witten, 1990).

| decoder | | dictionary | |
input	output	index	entry
		1	a
		2	b
		3	c
		4	d
1	a		
2	b	5	ab
5	ab	6	ba
7	aba	7	aba
3	c	8	abac
9	cc	9	cc
4	d	10	ccd
10	ccd	11	dc
12	ccdc	12	ccdc

Figure 5.8   A special case for the LZW decoder

Many popular data compression programs are implementations based on either LZ78 or LZW. Examples of programs based on LZ77 are ARJ[T], LHarc[T], PKZip[T], and UC2[T]; examples of programs based on LZ78, or rather on LZW, are ARC[T], PAK[T], and UNIX[T'] $ Compress; also .gif images are encoded using a version of LZW.

EXERCISES

1. In LZ77, the first l_1 positions are filled with l_1 copies of the first symbol of the input. Is it possible to have a different initialization?

2. In Figure 5.1, $l_1 = l_2 = 4 = 2^2$. In what respect does the choice of $l_1 = l_2 = 16 = 2^4$ simplify the implementation of the LZ77 algorithm?

3. In which situation does the LZ77 algorithm perform best? Worst?

4. Decode the sequence b31a23b30c21a32b using the LZ77 method.

5. Construct a table similar to Figure 5.2 to decode $a0221b0231c0120041a1d$ with LZSS.

6. Using LZ78 and a dictionary initialized with the letters a, b, c, decode the string encoded as 1 2 4 3 1 4 9 5 8 12 2.

7. What is the longest string that can be encoded as a triple with the LZ77 method? What possible problem can it cause?

8. In LZ78, a pair <0, s> is considered a special case, which indicates that the symbol s is not in the dictionary. Does this case have to be treated in a special way?

9. Encode with LZW the message $abababacccdccdccdca$ analyzed in Example 5.8.

BIBLIOGRAPHY

Bell, Timothy C., Better OPM/L text compression, *IEEE Transactions on Communications* COM-34 (1986), 1176–1182.

Bell, Timothy C., Cleary, John G., and Witten, Ian H., *Text compression*, Upper Saddle River, NJ: Prentice Hall, 1990.

Miller, Victor S., and Wegman, Mark N., Variations on a theme by Ziv and Lempel, in Apostolico, A., and Galil, Z. (eds.), *Combinatorial algorithms on words*, Berlin: Springer, 1985, 131–140.

Nelson, Mark, LZW data compression, *Dr. Dobb's Journal* 14 (1989), 29–37.

Schuegraf, E. J., and Heaps, H. S., A comparison of algorithms for data-base compression by use of fragments as language elements, *Information Storage and Retrieval* 10 (1974), 309–319.

Storer, James A., and Szymanski, Thomas G., Data compression via textual substitution, *Journal of the ACM* 29 (1982), 928–951.

Welch, Terry A., A technique for high-performance data compression, *Computer* 17 (1984), no. 6, 8–19.

Ziv, Jacob, and Lempel, Abraham, A universal algorithm for sequential data compression, *IEEE Transactions on Information Theory* IT-23 (1977), 337–343.

Ziv, Jacob, and Lempel, Abraham, Compression of individual sequences via variable-rate encoding, *IEEE Transactions on Information Theory* IT-24 (1978), 530–536.

Chapter 6

Sampling and Quantization

Computers are digital devices; that is, they operate with a language of 0s and 1s. On the other hand, most of the natural phenomena around us are continuous; they are constantly ongoing processes with continuous transitions between two different states. Leibniz wrote about the continuity principle as a way in which natural and social phenomena take their course. This was an expression of the Middle Age principle *natura non facit saltus,* "nature does not make jumps." That is, each process changes its states by smoothly going through all intermediate states when making a transition from state *A* to *B*.

The continuity principle means, for example, that there is no point of time when a body has no temperature. This temperature can be different at different moments, but it is always there and it changes with time continuously. So it is with other characteristics of the body. If we wanted to express these changes with numbers, we would have to use an infinity of numbers to represent the temperature of the body between two instants. However, the computer always has a limited range of numbers it can represent. Therefore, between any two numbers, another number can be found that cannot be represented by the computer, and yet there is always an infinity of instants between two different instants of time. Thus, there is an infinity of values for temperature between these two instants.

Such continuously changing information can be processed by an analog or continuous device. For example, continuous changes of voltage of a sensor can reflect continuous changes of temperature of a body. This, by the way, does not guarantee that no information is lost or distorted. An analog device can change its parameters due to power supply fluctuations or temperature variations. In addition, if a part of such a device is replaced, then the new part may affect the characteristics of the device, thereby adversely affecting the processing of information. Such problems are eliminated or greatly reduced if analog-to-digital (A/D) conversion is used. In this conversion, a continuous signal is transformed into a sequence of numbers, and because in many cases computers are involved along the way, the sequence is composed of binary numbers. This, however, leads to some problems of its own.

Temperature and voltage are examples of signals. A signal is a continuous function f in the time domain: For a value $y = f(t)$, the argument t of the function f represents time. If the *x* axis represents time, then the graph of f versus time is called a *waveform.*

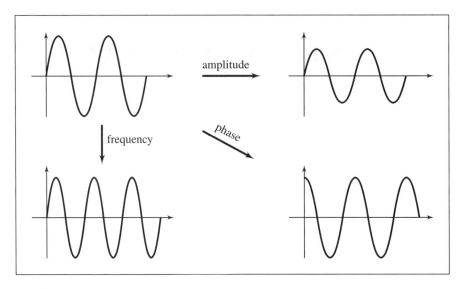

Figure 6.1   Independent changes of amplitude, frequency, and phase of a waveform

A wave has three characteristics that can be independently changed (modulated): the amplitude, frequency, and phase, which are illustrated in Figure 6.1 for the sinusoidal function. *Amplitude* is the intensity of the signal and it can be changed either by stretching or squeezing the waveform vertically. For example, with the increase of amplitude of a sound wave (measured in decibels) the sound becomes louder. *Frequency* indicates the number of times the waveform's period is repeated, and it can be changed either by stretching or squeezing the waveform horizontally. For example, increasing the frequency of a sound wave means an increase of its pitch. A change of *phase* means shifting the waveform to the right or to the left.

Numbers in the sequence obtained from the A/D conversion follow one another, unlike signal values in the source, which are continuous. This means that not all the signal values are recorded. It leads to the problem of proper *sampling*—that is, recording these values, which would allow the reconstruction of the original signal. Figure 6.2 illustrates samples taken at specific points of time t_0, t_1, t_2, and so forth.

Another problem in A/D processing is the precision of numbers. Since the signals can have any value within a certain range, then, in particular, they can be irrational numbers which would require an infinite number of digits after the decimal point to be recorded with the absolute precision. This, to be sure, is out of the question; therefore, the samples are always rounded, or *quantized*. As shown in Figure 6.2, the range of possible measurements is divided into smaller ranges, and the samples are recorded with some distortion due to rounding. As the result of sampling and quantization, the process in Figure 6.2a is recorded as the sequence of numbers that corresponds to the plot in Figure 6.2b. This illustration also indicates that the more samples we take and the more fine-grained the quantization used, then the more faithfully the stream of data is

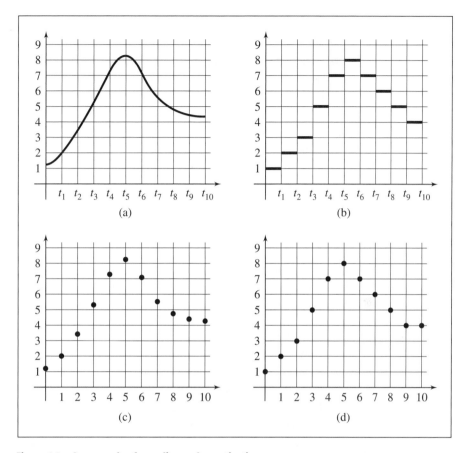

Figure 6.2   An example of sampling and quantization

recorded and the easier will be the process of reconstructing this original stream. However, if too many samples are taken or the rounding error reaches too big a precision, then the processing of information can be too slow and the amount of information collected can require too much storage. Therefore, a fine balance has to be struck between the efficiency and precision of continuous information processing. In the sections that follow, these issues are discussed separately with respect to sampling and quantizing.

6.1   Sampling

Sampling is the process of taking periodic measurements, or samples of a continuous signal. Usually, samples are taken at the regular time intervals—that is, every T seconds. The parameter T is called a *time step* (*sample interval*), and the parameter $1/T$ is called *sample frequency* (*sampling rate*). In this way, we obtain a *quantized signal* $f_*(n)$—that is, a function for which $f_*(n) = f(nT)$ for the time step T—so that the quantized signal $f_*(n)$ is a sequence of numbers that are the values of the function $f(t)$ in points $t = nT$.

Example 6.1

Figure 6.2a shows a plot of the signal $f(t)$ being quantized with a grid whose vertical lines represent moments at which samples are taken and horizontal lines represent measuring levels. If samples are taken at $t_0 = 0$ s, $t_1 = 1$ s, $t_2 = 2$ s and so on (i.e., $T = 1$ s), then the quantized signal $f_*(n) = \{1.1, 2, 3.45, 5.35, 7.2, 8.2, 7.1, 5.66, 4.87, 4.3, 4.2\}$ (Figure 6.2c). Quantization leads to rounding values of this sequence, whereby we obtain the sequence $f_*(n) = \{1, 2, 3, 5, 7, 8, 7, 6, 5, 4, 4\}$ (Figure 6.2c). This sequence represents the function in Figure 6.2b.

It appears that some information is lost during sampling so that the sampled signal contains less information than the original signal, and consequently, there is no way to recover the original signal from its samples. Although such a situation is possible, it does not have to occur.

To reconstruct the original signal exactly, a proper number of samples must be taken, and the *sampling theorem* (Nyquist's theorem) tells us what this number is. Simply stated, the theorem says that the sampling rate should be at least twice the highest frequency of the signal, or

sampling rate $\geq 2 \cdot$ highest signal frequency

Example 6.2

A significance of this theorem can be exemplified by a phenomenon we can observe when watching a movie. If a car drives slowly in the movie, then its wheels turn in the forward direction; however, when it drives fast, the wheels appear to turn backward. Let us recall that the movie evokes in the viewer an appearance of movement by showing 24 still pictures, or frames, in 1 second. The pictures are taken $1/24$ of a second apart so that they differ slightly, and by showing them in the fast sequence, the movements of the original scene can be brought to life on the screen. However, if some movements in the scene are very fast, then they are reconstructed in a distorted way. Let us look at the car whose wheels make the full turn in $4/24$ of a second (Figure 6.3a). By sampling this signal at the rate of 24 samples per second (i.e., by taking 24 pictures in 1 second), we create a movie which, when shown, properly reproduces the original movement of the wheels. If the wheels make a full turn in $2/24$ of a second (Figure 6.3b), then it can be seen that the wheels are turning, but it cannot be determined, just by looking at the wheels, in what direction they are turning. If it were not for the background in the scene, we would only know that the car is moving. Finally, if the wheels of the car make a full turn in less than $2/24$ of a second—say, in $1/18$ of a second (Figure 6.3c)—then, just by looking at the wheels, the movie would give an impression that the car is slowly moving backward.

This example also shows where the discrepancies begin. If the frequency of the signal (i.e., the number of times the wheel makes a full turn) is exactly one-half of the sampling rate, then the problems start, as shown in Figure 6.3b: There are 24 samples per second and the signal frequency is 12 (i.e., 12 full turns made in 1 second). On the other hand, in Figure 6.3a, the signal frequency is 6, which is fine, but in Figure 6.3c, it is 18, which is not good at all.

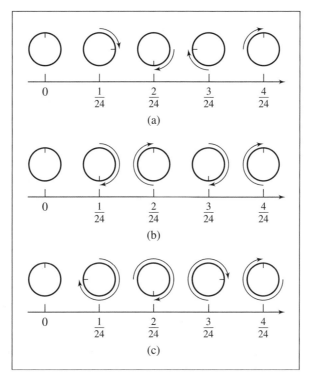

Figure 6.3 A wheel moving in a movie at the rate of (a) 6, (b) 12, and (c) 18 rotations a second

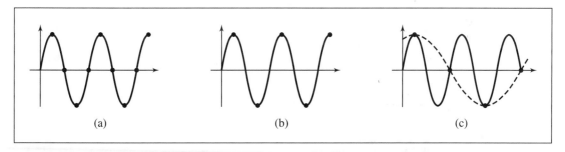

Figure 6.4 The sinusoidal signal is sampled at the rate (a) greater than, (b) equal to, and (c) smaller than twice its frequency

Figure 6.4 illustrates an impact of the sampling frequency on a continuous sinusoidal signal. If the sampling frequency meets the requirements of the sampling theorem, then the signal can be reconstructed from the sample sequence (Figure 6.4a). Usually, the signal can also be reconstructed when the sampling rate is exactly equal to the double signal frequency (Figure 6.4b). If the double signal frequency exceeds the sampling rate, then the reconstructed signal is distorted (Figure 6.4c).

A distortion introduced to the output and caused by sampling at the rate smaller than twice the signal's highest frequency is called *aliasing*. The signal reconstructed using samples in Figure 6.4c is shown with a dashed line. However, even if the conditions of the sampling theorem are met, an aliasing can occur due to the nature of filters which are used to prepare signals for digitizing. Therefore, in practical applications, sampling is made at a higher rate than twice the highest frequency of the signal.

6.2   Quantization

The sampling theorem tacitly assumes that the sample sequence is exact; that is, the measurements are taken and recorded with perfect precision. However, this is usually not the case. When taking samples, only some levels of measurement, called *reconstruction levels (quantization, quantizing, output levels),* are allowed and the values falling between the levels are represented by one of the neighbor level values. The process of assigning a particular sample to a particular level is called *quantization.* Only such quantized samples are later encoded and compressed for transmission.

It is convenient to model the quantization process of discrete sources with a continuous source by assuming that samples are taken at each point of time. For this case, the inputs are divided into intervals, and each value within an interval is represented by an endpoint of the interval. The endpoints are called *decision boundaries (levels, points).* The right endpoint of the rightmost interval is usually chosen to equal $+\infty$, and the left endpoint of the leftmost interval is $-\infty$.

Quantization is an inherently lossy operation because by rounding some measure of precision is irrecoverably lost. Quantization also allows for data compression if the reconstruction levels are efficiently encoded.

Example 6.3

If at the input we measure voltage and the range is from 0 to 20 V, then when using eight quantization levels, we may have the assignments of codewords to subranges as indicated in the table in Figure 6.5. According to this table, any input value falling between 2.5 and 5 V is encoded as 001.

voltage	binary codeword
0.0–2.5	000
2.5–5.0	001
5.0–7.5	010
7.5–10.0	011
10.0–12.5	100
12.5–15.0	101
15.0–17.5	110
17.5–20.0	111

Figure 6.5   Quantization of voltages from the range 0 through 20 V

This example indicates a problem we may encounter when trying to reconstruct an original signal using a sequence of codewords. To have a finer-grained distinction, we have to use more levels, which requires more reconstruction levels and thereby longer codewords. Since the codewords are now longer, the requirements to store the measurements are increased. Thus, an increase of precision means a decrease of compression rate.

Example 6.4   Filtered telephone signals have a maximum frequency of 3.5 kHz, which requires 7000 samples a second; however, in practice, this rate reaches 8000 samples/s. For these signals, $2^8 = 256$ quantization levels are used so that each sample is coded with eight bits. Therefore, 1 second of the telephone signal requires $8000 \cdot 8$ bits ≈ 8 KB of storage.

Scalar quantization is a process of quantizing each of the samples separately. When at least two samples are quantized at the same time, then the process is called *vector* (or *block*) *quantization*. We begin our discussion with scalar quantization.

6.2.1   Scalar Quantization

The scalar quantizer is characterized by a staircase function that relates input samples with output measurement values. There are two kinds of scalar quantizers. In a *midtread quantizer*, the values in the interval that includes zero are assigned zero. The quantizer is called midtread because zero is in the middle of a horizontal step, or a *tread*. If zero itself is a boundary level, then values from its left neighbor interval are assigned a negative value, and values from the right neighbor interval are assigned a positive number. This is the output given by a *midriser quantizer*, so called because zero is in the middle of a vertical interval, or a *riser* (Figure 6.6).

For L reconstruction levels $\{r_i\}$, there are $L + 1$ decision boundaries $\{d_i\}$. If the probability distribution is known—that is, for each input value x, the probability of

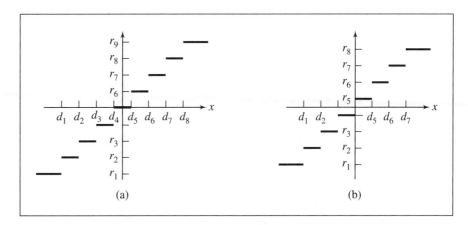

Figure 6.6   (a) A midtread quantizer and (b) a midriser quantizer

its occurrence $p(x)$ is defined—and if $x \in (d_{i-1}, d_i]$, then the quantizer Q can be expressed as a function

$$Q(x) = r_i = \hat{x} = x + e_Q$$

from which

$$e_Q = \hat{x} - x$$

where e_Q is the difference between quantized and unquantized values and is called *quantization (round-off) error* or *quantization noise,* and it indicates a distortion between the original sample value and the value produced by the quantizer. To measure this, a *distortion measure d(x, x)* is used, which is a nonnegative function indicating the magnitude of discrepancy between quantized and unquantized values. The most common distortion measure is the squared error distortion,

$$d(x, \hat{x}) = e_Q^2 = (\hat{x} - x)^2$$

The distortion measure is usually used to determine the reconstruction and decision levels. To that end, the following *average distortion* can be used

$$D = \int_{-\infty}^{\infty} d(x, \hat{x}) p(x) dx$$

If the probability distribution function $p(x)$ and the number of levels L are known, then the task of constructing an optimal quantizer consists of finding such decision boundaries $\{d_i\}$ and reconstruction levels $\{r_i\}$ that minimize the average distortion D.

If the reconstruction and decision levels are spaced evenly, then we have the simplest type of quantizer called a *uniform quantizer.* When the spacing between levels is not uniform, the quantizer is called *nonuniform.*

6.2.1.1   Uniform Quantization

For the uniform quantizer, the input and output intervals are of the same size

$$\Delta = d_i - d_{i-1}, \text{ for } 2 \leq i \leq L - 1$$
$$\Delta = r_i - r_{i-1}, \text{ for } 2 \leq i \leq L$$

where the interval Δ is called a *step size,* and reconstruction levels are the midpoints of decision levels; that is,

$$r_i = \frac{d_{i-1} + d_i}{2} = d_{i-1} + \frac{\Delta}{2}, \text{ for } 2 \leq i \leq L - 1$$

with

$$r_1 = d_1 - \frac{\Delta}{2}$$
$$r_L = d_{L-1} + \frac{\Delta}{2}$$

To assess the distortion, assume that the probability distribution function $p(x)$ is constant for each interval $(d_{i-1}, d_i]$ and equal to $p(d_i)$, which is a reasonable assumption for a large number L of quantization levels. Assume also that the number of samples less than d_1 and greater than d_{L-1} is negligible so that $p(d_1) = p(d_L) = 0$, $d_0 = -\infty$, and $d_L = +\infty$. Therefore, the average distortion

$$D = \int_{-\infty}^{\infty} d(x, \hat{x}) p(x) dx = \int_{-\infty}^{\infty} (r_i - x)^2 p(d_i) dx = \sum_{i=1}^{L} \int_{d_{i-1}}^{d_i} (r_i - x)^2 p(d_i) dx$$

$$D = -\sum_{i=2}^{L-1} \frac{(r_i - x)^3}{3} p(d_i) \bigg|_{d_{i-1}}^{d_i} = -\sum_{i=2}^{L-1} \left(\frac{(r_i - d_i)^3}{3} - \frac{(r_i - d_{i-1})^3}{3} \right) p(d_i)$$

Because

$$d_{i-1} = r_i - \frac{\Delta}{2}$$

$$d_i = r_i + \frac{\Delta}{2} \text{ for } 2 \le i \le L - 1$$

we obtain

$$D = -\sum_{i=2}^{L-1} \left(-\frac{\Delta^3/8}{3} - \frac{\Delta^3/8}{3} \right) p(d_i) = \frac{1}{12} \sum_{i=2}^{L-1} p(d_i) \Delta^3 = \frac{\Delta^2}{12}$$

since

$$\sum_{i=2}^{L-1} p(d_i) \Delta = \int_{-\infty}^{\infty} p(x) dx = 1$$

The formula $D = \frac{\Delta^2}{12}$ indicates that for a uniform quantizer the distortion measure increases with the square of interval size—that is, very quickly. Thus, as we may expect, the more decision levels are used in taking samples, the lower is the distortion. In particular, for a uniform quantizer, doubling the number of intervals (i.e., halving the step size Δ), reduces the distortion measure by the factor of 4.

6.2.1.1.1 Adaptive Quantization.

In the preceding sections, we discussed quantizers with fixed step sizes. However, it is possible to make the quantizer more flexible by having its step sizes adapt to the current values of samples.

Example 6.5

A simple adaptive quantizer suggested by James L. Flanagan and developed by P. Cumminskey and S. N. Jayant is a quantizer with one-word memory (Jayant, 1973). This is a uniform quantizer with the mean value = 0 in which the step size Δ_n is updated at every sample x_{n-1} depending on its value (but not on its sign), as in

$$\Delta_n = \Delta_{n-1} M(Q(|x_{n-1}|))$$

With this specification, a two-bit quantizer has four quantization levels, and thus, the function M has two possible values; in a three-bit quantizer, with eight quantization levels, M has four values. Figure 6.7 shows a three-bit quantizer with four values of M: $M_1 = 0.5$, $M_2 = 1.0$, $M_3 = 1.25$, and $M_4 = 1.5$, first at time $n - 1$ and then at time n, with a new step size Δ_n that depends on the value $|x_{n-1}|$. Of course, if $\Delta_{n-1} < |x_{n-1}| \le \Delta_{n-1}$, then $\Delta_n = \Delta_{n-1}$ since $M_2 = 1.0$. This example indicates that it is desirable to have the values of M in ascending order

$$1 > M_1 \le \ldots \le M_{L/2} > 1$$

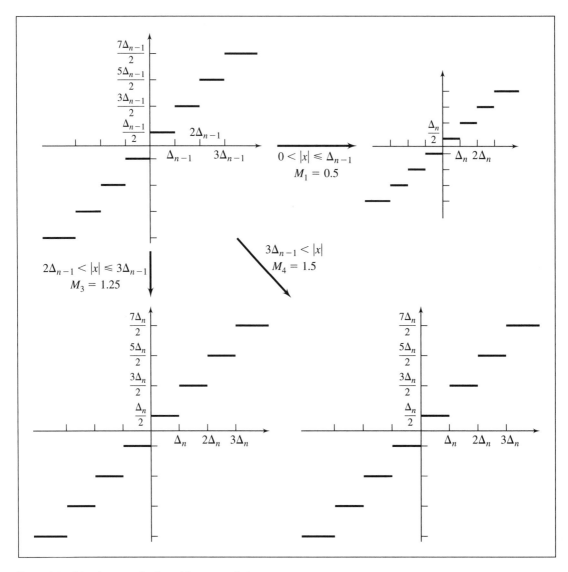

Figure 6.7   Adaptive quantization with one-word memory

It is also important that for each step size Δ_n

$$\Delta_{min} \le \Delta_n \le \Delta_{max}$$

These are practical constraints due to limited precision of computer arithmetic: When Δ_n is getting smaller and smaller, it reaches a value smaller than the smallest value that can be represented by the computer, and thus, it simply becomes zero, whereby all succeeding step sizes are also zero and the quantizer outputs only zeros. For a similar reason, Δ_n cannot become larger than the largest number representable by the computer.

6.2.1.2   *Nonuniform Quantization*

Although simple, uniform quantizers are usually inadequate. If, for example, a probability for sampling values from one interval is greater than sampling them from another interval, then it seems reasonable to assign more reconstruction levels to the former input interval than to the latter. With such a refinement, the distortion D can be decreased. In this way, we obtain reconstruction levels of different sizes and, hence, a nonuniform quantizer.

We would like to determine the reconstruction levels and the decision levels for a given L so that the quantization error D is minimized. Note that we are not making any assumption concerning the probability distribution function $p(x)$. To minimize the average distortion D, we find the necessary conditions by differentiating

$$D = \int_{-\infty}^{\infty} (r_i - x)^2 p(x) dx = \sum_{i=1}^{L} \int_{d_{i-1}}^{d_i} (r_i - x)^2 p(x) dx$$

with respect to the decision levels d_i and reconstruction levels r_i and by equating the obtained partial derivatives with zero:

$$\frac{\partial D}{\partial d_i} = (r_i - d_i)^2 p(d_i) - (r_{i+1} - d_i)^2 p(d_i) = 0 \text{ for } i = 1, \ldots, L - 1 \qquad (6.1)$$

$$\frac{\partial D}{\partial r_i} = 2 \int_{d_{i-1}}^{d_i} (r_i - x) p(x) dx = 0 \text{ for } i = 1, \ldots, L \qquad (6.2)$$

Note that we do not differentiate with respect to d_0 and d_L because they are constant values for endpoints for all possible input values.

If $p(d_i) \neq 0$, then (6.1) implies

$$d_i = \frac{r_i + r_{i+1}}{2} \text{ for } i = 1, \ldots, L - 1$$

which means that except for d_0 and d_L, each decision level d_i is the middle point between two reconstruction points r_i and r_{i+1}. From this we obtain

$$r_{i+1} = 2d_i - r_i \qquad (6.3)$$

Also, from (6.2) we obtain

$$\int_{d_{i-1}}^{d_i} (r_i - x) p(x) dx = 0 \qquad (6.4)$$

that is,

$$r_i = \frac{\displaystyle\int_{d_{i-1}}^{d_i} x p(x) dx}{\displaystyle\int_{d_{i-1}}^{d_i} p(x) dx} \text{ for } i = 1, \ldots, L - 1$$

which means that the reconstruction level r_i is the centroid (center of gravity) of the area of the probability distribution function $p(x)$ between d_{i-1} and d_i.

The set of Equations (6.3) and (6.4) are, generally, very difficult to solve in an analytical fashion, and the ease of solution hinges upon the choice of the probability distribution function $p(x)$. If the correct value of r_1 is found, then Equations (6.3) and (6.4) can be iteratively applied to find succeeding values of d_i and r_i. In this, we use the fact that (6.4) is an implicit equation for d_i in terms of r_i and d_{i-1}. If r_L found at the end of the process turns out to be the centroid of the area of $p(x)$ between d_{L-1} and $d_L = \infty$, then this proves that the sequence of d_is and r_is was properly determined. If not, the process has to start over with another r_1. Note that for a different number L of levels, d_1 is also different.

This algorithm was given independently by Stuart Lloyd and Joel Max. Here is an outline of the Lloyd-Max algorithm.[1]

LloydMaxAlgorithm()
> *choose r_1;*
> $d_0 = -\infty$;
> while *not success*
> > for i = 1 to L − 1
> > *compute d_i from (6.4)*;
> > > *compute r_{i+1} from (6.3)*;
> > if $\int_{d_{L-1}}^{d_{L=\infty}} (r_L - x)p(x)dx = 0$
> > > *success: accept the sequences $r_1, \ldots, r_L$, and $d_1, \ldots, d_{L-1}$;*
> > else *choose another r_1 and start over;*

Optimum decision and reconstruction levels for some four-level quantizers are shown in Figure 6.8.

6.2.2   Vector Quantization

In the preceding section, samples were quantized separately. A generalization of scalar quantization is *vector* (or *block*) *quantization*. In vector quantization, a stream of scalars is divided into blocks (vectors) x of N scalars, $x_i = [x_1, \ldots, x_N]^T$ and then all scalars in each block are quantized at the same time so that x is mapped to a vector $r_i = [r_1, \ldots, r_N]^T$, where $1 \le i \le L$, and L is the number of quantization levels. The set of L code vectors (*reference patterns* or *templates*) r_i is called a reconstruction *codebook*. To design a codebook, the N-dimensional space is divided into L *cells*, and

---

[1]Lloyd presented two methods, and this is what he calls Method 2. His Method 1 was later generalized by Linde, Buzo, and Gray, and this generalized form is discussed in Section 6.2.2.1. Lloyd mentions a paper reviewed in *Mathematical Reviews* in which J. Lukaszewicz and Hugo Steinhaus (1955) discuss a calibration method that uses gauge sets that are counterparts of quantization levels. The authors, however, do not provide any algorithm to find these levels; they only mention using predefined tables when a probability distribution is known.

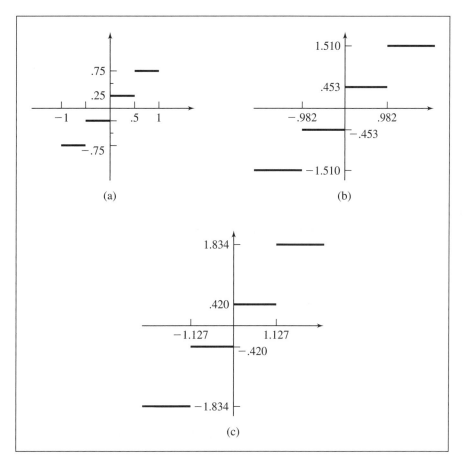

Figure 6.8 Parameters for an optimum nonuniform quantizer of four levels found with the Lloyd-Max algorithm when the probability distribution is (a) uniform, (b) Gaussian, (c) Laplacian

one code vector r_i is associated with each cell C_i. The quantization process Q consists now of assigning the code vector r_i to each vector x from C_i—that is, $Q(x) = r_i$.

If $N = 1$, then vector quantization reduces to scalar quantization. An example of vector quantization for $N = 2$ is shown in Figure 6.9. The two-dimensional space is divided into $L = 21$ cells (these cells constitute the so-called Voronoi diagram, which is a division of the plane into regions such that all points in one region are closer to a singled-out point than to any other singled-out point). The dots signify reconstruction levels. All vectors $[x_1, x_2]$ in a particular cell C are mapped to a vector $[r_1, r_2]$, which includes the coordinates of the dot in the cell C. Note that cells can be of different sizes and shapes, which is a property exploited by vector quantization. In scalar quantization, an interval between the two adjacent quantization levels can be of a different size, but being an interval, it is always of the same shape.

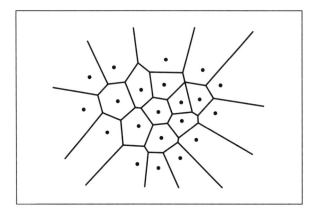

Figure 6.9   An example of quantization for $N = 2$ and $L = 21$

As in the case of scalar quantization, vector quantization also uses a *distortion measure* to assess the discrepancy between an input vector x and a code vector r. The most commonly used distortion measure is the squared-error distortion

$$d(x, r) = \sum_{i=1}^{N} (x_i - r_i)^2$$

An average distortion measure is defined as

$$D = \sum_{i=1}^{L} p(x \in C_i) \int_{x \in C_i} d(x, r_i) p(x) dx$$

where $p(x \in C_i)$ is the probability of vector x being in the cell C_i and the integral is taken over all components of x.

A quantizer is considered optimal if it meets the two necessary conditions.

Minimum distortion condition: The assignment of a code vector r_i to an input vector x results in the minimum distortion; that is,

$r_i = Q(x)$ iff $d(x, r_i) \le d(x, r_j)$ for all $j \ne i$, $1 \le j \le L$

Centroid condition: Each code vector r_i should minimize the average distortion D in each cell C_i; that is, each r_i minimizes the distortion

$$D_i \int_{x \in C_i} d(x, r_i) p(x) dx$$

The vector that meets this condition is called the *centroid* of the cell C_i.

These two conditions indicate the interdependence of code vectors and cells. The first condition does not make any explicit reference to cells, but it signifies that the cells are determined by a distortion measure d and code vectors r_i. The second condition says that for a distortion measure d we can determine the centroid (code vector) for each cell C_i.

A difficulty in direct practical application of these conditions lies in the fact that the minimum distortion condition requires a test for all input vectors x. Moreover, the multidimensional probability density function $p(x)$ may be unknown, which would prevent us from using the centroid condition. Therefore, in practice, a set of the so-called *training vectors* $\{x_k: 1 \leq k \leq M\}$ for some $M > L$ is used. For each cell C_i and M_i vectors in this cell, the average distortion D_i is defined as

$$D_i = \frac{1}{M_i} \sum_{s=1}^{M_i} d(x_s, r_i)$$

which becomes minimized for the squared-error distortion when

$$r_i = \frac{1}{M_i} \sum_{s=1}^{M_i} x_s$$

That is, for the squared-error distortion, an estimated centroid r_i of cell C_i is the average of all M_i training vectors in C_i.

6.2.2.1   The K-Means Algorithm

One method for determining a codebook was first described by Stuart Lloyd for the scalar case and by Edward Forgy for the vector case and is called the *K-means algorithm*. It is also called the *clustering algorithm* and—after Linde, Buzo, and Gray, who directly generalized Lloyd's Method 1—the *LBG algorithm*.

KmeansAlgorithm()
> *choose a set of initial code vectors r_i and a tolerance value e;*
> $m = 1$;
> $D^0 = \infty$;
> while *not success*
>> *divide the set of M training vectors x into L clusters K_i using the minimum distortion condition: $x \in K_i$ iff $d(x, r_i) \leq d(x, r_j)$ for all $j \neq i$, $1 \leq j \leq L$;*
>> *compute the average distortion $D^m = \frac{1}{M} \sum_{s=1}^{M} d(x_s, r_i)$;*
>> *where $x_s, r_i \in K_i$, i.e., code vector r_i is in the same group K_i as x_s;*
>> *in each cluster K_i, compute the centroid of the training vectors in K_i*
>> *and make this centroid the new code vector r_i in K_i;*
>> if $(D^{m-1} - D^m)/D^m < \varepsilon$
>>> *success;*
>> else *$m{+}{+}$ and try another iteration;*

Example 6.6   Consider the following stream of samples:

4 6 5 10 9 6 8 9 3 9 10 10 2 8 8 4 5 1 4 2

For $N = 2$, this stream is divided into ten vectors, all of them used as training vectors

[4 6] [5 10] [9 6] [8 9] [3 9] [10 10] [2 8] [8 4] [5 1] [4 2]

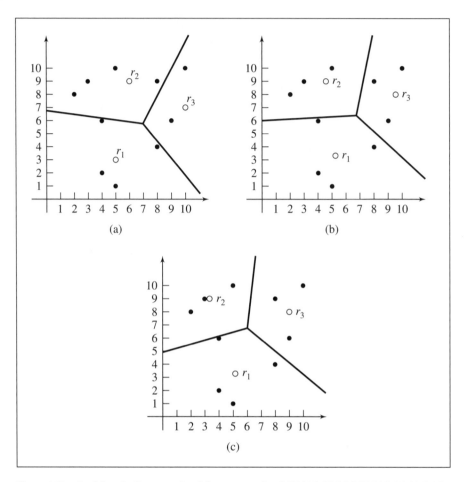

Figure 6.10 Applying the K-means algorithms to samples 4 6 5 10 9 6 8 9 3 9 10 10 2 8 8 4 5 1 4 2

that can be plotted on the Cartesian plane as shown in Figure 6.10a. To apply the K-means algorithm, let us set the number of levels to three, $L = 3$, and choose these three code vectors

$$r_1 = [5\ 3], r_2 = [6\ 9], r_3 = [10\ 7]$$

which are shown as open circles in Figure 6.10a. Using the squared-error distortion, we obtain the following three clusters

$$K_1 = \{[4\ 2][4\ 6][5\ 1][8\ 4]\}, K_2 = \{[2\ 8][3\ 9][5\ 10][8\ 9]\}, K_3 = \{[9\ 6][10\ 10]\}$$

Now we compute the average distortion

$$\begin{aligned}
D^1 = \frac{1}{10} (&((4-5)^2 + (2-3)^2) + ((4-5)^2 + (6-3)^2) + ((5-5)^2 \\
&+ (1-3)^2) + ((8-5)^2 + (4-3)^2) + ((2-6)^2 + (8-9)^2) \\
&+ ((3-6)^2 + (9-9)^2) + ((5-6)^2 + (10-9)^2) + ((8-6)^2 \\
&+ (9-9)^2) + ((9-10)^2 + (6-7)^2) + ((10-10)^2 + (10-7)^2))
\end{aligned}$$

$$D^1 = 6.9$$

and then centroids for each of the three clusters:

$$r_1 = \frac{1}{4}([4\ 2] + [4\ 6] + [5\ 1] + [8\ 4]) = \frac{1}{4}[21\ 13] = [5.25\ 3.25]$$

$$r_2 = \frac{1}{4}([2\ 8] + [3\ 9] + [5\ 10] + [8\ 9]) = [4.5\ 9]$$

$$r_3 = \frac{1}{2}([9\ 6] + [10\ 10]) = [9.5\ 8]$$

With the new centroids that become code vectors, the plot of training vectors is as in Figure 6.10b.

The second iteration of the main while loop begins with reclassification of the training vectors

$$K_1 = \{[4\ 2]\ [4\ 6]\ [5\ 1]\ [8\ 4]\},\ K_2 = \{[2\ 8]\ [3\ 9]\ [5\ 10]\},$$

$$K_3 = \{[8\ 9]\ [9\ 6]\ [10\ 10]\}$$

The first cluster remains the same, the second loses one vector, and the third cluster increase in size by one vector taken over from the previous second cluster. The new average distortion

$$D^2 = 4.8$$

is a substantial improvement over D^1. The new code vectors—that is, centroids of the three clusters—are now

$$r_1 = [5.25\ 3.25],\ r_2 = [3.33\ 9],\ r_3 = [9\ 8.33]$$

which results in the plot as in Figure 6.10c. None of the code vectors changes significantly, and the membership of the three clusters remains the same as before; the average distortion

$$D^3 = 4.28$$

It should now be obvious that the membership will remain the same if we continue execution of the algorithm, whereby the code vectors will not change their values.

Most of the cost in designing a codebook with the K-means algorithm concentrates on the classification step. If one scalar is coded with R bits, then in an N-dimensional

L	$\lg L$	N	bits per scalar	compression rate
32	5	8	0.625	12.8
32	5	16	0.3125	25.6
64	6	8	0.75	10.7
64	6	16	0.375	21.3
128	7	8	0.875	9.1
128	7	16	0.4375	18.3
256	8	8	1.0	8.0
256	8	16	0.5	16.0

Figure 6.11   **Examples of compression rates obtained with vector quantization**

quantizer, each vector requires RN bits. With that number of bits, 2^{RN} different vectors can be represented, which should also be the size of the codebook. In other words, each of the L code vectors is coded with the same number of bits $B = RN = \lg L$.

In the classification step, for each training vector, the distortion measure has to be computed once for each of the L code vectors; for M training vectors, this gives ML distortion evaluations in one iteration. Finding the squared error d takes N additions and multiplications. Therefore, the computational cost of performing one classification is equal to $NML = NM2^{RN}$ arithmetic operations, which indicates an exponential growth with the number of dimensions N (i.e., the number of scalars per vector) and the size of scalars R.

After the K-means algorithm is completed, the resulting code vectors are used to quantize all the sample vectors. To quantize a sample vector, the distortion measure has to be determined for each of the L code vectors, which requires performing $NL = N2^{RN}$ arithmetic operations per single quantization. This cost is rather high; on the other hand, dequantization is inexpensive because it requires performing only the codebook lookup.

The results of vector quantization can be very impressive, as shown in Figure 6.11. For the codebook of $L = 32 = 2^5$ codewords, five bits are needed per one codeword. If vectors contain eight scalar components ($N = 8$), then one scalar is coded with $5/8 = 0.625$ bits; doubling the dimension ($N = 16$) reduces the number of bits per scalar by a half, $5/16 = 0.3125$. If we define the compression level as the ratio of numbers of bits/scalar before and after quantization, we obtain a number that indicates how many times the number of bits required for one scalar decreases in comparison with the number of bits needed for the same scalar before quantization. Assuming that one scalar is originally coded with eight bits, for $N = 8$, the compression level $8/0.625 = 12.8$, so it takes 12.8 times less bits per scalar after quantization that before it.

6.2.2.2   Tree Codebook

In designing the codebook with the K-means algorithm, it was assumed that for each training vector the minimum distortion condition is tested for each code vector. This method, called a *full search,* is responsible for the high computational complexity of the algorithm. The number of operations can be reduced by imposing a certain structure on the codebook. One such possibility is using a tree structure, which renders a *tree codebook,* and the method is called the *binary search* or *hierarchical clustering.*

Assume that L, a number of code vectors, is a power of 2. First, we design with the K-means method the codebook with the two code vectors, r_0 and r_1. With these vectors, all training vectors are divided into two clusters, C_0 and C_1. Next, for each of the two clusters, a codebook is designed with the two code vectors r_{00} and r_{01} for the cluster C_0 and the code vectors r_{10} and r_{11} for the cluster C_1. The process is continued until in the last stage the total number of code vectors is equal to L (Figure 6.12).

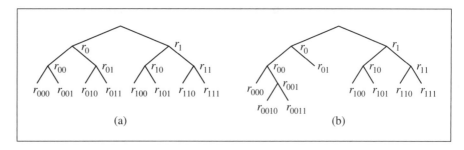

Figure 6.12   **(a) An example of a uniform tree codebook for $L = 2^3$; (b) a nonuniform tree codebook**

This method gives a substantial decrease in search complexity over full search. If, as before, N is the number of operations needed to find one distortion measure, then with $\lg L$ stages and M training vectors, the K-means algorithm performs $2NM\lg L$ operations in one iteration. The comparison of this number with the number of operations for the full search, $NM2^{RN}$, indicates a significant improvement by the factor of $NM2^{RN}/(2NM\lg L) = 2^{RN}/(2\lg L) = 2^{RN}/(2RN)$.

When quantizing a vector x, at each level i of the tree codebook, a distortion measure has to be computed for code vectors r_{i0} and r_{i1}, and if $d(x, r_{i0}) < d(x, r_{i1})$, then the bit 0 is sent as a part of the codeword for x. Next, at the level $i + 1$, the distortion measure is found for x and the two descendants of r_{i0}, namely, r_{i00} and r_{i01}; otherwise, 1 is sent and then x follows the r_{i1} branch of the tree codebook. In this approach, one single quantization requires performing $2N\lg L$ operations, which again is a significant improvement over the same process for the full search case: $N2^{RN}/(2N\lg L) = 2^{RN}/(2RN)$.

This method requires storing twice as many code vectors as in the full search case. Because the tree codebook is a complete binary tree, it has L leaves and $L - 1$ nonleaves, the latter containing the additional code vectors not required by the previous version of the K-means method.

The tree in Figure 6.12a is called *uniform* because of its uniform branching: Each nonleaf has two subtrees of the same height because at each stage all clusters are divided into two subclusters. This may lead to having clusters with very few vectors, possibly even with one vector. In such a case, further subdivisions of the clusters will not reduce the distortion measure. This would increase unnecessarily the length of codewords for some clusters. To avoid this situation, for each cluster a total distortion is determined. The cluster with the largest total distortion is divided into two subclusters. This process typically render a *nonuniform* tree, as shown in Figure 6.12b. For nonuniform trees, the assumption of L being a power of 2 is no longer needed.

An extension of the binary search method is *tree-searched* quantization, in which trees are not limited to binary trees.

6.3   Appendix: Probability Distribution Functions

If S is a source of sample values, then a *random variable X* is defined as a function

$$X: S \rightarrow \text{R}$$

where R is the set of real numbers. We use the notation $p(X = x_i)$ to indicate the probability with which a random variable X is equal to x_i.

For a discrete source $S = \{x_1, \ldots, x_N\}$, we define an *expected value* as

$$E[X] = \sum x_i p(X = x_i)$$

For continuous sources, an expected value is defined as

$$E[X] = \int_{-\infty}^{\infty} x p(x) dx$$

where p is a probability distribution function (see below).

The *variance* $\sigma^2 = E[(X - \mu)^2] = E[X^2] - \mu^2$, where the mean $\mu = E[X]$.

There are many commonly used *probability distribution functions*. Here are some examples:

Uniform
$$p(x) = \begin{cases} \dfrac{1}{b-a} & \text{for } a \le x \le b \\ 0 & \text{otherwise} \end{cases}$$

Gaussian
$$p(x) = \frac{1}{\sqrt{2\pi\sigma^2}} e^{-(x-\mu)^2/(2\sigma^2)}$$

Laplacian
$$p(x) = \frac{1}{\sqrt{2\sigma^2}} e^{-\sqrt{2}|x|/\sigma}$$

Plots of these functions are shown in Figure 6.13, where $\sigma = 1$ and $\mu = 0$.

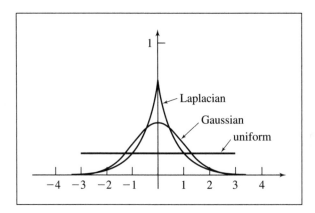

Figure 6.13   Plots of some probability distribution functions

EXERCISES

1. If we look at Figure 6.3, then we may have an impression that the sampling theorem is defeated when wheels turn very fast. For example, if they turn, say, 30 times a second, then the movie shows the wheels turning forward. Does this observation undermine this theorem?

2. It was observed in Section 6.1 that a function can *usually* be reconstructed if the sampling rate is exactly equal to the double signal frequency (Figure 6.4b). In what cases is this observation not true?

3. In high-fidelity digital recording with the maximum frequency of 20 kHz, the sampling rate equals 44.1 KHz. How much memory is needed to store 1 hour of music if the number of quantization levels is a. 2^8? b. 2^{16}?

4. How can the for loop in the LloydMaxAlgorithm() be optimized? Can it always be done?

5. What is the relation of the minimum distortion condition and centroid condition defined for an optimal vector quantizer to a scalar quantizer that uses the squared error distortion measure? Consider a relation of these conditions to formulas (6.3) and (6.4).

6. What is the significance of using the number 1 as the upper and lower bounds in the condition for the one-word adaptive quantizer from Section 6.2.1.1.1

   $$1 > M_1 \leq \ldots \leq M_{L/2} > 1$$

   What happens if at least one of these bounds is not required?

7. Apply the K-means algorithm to the samples in Example 6.5 using only two code vectors: a. [6 9] [10 7] b. [5 3] [10 7]. Does it matter what code vectors are initially chosen? What happens if one of the code vectors is much larger (or smaller) than any of the samples? Consider four initial code vectors: [5 3] [6 9] [10 7] [20 20] (the first three are the same as in Example 6.5).

BIBLIOGRAPHY

Abut, Hüseyin (ed.), *Vector quantization*, New York: IEEE Press, 1990.

Davisson, Lee D., and Gray, Robert M. (eds.), *Data compression*, Stroudsburg, PA: Dowden, Hutchinson & Ross, 1976.

Forgy, Edward W., Cluster analysis of multivariate data: Efficiency vs. interpretability of classifications, *Biometrics* 21 (1965), 768.

Gersho, Allen, and Gray, Robert M., *Vector quantization and signal compression*, Boston: Kluwer, 1992.

Jayant, S. Nuggehally, Adaptive quantization with a one word memory, *Bell System Technical Journal* 52 (1973), 1119–1144.

Jayant, S. Nuggehally (ed.), *Waveform quantization and coding*, New York: IEEE Press, 1976.

Jayant, S. Nuggehally, and Noll, Peter, *Digital coding of waveforms: Principles and applications in speech and video*, Englewood Cliffs, NJ: Prentice Hall, 1984.

Lim, Jae S., *Two-dimensional signal and image processing*, Englewood Cliffs, NJ: Prentice Hall, 1990.

Linde, Yoseph, Buzo, Andrés, and Gray, Robert M., An algorithm for vector quantizer design, *IEEE Transactions on Communication* COM-28 (1980), 84–95 [also in Abut, 1990].

Lloyd, Stuart P., Least squares quantization in PCM, *IEEE Transactions on Information Theory* IT-28 (1982), 129-137 [it originally appeared as a 1957 Bell Lab internal research report].

Lukaszewicz, J., and Steinhaus, H., O mierzeniu przez kalibrowanie [On measuring by calibration], *Zastosowania Matematyki* (1955), 225–231.

Lynch, Thomas J., *Data compression: Techniques and applications*, New York: Van Norstrand Reinhold, 1985.

Makhoul, John, Roucos, Salim, and Gish, Herbert, Vector quantization in speech coding, *Proceedings of the IEEE* 73 (1985), 1551–1588 [also in Abut, 1990].

Max, Joel, Quantizing for minimum distortion, *IRE Transactions on Information Theory* 6 (1960), 7–12 [also in Davisson and Gray, 1976].

Chapter 7

Predictive Coding

In scalar quantization, samples were quantized separately without regard to their intercorrelation. This was also the case in vector quantization, where several samples were coded at a time, but inclusion of these samples in one vector was determined by their physical adjacency in the body of data. In many situations, however, physical adjacency of samples also means that their values are similar. In an audio wave, values of adjacent samples do not usually vary by much; in images, neighboring pixels are of similar intensity and color most of the time. This interconnection can be exploited in coding the samples. In predictive coding, the value of each sample is predicted based on the values of a number of neighboring samples. This predicted value represents redundant information that can be omitted; therefore, instead of encoding a sample itself, the difference (prediction error) between its value and the predicted value is encoded. The receiver uses the quantized difference to reconstruct the original sample by computing its predicted value from already decoded sample values and adding them to the encoded prediction error. One technique based on this observation is delta modulation.

7.1 Delta Modulation

Delta modulation (DM) is the simplest method of predictive coding. Let the quantization step used by the quantizer be equal to Δ, and let $\hat{x}_n$ represent the value of x_n reconstructed by DM. DM does not quantize the sample value x_n, but instead it quantizes the difference between this value and the reconstructed value x_{n-1} of the preceding sample x_{n-1}; that is, DM quantizes the *difference signal (prediction error)*

$$e_n = x_n - \hat{x}_{n-1}$$

The difference e_n is first quantized according to the sign function

$$\hat{e}_n = \text{sign}(e_n) = \begin{cases} 1 & \text{if } e_n > 0 \\ -1 & \text{otherwise} \end{cases}$$

and then sent by the transmitter. The receiver uses a received quantized value $\hat{e}_n$ and a previously reconstructed sample value to reconstruct the sample value corresponding to the received value,

$$\hat{x}_n = \hat{x}_{n-1} + \hat{e}_n \cdot \Delta \tag{7.1}$$

Note that there are only two possible values to be transmitted: 1 if the quantized difference $\hat{e}_n$ is positive or -1 if $\hat{e}_n$ is negative or zero. Therefore, only one bit is needed to convey this information. The receiver uses this bit to construct a staircase representation of the original samples.

It is important to emphasize that the difference signal $e_n = x_n - \hat{x}_{n-1}$, and not $e_n = x_n - x_{n-1}$. This is the difference between a value x_n and the *prediction* $\hat{x}_{n-1}$ (Figure 7.1b) of its predecessor x_{n-1}, not between x_n and the predecessor itself (Figure 7.1a). If the latter were the case, then, for example, for a slowly growing input waveform, the reconstructed function would grow too fast by adding Δ at every step. By using prediction $\hat{x}_{n-1}$ in finding the difference e_n, it is easy to see how the reconstructed function should be drawn: The current step of the staircase function is always drawn in the direction of the input waveform.

There are two types of quantization errors in DM, and they cannot be reduced at the same time. The first error is the *slope overload* distortion which occurs when the quantization step Δ is too small to match a change of a steep slope of the input waveform (Figure 7.2a). The increase of the value of Δ leads to the decrease of the slope overload (Figure 7.2b). The second type of quantization error is the *granular noise* (*granularity*) when the step size is too large in comparison to small changes, or no changes, of the input waveform. In this case, the decrease of Δ leads to a better match of input and the resulting staircase function. We shall also use as a measure of modulator effectiveness the *cumulative prediction error*

$$E_k = \sum_{i=0}^{k} |x_i - \hat{x}_i|$$

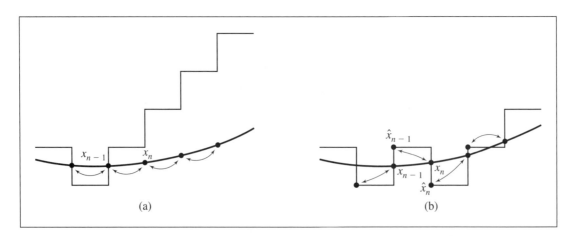

(a)   (b)

Figure 7.1   **The difference signal e_n in delta modulation computed (a) as $e_n = x_n - x_{n-1}$ and (b) $e_n = x_n - \hat{x}_{n-1}$; the values used in finding e_n are connected with a double-headed arrow**

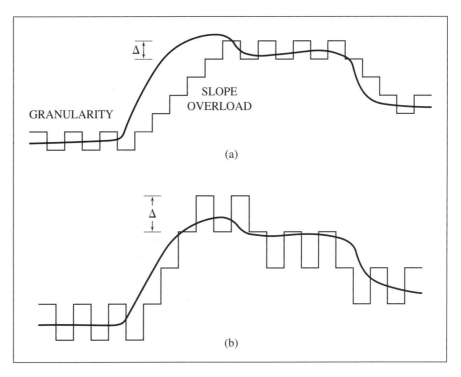

GRANULARITY

SLOPE
OVERLOAD

(a)

(b)

Figure 7.2   The quantization error in delta modulation

which is a sum total of magnitudes of differences between actual and reconstructed sample values.

7.1.1   Adaptive Delta Modulation

To decide on a proper size of the quantization step Δ, it is very difficult to find a compromise between the requirement to reduce slope overload and granularity since these requirements are contradictory. To rectify the problem, an adaptive DM system is needed that changes the step size according to the change of input.

Adaptive DM looks at m most recently transmitted bits and sets the value of Δ using a *step size multiplier* whose value is the function of the m bits, as in

$$\Delta_n = M_n \Delta_{n-1}$$

With only the two most recent bits, a possible slope overload is detected if the bits are the same, and a possible granularity is detected if the bits are different. If more than two bits are used, then the decision concerning one of these two problems can be made more reasonably.

Example 7.1

One example is a DM given by Song, Garodnick, and Schilling (1971). In this DM, a step size is increased by 50% if the difference $\hat{e}_n$ remains the same and decreased by 50% if $\hat{e}_n$ does change

n	x_n	$\hat{e}_n$	Δ_n	$\hat{x}_n$
		1	5	5
0	5	−1	2.5	2.5
1	5	1	1.25	3.75
2	5	1	1.875	5.625
3	7	1	2.8125	8.4375
4	15	1	4.2188	12.6563
5	30	1	6.3281	18.9844
6	45	1	9.4922	28.4766
7	50	1	14.2383	42.7148
8	48	1	21.3574	64.0723
9	44	−1	10.6787	53.3936
10	40	−1	16.0181	37.3755
11	40	1	8.009	45.3845
12	42	−1	4.0045	41.38
13	47	1	2.0023	43.3823
14	50	1	3.0034	46.3857
15	47	1	4.5051	50.8907
16	32	−1	2.2525	48.6382
17	28	−1	3.3788	45.2594
18	25	−1	5.0682	40.1912
19	25	−1	7.6023	32.5888
20	23	−1	11.4035	21.1854
21	15	−1	17.1052	4.0801
22	10	1	8.5526	12.6327
23	5	−1	4.2763	8.3564
24	5	−1	6.4145	1.942
25	8	1	3.2072	5.1492
26	10	1	4.8108	9.96
27	15	1	7.2163	17.1763
28	17	−1	3.6081	13.5682
29	20	1	1.8041	15.3722
30	19	1	2.7061	18.0783
31	19	1	4.0592	22.1375

(a)

Figure 7.3   (a) A table indicating changes of variables used in the adaptive delta modulator in Example 7.1

$$\hat{e}_n = \text{sign}(e_n) = \text{sign}(x_n - \hat{x}_{n-1})$$

$$\Delta_n = \begin{cases} \Delta_{min} & \text{if } 0 < \Delta_{n-1} < \Delta_{min} \\ -\Delta_{min} & \text{if } -\Delta_{min} < \Delta_{n-1} < 0 \\ \Delta_{n-1} \left| \hat{e}_n + \frac{1}{2}\hat{e}_{n-1} \right| & \text{otherwise} \end{cases}$$

$$\hat{x}_n = \hat{x}_{n-1} + \hat{e}_n \Delta_n$$

where Δ_{min} is the minimum quantization step (cf. Lei, Scheinberg, and Schilling, 1977). Note that the step size multiplier $\left| \hat{e}_n + \frac{1}{2}\hat{e}_{n-1} \right|$ can be either 0.5 or 1.5. If $\Delta_{n-1} < \Delta_{min}$, the quantization step is reset to the minimum value. An example is shown in Figure 7.3a–b for the set of samples

$$\{5\,5\,5\,7\,15\,30\,45\,50\,48\,44\,40\,40\,42\,47\,50\,47\,32\,28\,25\,25\,23\,15\,10\,5\,5\,8\,10\,15\,17\,20\,19\,19\}$$

The quantization step is increased if the staircase function is left behind so that the function can quickly reach the rate of change of the input waveform. Every time after it crosses this waveform, the quantization step is reduced so that the staircase function can be close to the waveform's slow change. Compare it to the output produced by the nonadaptive delta modulator with $\Delta = 5$ (Figure 7.3c).

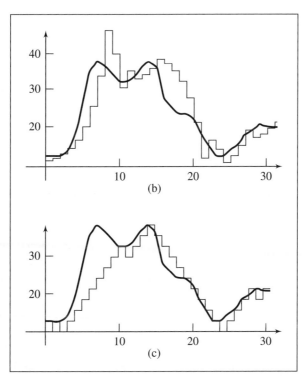

Figure 7.3 **(b) The output of this adaptive delta modulator, and (c) the output of the nonadaptive delta modulator**

7.1.2   Delayed Coding and Delta Modulation

Adaptive DM discussed in the previous section uses the knowledge about the past to adjust the step size Δ. However, adaptation may be greatly improved if knowledge about the future samples is also included in determining the best value of Δ for the currently processed sample. This process is called *delayed coding* (Newton, 1970; Cutler, 1971). Delayed coding can be used in a variety of contexts, particularly in quantization. We shall discuss it only in the context of delta modulation.

Delayed coding uses a buffer of k future samples and evaluates the best combination of $k + 1$ step sizes that allows for the optimal reproduction of the current sample and the samples included in the buffer. If the buffer includes only one sample, then unlike before, the decision on what should be the value of $\hat{e}_n$, and thus of $\hat{e}_n \cdot \Delta$, to find $\hat{x}_n$ is not based only on the difference $x_n - \hat{x}_{n-1}$—that is, on the knowledge of the current sample x_n and the past quantized sample $\hat{x}_{n-1}$—but also on the knowledge of the future sample x_{n+1} included in the buffer. Now that it is tested, what is the best combination of the values for $\hat{e}_n$ and $\hat{e}_{n+1}$ so that the cumulative prediction error $|x_n - \hat{x}_n| + |x_{n+1} - \hat{x}_{n+1}|$ is minimal? Because there are two values for both $\hat{e}_n$ and $\hat{e}_{n+1}$, the cumulative prediction error needs to be checked for four cases. For the buffer of k future samples, that requires testing 2^{k+1} combinations of values for $\hat{e}_n, \ldots, \hat{e}_{n+k}$ and the cumulative prediction errors $\sum_{i=0}^{k} |x_{n+i} - \hat{x}_{n+i}|$ corresponding to them.

Example 7.2

For the set of samples

$$\{5\ 5\ 5\ 7\ 15\ 30\ 45\ 50\ 48\ 44\ 40\ 40\ 42\ 47\ 50\ 47\ 32\ 28\ 25\ 25\ 23\ 15\ 10\ 5\ 5\ 8\ 10\ 15\ 17\ 20\ 19\ 19\}$$

x_{-1} and Δ both initialized to 5 and only one future sample used in delayed coding, we want to choose $\hat{e}_0$ so that both x_0 and x_1 are quantized optimally. For the choice $\hat{e}_0 = 1$, we have $\hat{x}_0 = 10$, for which the error $|x_0 - \hat{x}_0| = 5$; for $\hat{e}_0 = 1$, we try $\hat{e}_1 = 1$, which leads to $\hat{x}_1 = 15$ and the error $|x_1 - \hat{x}_1| = 10$; thus, the cumulative prediction error $E_1 = 5 + 10 = 15$. Still for $\hat{e}_0 = 1$, we try $\hat{e}_1 = -1$, which gives $\hat{x}_1 = 5$ and the distortion $|x_1 - \hat{x}_1| = 0$; thus, the cumulative distortion $E_1 = 5 + 0 = 5$. Then we check the same two possibilities for $\hat{e}_1$ with $\hat{e}_0 = -1$, which renders the cumulative prediction error equal to 5 and 15. At that stage, any choice for $\hat{e}_0$ (1 or -1) is acceptable, but we chose 1 first, and because the choice of -1 does not improve the cumulative prediction error, $\hat{e}_0$ becomes 1. Then, the sample from the buffer becomes current and a new sample is put in the buffer. The process of finding $\hat{e}_i$ and cumulative prediction errors for the first four samples is shown in Figure 7.4a. The output produced by using only one sample in prediction is depicted in Figure 7.4b. The cumulative prediction error $E_{31} = 164$ (for all the samples), and it is the same as for regular DM obtained with (7.1) without using any delayed coding. However, if two samples are used, then E_{31} drops to 122 (Figure 7.4c) and stays the same regardless of the number of future samples used in the forecast.

There is no restriction on using delayed coding only to DM with fixed step sizes. If step sizes are adjusted using past samples, they can also be adjusted by including future samples.

n	$\hat{x}_{n-1}$	x_n	$\hat{e}_n - \Delta$	$\hat{x}_n$	pred. error	x_{n+1}	$\hat{e}_n \cdot \Delta$	$\hat{x}_{n+1}$	pred. error	cumulative pred. error
0	5	5	5	10	5	5	5	15	10	15
0	5	5	**5**	**10**	5	5	−5	5	0	**5**
0	5	5	−5	0	5	5	5	5	0	5
0	5	5	−5	0	5	5	−5	−5	10	15
1	10	5	5	15	10	5	5	20	15	25
1	10	5	5	15	10	5	−5	5	5	15
1	10	5	**−5**	**5**	0	5	5	10	5	**5**
1	10	5	−5	5	0	5	−5	0	5	5
2	5	5	5	10	5	7	5	15	8	13
2	5	5	**5**	**10**	5	7	−5	5	2	**7**
2	5	5	−5	0	5	7	5	5	2	7
2	5	5	−5	0	5	7	−5	−5	2	17
3	10	7	5	15	8	15	5	20	5	13
3	10	7	5	15	8	15	−5	10	5	13
3	10	7	**−5**	**5**	2	15	5	10	5	**7**
3	10	7	−5	5	2	15	−5	0	15	17
….	….	….	….	….	….	….	….	….	….	….

(a)

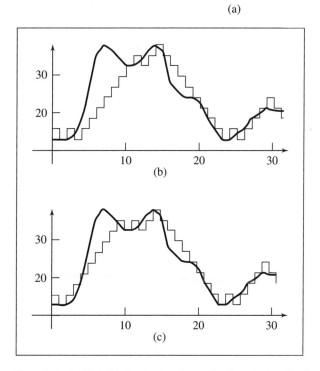

Figure 7.4 (a) The table illustrating the application of delayed coding in delta modulation that uses one future sample in finding the step size. The minimum cumulative prediction error, the chosen step sizes, and the generated quantized values for the current sample are shown in boldface (b) The output of the delta modulator that uses one future sample and (c) two future samples

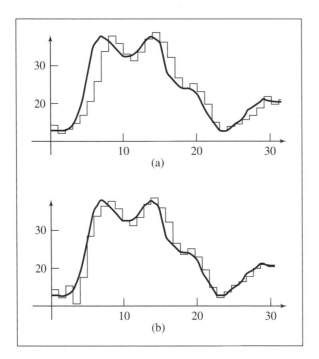

Figure 7.5   Adaptive DM from Example 7.1 amplified by the delayed coding technique using (a) one future sample and (b) three future samples

Example 7.3

The delta modulator defined in Example 7.1 produces an output shown in Figure 7.3b in which the cumulative prediction error for all samples equals 187. If only one sample is used in prediction, the cumulative error drops to 78 (Figure 7.5a) and remains the same for the case when two future samples are used, but for three or four future samples, the cumulative error is again decreased to 58 (Figure 7.5b).

7.2   Differential Pulse Code Modulation

In DM, $\hat{x}_{n-1}$ is the prediction of a sample x_n; that is, for the predicted value x_n^* of sample x_n

$$x_n^* = \hat{x}_{n-1}$$

so that the value of the sample x_n is reconstructed with its immediate quantized predecessor. In *differential pulse code modulation* (*DPCM*), a prediction of the current sample value is found by using more than one previously processed sample value. Therefore, DPCM can be considered a generalization of DM.

The predicted value x_n^* of sample x_n is considered in DPCM to be a linear function of its N predecessors

$$x_n^* = \sum_{i=1}^{N} a_i \hat{x}_{n-i}$$

where α_i are *predictor coefficients* or weights (weighting factors). The number N (i.e., the number of previous samples included in predicting the value of the current sample) indicates the *order* of the predictor. The prediction error

$$e_n = x_n - x_n^*$$

is then quantized as

$$\hat{e}_n = Q(e_n)$$

and sent over the transmission line (Figure 7.6). The receiver uses $\hat{e}_n$ and the prediction of x_n, which is x_n^*, to reconstruct

$$\hat{x}_n = x_n^* + \hat{e}_n$$

which is the DPCM receiver's approximation of the input value x_n. To that end, the prediction x_n^* is reconstructed by the receiver using previously obtained quantized prediction error values and reconstructed sample values.

To design a predictor, we have to find the optimal predictor coefficients. Optimality means making the cumulative prediction error as small as possible, where the measure of discrepancy depends on an assumed criterion. Usually, the squared error is used. To concentrate only on designing the predictor, it is assumed that the predictor operates on the original data; that is, no quantization is used. If linear prediction is of the form

$$x_n^* = \sum_{i=1}^{N} \alpha_i x_{n-i}$$

then the problem of designing the predictor consists in minimizing the variance of the difference sequence

$$\sigma^2 = E[(x_n - x_n^*)^2] = E[(x_n - \sum_{i=1}^{N} \alpha_i x_{n-i})^2]$$

where E is the expected value. To find the minimum σ^2, we find partial derivatives and equate them to zero

$$\frac{\partial \sigma^2}{\partial \alpha_k} = -2E[(x_n^* - \sum_{i=1}^{N} \alpha_i x_{n-i})x_{n-k}] = 0, \quad \text{for } 1 \leq k \leq N$$

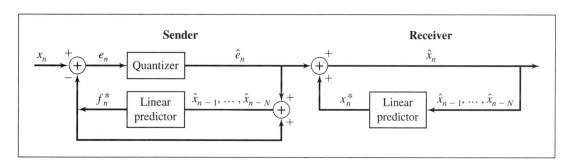

Figure 7.6   A block diagram of DPCM

from which

$$E[(x_n - x_n^*)x_{n-k}] = E[(x_n x_{n-k} - x_n^* x_{n-k})] = 0$$

that is,

$$E[x_n x_{n-k}] = E[x_n^* x_{n-k}] \tag{7.2}$$

Using the definition of the autocorrelation function of x_n

$$R_{xx}(k) = E[x_n x_{n+k}]$$

and the fact that $R_{xx}(k) = R_{xx}(-k)$, (7.2) can be rewritten as

$$R_{xx}(k) = E[x_n x_{n-k}] = E[x_n^* x_{n-k}]$$

$$= \sum_{i=1}^{N} \alpha_i E[x_{n-k} x_{n-i}] = \sum_{i=1}^{N} \alpha_i E[x_n x_{n-i+k}] = \sum_{i=1}^{N} \alpha_i R_{xx}(i - k)$$

for $1 \le k \le N$ or, in a more explicit form, as

$$R_{xx}(1) = \alpha_1 R_{xx}(0) + \alpha_2 R_{xx}(1) + \alpha_3 R_{xx}(2) + \ldots + \alpha_N R_{xx}(N - 1)$$
$$R_{xx}(2) = \alpha_1 R_{xx}(1) + \alpha_2 R_{xx}(0) + \alpha_3 R_{xx}(1) + \ldots + \alpha_N R_{xx}(N - 2)$$
$$R_{xx}(3) = \alpha_1 R_{xx}(2) + \alpha_2 R_{xx}(1) + \alpha_3 R_{xx}(0) + \ldots + \alpha_N R_{xx}(N - 3)$$

$$\cdots$$

$$R_{xx}(N) = \alpha_1 R_{xx}(N - 1) + \alpha_2 R_{xx}(N - 2) + \alpha_3 R_{xx}(N - 3) + \ldots + \alpha_N R_{xx}(0)$$

which is a set of equations to be simultaneously solved for $\alpha_1, \alpha_2, \ldots, \alpha_N$. The equations are called *normal equations*, *Wiener-Hopf equations*, or *Yule-Walker equations*.

Example 7.4   Consider the set of $M = 31$ sample values

data = $\{5\ 6\ 5\ 6\ 5\ 7\ 4\ 8\ 3\ 9\ 2\ 10\ 1\ 9\ 2\ 8\ 6\ 6\ 6\ 10\ 1\ 10\ 1\ 6\ 1\ 6\ 1\ 3\ 5\ 7\ 9\}$

See Figure 7.7a. We shall use predictors for $N = 1$, 2, and 3. To compare the three predictors, the following *prediction gain* (measured in decibels, dB) is used

$$\text{PGain} = \sum_{i=1}^{M} x_i^2 \Big/ \sum_{i=1}^{M} (x_i - x_i^*)^2$$

We also use the definition

$$R_{xx}(k) = E[x_n x_{n+k}] = \frac{1}{M - k} \sum_{i=1}^{M-k} x_i x_{i+k}$$

For $N = 1$,

$$R_{xx}(1) = \alpha_1 R_{xx}(0)$$

$$R_{xx}(0) = \frac{1}{31}(5 \cdot 1^2 + 2 \cdot 2^2 + 2 \cdot 3^2 + 1 \cdot 4^2 + 4 \cdot 5^2 + 7 \cdot 6^2 + 2 \cdot 7^2 + 2 \cdot 8^2$$
$$+ 3 \cdot 9^2 + 3 \cdot 10^2)$$
$$= 1168/31 = 37.68$$

$$R_{xx}(1) = \frac{1}{30}(5 \cdot 6 + 6 \cdot 5 + 5 \cdot 6 + 6 \cdot 5 + 5 \cdot 7 + 7 \cdot 4 + 4 \cdot 8 + 8 \cdot 3 + 3 \cdot 9$$
$$+ 9 \cdot 2 + 2 \cdot 10 + 10 \cdot 1 + 1 \cdot 9 + 9 \cdot 2 + 2 \cdot 8 + 8 \cdot 6 + 2 \cdot (6 \cdot 6)$$
$$+ 6 \cdot 10 + 10 \cdot 1 + 1 \cdot 10 + 10 \cdot 1 + 2 \cdot (1 \cdot 6 + 6 \cdot 1) + 1 \cdot 3$$
$$+ 3 \cdot 5 + 5 \cdot 7 + 7 \cdot 9)$$
$$= 707/30 = 23.57$$

$$\alpha_1 = R_{xx}(1)/R_{xx}(0) = 23.57/37.68 = 0.6255$$

Therefore, the predictor will use the equation

$$x_n^* = 0.6255 x_{n-1}$$

and the transmitted values are difference signals

$$e_n = x_n - x_n^*$$

These values, however, have a wider range than the original values; the latter range between 1 and 10, and the difference signals range between -5.3 and 9.4.

For the second order predictor, when $N = 2$,

$$R_{xx}(1) = \alpha_1 R_{xx}(0) + \alpha_2 R_{xx}(1)$$
$$R_{xx}(2) = \alpha_1 R_{xx}(1) + \alpha_2 R_{xx}(0)$$

Finding $R_{xx}(2) = \frac{1}{29} \cdot 1000 = 34.48$ and solving these equations for α_1 and α_2 result in

$$\alpha_1 = 0.0871 \text{ and } \alpha_2 = 0.8607$$

Therefore, the predicted values are

$$x_n^* = 0.0871 x_{n-1} + 0.8607 x_{n-2}$$

For the third order predictor, when $N = 3$, the set of equations is

$$R_{xx}(1) = \alpha_1 R_{xx}(0) + \alpha_2 R_{xx}(1) + \alpha_3 R_{xx}(2)$$
$$R_{xx}(2) = \alpha_1 R_{xx}(1) + \alpha_2 R_{xx}(0) + \alpha_3 R_{xx}(1)$$
$$R_{xx}(3) = \alpha_1 R_{xx}(2) + \alpha_2 R_{xx}(1) + \alpha_3 R_{xx}(0)$$

which with $R_{xx}(3) = \frac{1}{28} \cdot 662 = 23.64$ gives

$$\alpha_1 = 0.0358, \alpha_2 = 0.8555, \alpha_3 = 0.0596$$

and the values are predicted according to the equation

$$x_n^* = 0.0358 x_{n-1} + 0.8555 x_{n-2} + 0.0596 x_{n-3}$$

Figure 7.7b-d shows plots for *differences* between original values and predicted values for all three predictor orders. We can observe a significant difference between the predictor of the first order and predictors of higher orders. The predictor of the first order produces values that are very similar to the original values (Figure 7.7b). Predictors of the second and third orders are flattened in comparison with the predictor of the first order. The prediction gains are 1.67, 7.84, and 7.80. Thus, there is a significant improvement by going from $N = 1$ to $N = 2$, but the difference between the second and third order predictors is negligible.

7.2.1 Adaptive Differential Pulse Code Modulation

In the foregoing discussion, DPCM was using a fixed set of predictor coefficients. Example 7.4 suggests that different coefficients should be used for different segments of samples, which leads to the concept of adaptive DPCM. There are at least two components of adaptive DPCM that can be modified: predictor coefficients and quantization levels. Adaptive DPCM can be based on adjusting only one of these two components, but it is possible to modify both. The problem of adaptive quantization was presented in Section 6.2.1.1; therefore, only adaptive prediction needs to be discussed.

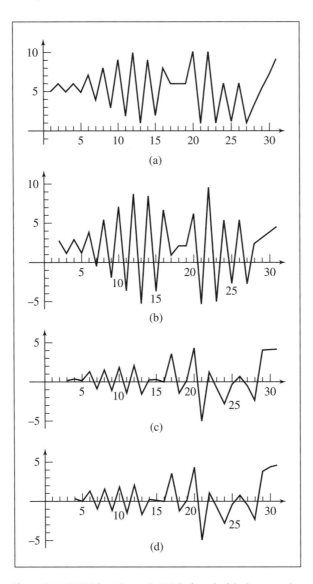

Figure 7.7 DPCM from Example 7.4 designed with the normal equations: (a) graph of samples; graph of *differences* between original values and predicted values for the predictor of (b) the first order, (c) the second order, and (d) the third order

7.2.1.1 *Adaptive Prediction*

DPCM with the adaptive predictor periodically modifies the predictor coefficients so that they reflect the changes in the stream of input samples. One such adaptive DPCM method was proposed by Atal and Schroeder (1970). The set of equations

$$\frac{\partial \sigma^2}{\partial \alpha_k} = -2E\left[\left(x_n^* - \sum_{i=1}^{N} \alpha_i x_{n-i}\right)x_{n-k}\right] = 0, \qquad \text{for } 1 \leq k \leq N$$

is solved for all the samples in a 5-millisecond time segment so that the predictor is optimum (with respect to the squared error) during this period of time. Because the authors sampled speech signals at the rate of 6.67 kHz, $N = 33$. The coefficients computed once every 5 ms are sent to the receiver along with the difference signals so that the receiver can be reset every 5 ms.

The problem is that this approach requires a buffer of samples to find the values of predictor coefficients. This also leads to the transmission delay since the coefficients have to be known before the data are sent. Moreover, additional information (side information) needs to be transmitted, such as predictor coefficients. This is due to the fact that adaptation is made on the basis of the encoder's input that is not available to the receiver. This is also called the *forward adaptation*.

To rectify the problem, predictor coefficients are estimated based on quantized and transmitted data. This is an output of the encoder; therefore, it is also available to the receiver, which eliminates the need of transmitting any additional information beyond pure data. This type of adaptation is called *backward adaptation*.

Consider the expression for the squared error for the first order predictor

$$e_n^2 = (x_n - x_n^*)^2 = (x_n - \alpha_1 \hat{x}_{n-1})^2$$

The plot of the prediction error e_n^2 versus predictor coefficient α_1 is shown in Figure 7.8. The derivative of e_n^2 at the optimum α_{opt} is zero, which signifies the minimum value of the error e_n^2. The derivative of e_n^2 at a point α_1 to the left of α_{opt} is *negative*. In this case, to bring α_1 closer to α_{opt}, α_1 has to be increased; that is, a *positive* value should be added to α_1 to correct it (i.e., to adapt it). This correction is positive—that is, opposite to the sign of the derivative. Similarly, if $\alpha_1 > \alpha_{opt}$, the derivative at α_1 is *positive*, and the adaptation of α_1 is done be subtracting a value from it, which is also a sign opposite that of the derivative.

In the method of the *steepest descent* (*gradient search*), an adaptation of the predictor coefficient α_1 at time $n + 1$ is done by adding a value proportional to the negative of the derivative of e_n^2 to the coefficient α_1's value at time n:

$$\alpha_1(n+1) = \alpha_1(n) - \beta \frac{\partial e_n^2}{\partial \alpha_1} \approx \alpha_1(n) - \beta \frac{\partial \hat{e}_n^2}{\partial \alpha_1}$$

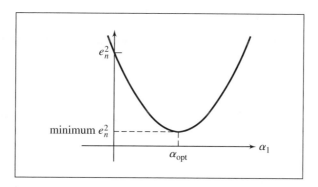

Figure 7.8   The graph of the predictor error e_n^2 versus predictor coefficient α_1.

where β, called a *gradient coefficient*, is used to control the adaptation rate (the coefficient β is often a constant), and the *gradient* of the function f defined in an n-dimensional space is a vector composed of n partial derivatives

$$\nabla f = \left[\frac{\partial f}{\partial x_1}, \ldots, \frac{\partial f}{\partial x_n} \right]^T$$

One way of estimating the gradient of the function e_n^2 is given by the *least mean square* algorithm (Widrow et al., 1976). Since

$$\frac{\partial \hat{e}_n^2}{\partial \alpha_1} \approx \frac{\partial e_n^2}{\partial \alpha_1} = -2(x_n - \alpha_1 \hat{x}_{n-1})\hat{x}_{n-1} = -2e_n \hat{x}_{n-1}$$

we obtain

$$\alpha_1(n+1) = \alpha_1(n) + 2\beta e_n \hat{x}_{n-1} \approx \alpha_1(n) + 2\beta \hat{e}_n \hat{x}_{n-1}$$

which is the value to be used in

$$e_n = (x_n - \alpha_1(n)\hat{x}_{n-1})$$

For an N order predictor, the squared prediction error is

$$e_n^2 = \left(x_n - \sum_{i=1}^{N} \alpha x_{n-i} \right)^2$$

from which we obtain N derivatives with respect to the coefficients α_k

$$\nabla e_n^2 = \left[\frac{\partial e_n^2}{\partial \alpha_1}, \ldots, \frac{\partial e_n^2}{\partial \alpha_N} \right]^T$$

which is the gradient of the function e_n^2. Each derivative

$$\frac{\partial \hat{e}_n^2}{\partial \alpha_k} \approx \frac{\partial e_n^2}{\partial \alpha_k} = -2(x_n - \alpha_k \hat{x}_{n-k})\hat{x}_{n-k} = -2e_n \hat{x}_{n-k}$$

and thus,

$$a_k(n+1) = a_k(n) + 2\beta e_n \hat{x}_{n-k} \approx a_k(n) + 2\beta \hat{e}_n \hat{x}_{n-k}$$

Example 7.5

Let us use the data samples from Example 7.4:

data = $\{5\ 6\ 5\ 6\ 5\ 7\ 4\ 8\ 3\ 9\ 2\ 10\ 1\ 9\ 2\ 8\ 6\ 6\ 6\ 10\ 1\ 10\ 1\ 6\ 1\ 6\ 1\ 3\ 5\ 7\ 9\}$

with $\beta = 0.0001$. We assume that no quantization is used; therefore, the first order adaptive predictor uses the formulas

$$e_n = (x_n - \alpha_1(n)x_{n-1})$$
$$\alpha_1(n+1) = \alpha_1(n) + 2\beta e_n x_{n-1}$$

To begin the process, $\alpha_1(1)$ is set to 0.6. Adaptation is not very good, and the prediction gain is merely 1.66. There is a significant improvement for the second order adaptive predictor, with initializations $\alpha_1(2) = 0.09$ and $\alpha_2(2) = 0.9$, PGain = 7.85. The third order predictor is about the same, with $\alpha_1(3) = 0.04$, $\alpha_2(3) = 0.9$, and $\alpha_3(3) = 0.06$, PGain = 7.78. The adaptive predictor from this example, however, fares slightly worse than DPCM from Example 7.4 based on the normal equations. It is important to notice that the efficiency of the algorithm hinges upon the choice of the parameter β. If $\beta = 0.001$, then PGain is 1.59, 6.94, and 6.72 for the three analyzed orders, but it drops dramatically when $\beta = 0.01$, in which case PGain is 1.08, 0.61, and 0.01, respectively.

EXERCISES

1. In what situation can the step size Δ_n reach the minimum step size Δ_{min}?

2. In the adaptive DM method given by Winkler (1963), the step size is given by

$$\Delta_n = \begin{cases} 2\Delta_{n-1} & \text{if } \hat{e}_n = \hat{e}_{n-1} = \hat{e}_{n-2} \\ .5\Delta_{n-1} & \text{if } \hat{e}_n \neq \hat{e}_{n-1} \text{ and } 2\Delta_{n-1} > \Delta_{min} \\ \Delta_{n-1} & \text{otherwise} \end{cases}$$
$$\hat{x}_n = \hat{x}_{n-1} + \hat{e}_n \Delta_n$$

Winkler's DM reduces the quantization step Δ by a half upon the change of sign of $\hat{e}_n$; if $\hat{e}_n$ changed the last time, Δ remains the same, but if $\hat{e}_n$ remained the same for the last two times, which is a sure sign of slope overload, Δ is doubled. Draw an output of Winkler's DM using the waveform from Figure 7.3.

3. For an adaptive DM defined as

$$\Delta_n = \begin{cases} M_1 \Delta_{n-1} & \text{if } \hat{e}_n = \hat{e}_{n-1} \\ M_2 \Delta_{n-1} & \text{otherwise} \end{cases}$$

and the condition $M_1 = 1/M_2 = M$ (Jayant 1970), draw the output for
   a. $M = 1.2$,
   b. $M = 1.5$,
   c. $M = 2$

using the input from Figure 7.3.

4. Create a table similar to the table in Figure 7.4a for the case when two samples are used in prediction. Do that only for the first sample.

BIBLIOGRAPHY

Atal, B. S., and Schroeder, M. R., Adaptive predictive coding of speech signals, *Bell System Technical Journal* 49 (1970), 1979–1986 [also in Jayant, 1976].

Cutler, C. Chapin, Delayed encoding: Stabilizer for adaptive coders, *IEEE Transactions on Communications* COM-19 (1971), 898–907 [also in Jayant, 1976].

Jayant, S. N., Adaptive deltamodulation with a one-bit memory, *Bell System Technical Journal* (1970), 321–342.

Jayant, S. Nuggehally (ed.), *Waveform quantization and coding*, New York: IEEE Press, 1976.

Lei, Tsu Luen R., Scheinberg, Norman, and Schilling, Donald L., Adaptive delta modulation systems for video encoding, *IEEE Transactions on Communications* COM-25 (1977), 1302–1314.

Newton, C. M. B., Delta modulation with slope-overloaded prediction, *Electronics Letters* 6 (1970), 272–274.

Song, Ching-Long, Garodnick, Joseph, and Schilling, Donald C., A variable-step-size robust delta modulator, *IEEE Transactions on Communication Technology* COM-19 (1971), 1033–1044 [also in Davisson and Gray (eds.), *Data compression*, Stroudsburg, PA: Dowden, Hutchinson & Ross 1976].

Widrow, Bernard, McCool, John M., Larimore, Michael G., and Johnson, C. Richard, Stationary and nonstationary learning characteristics of the LMS adaptive filter, *Proceedings of the IEEE* 64 (1976), 1151–1162.

Winkler, Marion R., High information delta modulation, *IEEE International Convention Record* (1963), Part 8, 260–265.

Chapter 8

Transform Coding

In many situations, operating on some data used in their original form is inconvenient because of the nature of operations involved or the nature of results returned. For example, addition is easier than multiplication, and therefore, it may be more convenient to replace one operation by another. However, the data have to be transformed from one form to another so that the easier operation makes sense in a particular context. For example, numbers can be transformed into their logarithms so that they can be added instead of multiplied, but the result then has to be converted into a form that makes it identical to the result obtained with multiplication only, without logarithmic transformation. In the case of a logarithm, this amounts to establishing an isomorphic mapping between relational domains $(\mathbb{R}^+, *)$ and $(\mathbb{R}, +)$ because a logarithm is a one-to-one function from the domain of positive real numbers $\mathbb{R}^+$ onto the range of real numbers $\mathbb{R}$ and $\log(x * y) = \log x + \log y$. In effect, a logarithm can be considered a way of transforming the operation (or function) of multiplication into addition in such a way that whatever is done with addition can be transformed back (say, by using a logarithm table lookup or by using the exponential function) to the original relational domain (Figure 8.1). In the context of data compression, data transformation should allow for quicker and more efficient data transmission than in the case of transmitting the data in the original form. However, as we shall see, the transformation functions applied in this case transform a cluster of data into another cluster which lends itself for efficient transmission.

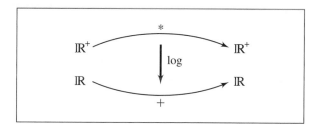

Figure 8.1   A correspondence established with the logarithmic function between relational domains ($\mathbb{R}^+$, $*$) and ($\mathbb{R}, +$)

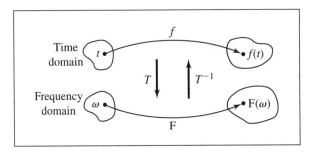

Figure 8.2   Creating the transform _F_ of function _f_ with a transformation function _T_

Another reason for transforming the data is that in the transformed form certain dependencies can be seen better than without transformation. For example, information shown on the oscilloscope in the time domain may be insufficient because it shows a dependence of the wave amplitude on time (i.e., how the wave changes over time). For audio signals, this form is inconvenient for predicting the sound of the signal. More information can be retrieved if we use the signal's frequency domain representation that shows the frequency versus its amplitude and phase. Therefore, we want to convert the time domain function $f(t)$ to the frequency domain function $T(f) = F(\omega)$ so that the _transformation function T_ is uniquely defined. A _transform_ of a function _f_ with a certain domain and range is a function F with a certain domain and range, which is uniquely defined and uniquely associated with _f_ (Figure 8.2). For example, multiplication is a transform of addition if a logarithm is the transformation function.

There is also another goal in data transformation. The transformed data should be uncorrelated, whereby most or, ideally, all of the signal energy is concentrated in a small portion of the output sequence. In this way, only the elements saturated with energy need be transmitted. This is the idea behind transform coding, which is a process of encoding signals into a sequence of data that, ideally, are not correlated.

8.1   Defining a Transform

Definition 8.1   A _one-dimensional discrete transform_ F of function _f_ is given by the general formula

$$F(k) = \sum_{n=0}^{N-1} f(n)a(k, n) \text{ for } k = 0, 1, \ldots, N - 1$$

where $a(k, n)$ is called a _forward transformation kernel_. An inverse transform _f_ of F is given by

$$f(n) = \sum_{k=0}^{N-1} F(k)b(k, n) \text{ for } n = 0, 1, \ldots, N - 1$$

in which $b(k, n)$ is called an _inverse transformation kernel_.

First, note that each value of the transform $F(k)$ depends on the values of $f(n)$ defined for all the arguments n included in the domain of function f. Moreover, if $[f] = [f(0) f(1) \ldots f(N-1)]^T$ is a signal vector, then the vector $[F] = [F(0) F(1) \ldots F(N-1)]^T$ represents its transform given by

$$[F] = T[f]$$

where $T = [a(k, n)]$ is a two-dimensional $N \times N$ *transformation matrix*. T should be an orthogonal matrix, whereby the energy of the signal is preserved in the energy of the transform, where energy preservation is determined by

$$\sum_k |f(k)|^2 = \sum_k |F(k)|^2$$

The validity of this equation can be shown by observing that

$$[f]^T[f] = (T^T[F])^T (T^T[F]) = [F]^T T T^T [F] = [F]^T[F]$$

The elements of the matrix $[F]$ are called *transform coefficients*; these coefficients are first quantized and then transmitted over the transmission line. On the receiving side, the original signal is decoded by recovering the original vector $[f]$ with the transformation

$$[f] = T^{-1}[F]$$

where $T^{-1} = [b(k, n)]$.

All the definitions can be extended to two dimensions, which is important for compression of images. In this case, a set of samples, such as image samples, is represented by a two-dimensional square array of N^2 intensity samples over the image surface, and these samples are described by a function $f(m, n)$ for the image coordinates $m, n = 0, 1, \ldots, N-1$; now Definition 8.1 can be extended to two dimensions.

Definition 8.2

A *two-dimensional discrete forward transform* is of the form

$$F(k, l) = \sum_{m=0}^{N-1} \sum_{n=0}^{N-1} f(m, n) a(k, l, m, n) \text{ for } k, l = 0, 1, \ldots, N-1$$

where $a(k, l, m, n)$ is called the *forward transform kernel*, and the variables k and l are called *spatial frequencies*. The corresponding *reverse transform* is of the form

$$\bar{f}(m, n) = \sum_{k=0}^{N-1} \sum_{l=0}^{N-1} F(k, l) b(k, l, m, n) \text{ for } m, n = 0, 1, \ldots, N-1$$

where $b(k, l, m, n)$ is called the *reverse transform kernel*.

Definition 8.3

A forward transform

$$F(k, l) = \sum_{m=0}^{N-1} \sum_{n=0}^{N-1} f(m, n) a(k, l, m, n) \text{ for } k, l = 0, 1, \ldots, N-1$$

is called *separable* if its kernel is separable; that is, if

$$a(k, l, m, n) = a_1(k, m) a_2(l, n)$$

for two one-dimensional kernels $a_1(k, m)$ and $a_2(l, n)$.

If a two-dimensional transform is separable, then it can be found by consecutive application of two one-dimensional transforms; that is, the two-dimensional transform can be built from the knowledge of two one-dimensional transforms. Also, the number of multiplications and additions can be reduced from $O(N^4)$ from the original version to $O(N^3)$ in the separable case. Note that for $k, l = 0, 1, \ldots, N-1$

$$F(k, l) = \sum_{m=0}^{N-1} \sum_{n=0}^{N-1} f(m, n) a(k, l, m, n) = \sum_{m=0}^{N-1} \sum_{n=0}^{N-1} f(m, n) a_1(k, m) a_2(l, n)$$

$$= \sum_{m=0}^{N-1} a_1(k, m) \sum_{n=0}^{N-1} f(m, n) a_2(l, n)$$

If, therefore, for each value of m we take a one-dimensional transform

$$\sum_{n=0}^{N-1} f(m, n) a_2(l, n)$$

where $l = 0, 1, \ldots, N-1$, then we obtain a two-dimensional transform

$$F(m, l) = \sum_{n=0}^{N-1} f(m, n) a_2(l, n)$$

along each column m. The two-dimensional transform

$$F(k, l) = \sum_{m=0}^{N-1} a_1(k, m) F(m, l)$$

results in turn from taking a transform along each row l of $F(m, l)$, as in Figure 8.3.

Definition 8.4   A forward kernel is called *symmetric* if

$$a(k, l, m, n) = a_1(k, m) a_1(l, n)$$

It is sometimes more convenient to express a transform in the form of a matrix. For a separable and symmetric kernel $a(k, l, m, n)$, the formula (8.1) for the forward transform $[F]$ is given by the equation

$$[F] = [F(k, l)] = [a_1(p, s)][f(m, n)][a_1(p, s)] = T[f]T$$

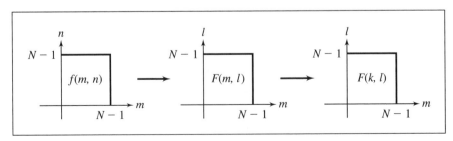

Figure 8.3   Finding the two-dimensional transform using one-dimensional transformations

where $[f] = [f(m, n)]$ is an $N \times N$ matrix of samples, $T = [a_1(p, s)]$ is a symmetric transformation matrix and $[F]$ is an $N \times N$ transform matrix obtained as the result of transformation. If the inverse transform kernel is separable and symmetric—that is, if

$$b(k, l, m, n) = b_1(k, m)b_1(l, n)$$

and the inverse of T, $T^{-1} = [b_1(k, m)]$—then multiplying both sides of (8.2) from the left and from the right by the inverse T^{-1} renders

$$T^{-1}[F]T^{-1} = T^{-1}T[f]TT^{-1} = [f]$$

In this way, an image $[f]$ given as a matrix in the spatial domain is converted with the transformation matrix T into a transform $[F]$ given as a two-dimensional matrix in the frequency domain (spatial frequency).

The reason for transforming $[f]$ into $[F]$ is that all elements of the transform matrix $[F]$ are not of equal importance. Because most of the energy of the matrix is concentrated around the left upper corner, the other elements can for practical purposes be neglected (i.e., treated as equal to 0). In this way, some information is lost, but the amount of the lost information is (should be) insignificant compared to the information retained so that the reconstruction of the original information is possible to an acceptable degree of accuracy.

8.2   Interpretation of Transforms

The transform can be interpreted in several ways, and we are going to present two such interpretations: a transform as a way of rotating coordinate axes and a transform as a way of decomposing a set of samples into a sum of basis vectors.

8.2.1   Transforms and Rotation of Axes

Consider an 8×8 image on Figure 8.4a in which numbers represent shades of gray on the scale of 16 levels, 0 through 15. The image is divided into 2×1 blocks to be a subject of a 2×2 transformation T. The numbers are also plotted on Figure 8.4b. The numbers next to points indicate the number of blocks corresponding to the particular point. If the image were made randomly, then any number 0 through 15 would have an equal chance to appear at any point of the image, and the plot would show the points almost uniformly scattered in the square $[0\ 15] \times [0\ 15]$. However, the image, which presents a bent crest, displays orderly behavior in that most of the time the numbers in the 2×1 blocks are the same or nearly the same: Twenty-two blocks contain a pair of the same numbers, twelve blocks include two 1s, four include two 6s, four two 8s, and two include two 10s. The points corresponding to these blocks are located on the diagonal of the plane. There are only three blocks with widely different numbers (1 and 6), and the numbers included in the remaining blocks are not very different so that they are plotted near the diagonal. Thus, most of the points are at the diagonal or in its neighborhood, which indicates that the numbers included in

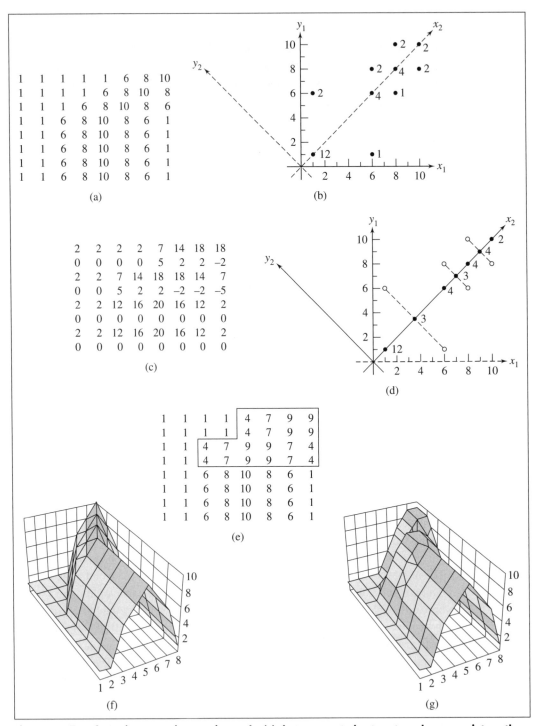

Figure 8.4   Transformation as rotation: matrix samples (a) that represent a bent crest are shown as points on the Cartesian plane (b); (c) the matrix (a) after transformation; (d) the points of the transformed matrix; (e) the reconstructed matrix with an inverse transformation after setting to zero coordinate y_2 for each point in (d); (f–g) three-dimensional representations of matrices (a) and (e)

the blocks that compose the picture are highly correlated. Now, let us rotate the co-ordinate axes by 45°. This can be accomplished by transforming each block to a new block by using a rotation matrix,

$$\begin{bmatrix} \cos 45° & \sin 45° \\ -\sin 45° & \cos 45° \end{bmatrix} = \frac{1}{\sqrt{2}}\begin{bmatrix} 1 & 1 \\ -1 & 1 \end{bmatrix}$$

as in

$$\begin{bmatrix} c \\ d \end{bmatrix} = \frac{1}{\sqrt{2}}\begin{bmatrix} 1 & 1 \\ -1 & 1 \end{bmatrix}\begin{bmatrix} a \\ b \end{bmatrix}$$

where the block $[c\ d]^T$ is a counterpart of a block $[a\ b]^T$ in the new coordinate system. For example,

$$\frac{1}{\sqrt{2}}\begin{bmatrix} 1 & 1 \\ -1 & 1 \end{bmatrix}\begin{bmatrix} 1 \\ 1 \end{bmatrix} = \frac{1}{\sqrt{2}}\begin{bmatrix} 2 \\ 0 \end{bmatrix}$$

$$\frac{1}{\sqrt{2}}\begin{bmatrix} 1 & 1 \\ -1 & 1 \end{bmatrix}\begin{bmatrix} 1 \\ 6 \end{bmatrix} = \frac{1}{\sqrt{2}}\begin{bmatrix} 7 \\ 5 \end{bmatrix}$$

That is, $[1\ 1]^T$ is transformed to $\frac{1}{\sqrt{2}}[2\ 0]^T = \left[\frac{2}{\sqrt{2}}\ 0\right]^T$, and $[1\ 6]^T$ is transformed to $\frac{1}{\sqrt{2}}[7\ 5]^T = \left[\frac{7}{\sqrt{2}}\ \frac{5}{\sqrt{2}}\right]^T$. In effect, the image in Figure in 8.4a is transformed into the image 8.4c after applying the transformation to each block of the image in 8.4a. Note that the numbers in the image 8.4c should all be divided by $\sqrt{2}$. It can be observed that the second number of each block is zero or close to zero since the points corresponding to the transformed blocks are located in the proximity of the x_2 axis. The first number of each block, however, increased; that is, the energy of the image is now concentrated in the first elements of the blocks. The total energy of the image remains the same before and after transformation, where the total energy is the sum of the energies along both axes:

$$\sum x_1^2 + \sum y_1^2 = (14 \cdot 1^2 + 7 \cdot 6^2 + 7 \cdot 8^2 + 4 \cdot 10^2) + (13 \cdot 1^2 + 7 \cdot 6^2 + 8 \cdot 8^2$$
$$+ 4 \cdot 10^2)$$
$$= 1114 + 1177 = 2291$$

$$\sum x_2^2 + \sum y_2^2 = \frac{1}{(\sqrt{2})^2}((12 \cdot 2^2 + 3 \cdot 7^2 + 4 \cdot 12^2 + 3 \cdot 14^2 + 4 \cdot 16^2 + 4 \cdot 18^2$$
$$+ 2 \cdot 20^2) + (22 \cdot 0^2 + 3 \cdot 5^2 + 7 \cdot 2^2))$$
$$= \frac{1}{2}(4374 + 103) = 2291$$

If so, then at the cost of some distortion, the transformed points can be all projected onto the x_2 axis, whereby the second elements of each block become equated with zero (Figure 8.4d). In this way, only the first number in each block needs to be transmitted, which amounts to transmitting only half the original amount of numbers. That the resulting distortion does not significantly distort the picture can be seen in Figure 8.4e in which the original image is reconstructed by rotating each transformed point by 45^3 to the right—that is, by applying the inverse transformation

$$\begin{bmatrix} \cos 45° & -\sin 45° \\ \sin 45° & \cos 45° \end{bmatrix} = \frac{1}{\sqrt{2}}\begin{bmatrix} 1 & -1 \\ 1 & 1 \end{bmatrix}$$

as in

$$\begin{bmatrix} a \\ b \end{bmatrix} = \frac{1}{\sqrt{2}}\begin{bmatrix} 1 & -1 \\ 1 & 1 \end{bmatrix}\begin{bmatrix} c \\ d \end{bmatrix}$$

to each transformed block. For example,

$$\frac{1}{\sqrt{2}}\begin{bmatrix} 1 & -1 \\ 1 & 1 \end{bmatrix}\frac{1}{\sqrt{2}}\begin{bmatrix} 2 \\ 0 \end{bmatrix} = \begin{bmatrix} 1 \\ 1 \end{bmatrix}$$

$$\frac{1}{\sqrt{2}}\begin{bmatrix} 1 & -1 \\ 1 & 1 \end{bmatrix}\frac{1}{\sqrt{2}}\begin{bmatrix} 7 \\ 5 \end{bmatrix} = \begin{bmatrix} 1 \\ 6 \end{bmatrix}$$

The distorted area of the image is marked in Figure 8.4e.

This example illustrates the goal of using a transform, which involves concentrating the maximum energy of an image in a minimum number of components in the transformed image.

A rotation of axes also leads to decorrelation of the block components or at least to a significant decrease of correlation of the components. As Figure 8.4b indicates, when a value on the x_1 axis is given, then in most cases the corresponding y_1 value can be safely guessed because the x_1 values are equal or almost equal to the y_1 values. However, the situation changes drastically in the new coordinate axes. Now, x_2 values correspond to small y_2 values—which is an indication of shifting energy from y_2 values to x_2 values, and y_2 values can correspond to any x_2 value. That is, the values in one block have been decorrelated, or made less dependent on each other. (We have to be careful with the terminology since independence, or stochastic independence, is not identical to uncorrelation: Block components can be uncorrelated and yet stochastically dependent.)

8.2.2   Transforms and Basis Matrices

It can be observed that each matrix of image samples can be presented in the form of identity expansion by using a set of orthogonal matrices, as in

$$X = \sum_{m=0}^{M-1} \sum_{n=0}^{N-1} X(m, n)[e(m, n)]$$

where $[e(m, n)]$ is an $M \times N$ matrix with 1 in the position (m, n) and 0 in the remaining positions. That is, the sample matrix X is a composition of basis vectors multiplied by coefficients (weights) that are the matrix's components. For example,

$$\begin{bmatrix} a \\ b \end{bmatrix} = a\begin{bmatrix} 1 \\ 0 \end{bmatrix} + b\begin{bmatrix} 0 \\ 1 \end{bmatrix}$$

That is, the vector $[a \ b]^T$ is transformed into itself using an identity transform,

$$\begin{bmatrix} a \\ b \end{bmatrix} = \begin{bmatrix} 1 & 0 \\ 0 & 1 \end{bmatrix}\begin{bmatrix} a \\ b \end{bmatrix}$$

which suggests that other transforms can also be considered matrices of basis vectors with which the sample matrices are decomposed. As an example, consider the Hadamard transformation (to be discussed in Section 8.4) applied to the sample vector $X = [2 \ 5]^T$

$$Y = \frac{1}{\sqrt{2}}\begin{bmatrix} 1 & 1 \\ 1 & -1 \end{bmatrix}\begin{bmatrix} 2 \\ 5 \end{bmatrix} = \frac{1}{\sqrt{2}}\begin{bmatrix} 7 \\ -3 \end{bmatrix}$$

Because the inverse of the Hadamard matrix is the matrix itself, the original vector X can be recovered by applying the inverse transformation

$$X = \frac{1}{\sqrt{2}}\begin{bmatrix} 1 & 1 \\ 1 & -1 \end{bmatrix}\frac{1}{\sqrt{2}}\begin{bmatrix} 7 \\ -3 \end{bmatrix} = \begin{bmatrix} 2 \\ 5 \end{bmatrix}$$

The rows of the Hadamard transformation matrix can thus be considered basis vectors with the components of the vector Y being coefficients of these vectors so that the vector

$$X = \frac{7}{\sqrt{2}}\left(\frac{1}{\sqrt{2}}\begin{bmatrix} 1 \\ 1 \end{bmatrix}\right) - \frac{3}{\sqrt{2}}\left(\frac{1}{\sqrt{2}}\begin{bmatrix} 1 \\ -1 \end{bmatrix}\right)$$

That is, X is a composition of basis vectors weighted with the coefficients included in the transform Y. Forward transformation of sample vector X (i.e., the process of finding the transform Y) is a process of analysis that consists in finding the components of the sample vector in terms of the basis vectors. The coefficients in Y specify the amount of each component in X. The inverse transformation is the process of synthesis in which the original signal X is reconstructed from the transform coefficients contained in Y. The coefficients specify the amount of each basis vector that has to be included in the reconstructed sample vector X.

If data are now sampled as 2×2 matrices, then the transformation has to be performed either by using a 4×4 transformation matrix, or if the matrix is separable and symmetric, the transformation is performed twice with the same 2×2 transformation matrix: first for rows and then for columns of the sample matrix. Let us consider the second case first. Our task is to find a Hadamard transform for the sample matrix

$$X = \begin{bmatrix} 2 & 3 \\ 5 & -2 \end{bmatrix}$$

that is, to find the matrix

$$Y = \frac{1}{\sqrt{2}}\begin{bmatrix} 1 & 1 \\ 1 & -1 \end{bmatrix}\begin{bmatrix} 2 & 3 \\ 5 & -2 \end{bmatrix}\frac{1}{\sqrt{2}}\begin{bmatrix} 1 & 1 \\ 1 & -1 \end{bmatrix} = \frac{1}{2}\begin{bmatrix} 7 & 1 \\ -3 & 5 \end{bmatrix}\begin{bmatrix} 1 & 1 \\ 1 & -1 \end{bmatrix} = \frac{1}{2}\begin{bmatrix} 8 & 6 \\ 2 & -8 \end{bmatrix}$$

$$= \begin{bmatrix} 4 & 3 \\ 1 & -4 \end{bmatrix}$$

(8.3)

The original sample matrix X can be reconstructed by following the same steps with the roles of X and Y reversed,

$$X = \frac{1}{\sqrt{2}}\begin{bmatrix} 1 & 1 \\ 1 & -1 \end{bmatrix}\begin{bmatrix} 4 & 3 \\ 1 & -4 \end{bmatrix}\frac{1}{\sqrt{2}}\begin{bmatrix} 1 & 1 \\ 1 & -1 \end{bmatrix} = \begin{bmatrix} 2 & 3 \\ 5 & -2 \end{bmatrix}$$

The 2×2 matrix X can be viewed as a point in the four-dimensional space, and thus, it can be represented with a weighted sum of basis vectors of that space. These vectors, to be sure, should also be points in the four-dimensional space. We can use the just-applied 2×2 Hadamard matrix to find these basis vectors. The matrix that consists of two basis vectors was applied twice in the course of finding the transform Y in multiplication. Therefore, we can find the four-dimensional basis vectors by multiplying a horizontally oriented two-dimensional basis vectors by vertically oriented sets of the same vectors, as in Figure 8.5. Again, if the components of the transformed

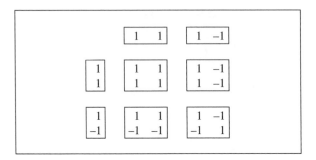

Figure 8.5   Creating four basis matrices using two basis vectors

matrix Y are interpreted as weights for basis vectors, then the matrix X can be decomposed into the sum of four weighted basis matrices,

$$X = \begin{bmatrix} 2 & 3 \\ 5 & -2 \end{bmatrix} = \frac{1}{2}\left(4\begin{bmatrix} 1 & 1 \\ 1 & 1 \end{bmatrix} + 3\begin{bmatrix} 1 & -1 \\ 1 & -1 \end{bmatrix} + 1\begin{bmatrix} 1 & 1 \\ -1 & -1 \end{bmatrix} - 4\begin{bmatrix} 1 & -1 \\ -1 & 1 \end{bmatrix} \right)$$

If the transformation matrix is not separable, then points in the four-dimensional space have to be represented as four-component vectors, and the transformation matrix has to be applied once; therefore, it must be a 4×4 matrix. 2×2 matrices of samples are converted into vertical arrays by stacking all their components on top of one another. For example, our example matrix X turns into a vector $[2 \ 3 \ 5 \ -2]^T$, and the transformation now looks like this

$$Y = \frac{1}{\sqrt{4}}\begin{bmatrix} 1 & 1 & 1 & 1 \\ 1 & -1 & 1 & -1 \\ 1 & 1 & -1 & -1 \\ 1 & -1 & -1 & 1 \end{bmatrix}\begin{bmatrix} 2 \\ 3 \\ 5 \\ -2 \end{bmatrix} = \begin{bmatrix} 4 \\ 3 \\ 1 \\ -4 \end{bmatrix} \tag{8.4}$$

Therefore, the decomposition of X into basis vectors extracted directly from the Hadamard matrix now becomes

$$X = \begin{bmatrix} 2 \\ 3 \\ 5 \\ -2 \end{bmatrix} = \frac{1}{2}\left(4\begin{bmatrix} 1 \\ 1 \\ 1 \\ 1 \end{bmatrix} + 3\begin{bmatrix} 1 \\ -1 \\ 1 \\ -1 \end{bmatrix} + 1\begin{bmatrix} 1 \\ 1 \\ -1 \\ -1 \end{bmatrix} - 4\begin{bmatrix} 1 \\ -1 \\ -1 \\ 1 \end{bmatrix} \right)$$

which is simply another way of representing the same decomposition as with the use of basis matrices.

8.3   The Karhunen-Loève Transform

The transform was proposed by Harold Hotelling (1933) as the *principal component transform* and then developed by Kari Karhunen (1947) and Michel Loève (1948). It is also called the *Hotelling* or *eigenvector transform*. The transform is based on statistical properties of the image, which requires introducing some definitions.

In what follows, we assume that vectors of samples are realizations of a stochastic process. That is, each such vector $[f] = [x_0 \ x_1 \dots x_{N-1}]^T$ is a random event, where components x_k of the vector can be complex or real or just natural numbers, and they are also random. For example, a vector of audio samples after transmission can be distorted by the transmission channel due to electrical noise or atmospheric disturbances, and it cannot be predicted with perfect accuracy what the receiver gets after transmission; however, the average properties of a sequence of such vectors can still be studied.

In the context of data compression, a stream of samples can be divided into blocks so that each block is a vector of sample values. Our aim is to find a way of transmitting these blocks in an uncorrelated form. In the case of images, a sampled image can be divided into a set of M 8×8 blocks resulting in a sequence of blocks $[f^0], \ldots, [f^{M-1}]$, each $[f^k] = [f_{00}^k \; f_{01}^k \ldots, f_{i0}^k \ldots f_{i7}^k \ldots f_{77}^k]^T$ being a vector of 64 samples of block k. The image can also be divided into layers corresponding to, for instance, different basic colors so that $[f^k]$ would be a vector including samples for color c for each pixel of the image.

Definition 8.5   An *average value* of a random vector $X = [x_0 \ldots x_{N-1}]^T$ is defined as

$$E[X] = \overline{X} = \frac{1}{M} \sum_{k=0}^{M-1} X^k$$

where $X^0, \ldots, X^{M-1}$ is a sequence of sample vectors.

Definition 8.6   The *autocorrelation (sparse) matrix* of a random vector X is a matrix $E[XX^T]$.

For a certain sequence of sample vectors $X^0, \ldots, X^{M-1}$, the autocorrelation matrix can be estimated for the random vector X using the formula

$$E[XX^T] = \frac{1}{M} \sum_{k=0}^{M-1} X^k (X^k)^T = \left[\frac{1}{M} \sum_{k=0}^{M-1} X_l^k X_m^k \right]_{lm} \quad \text{for } l, m = 0, \ldots, N-1$$

Definition 8.7   The *covariance matrix* of a discrete variable X is defined as

$$Cov(X) = E[(X - E[X])(X - E[X])^T]$$

For computational purposes, it is more convenient to use a different form of this definition. If we have a sequence of sample vectors $X^0, X^1, \ldots, X^{M-1}$, then

$$Cov(X) = E[(X - \overline{X})(X - \overline{X})^T] = \frac{1}{M} \sum_{k=0}^{M-1} (X^k - \overline{X})(X^k - \overline{X})^T$$

$$= \frac{1}{M} \sum_{k=0}^{M-1} (X^k - \overline{X})((X^k)^T - \overline{X}^T)$$

$$= \frac{1}{M} \sum_{k=0}^{M-1} X^k (X^k)^T - \frac{1}{M} \sum_{k=0}^{M-1} X^k \overline{X}^T - \frac{1}{M} \sum_{k=0}^{M-1} \overline{X}(X^k)^T + \frac{1}{M} \sum_{k=0}^{M-1} \overline{X}\,\overline{X}^T$$

$$= E[XX^T] - \left(\frac{1}{M} \sum_{k=0}^{M-1} X^k \right) \overline{X}^T - \overline{X} \frac{1}{M} \sum_{k=0}^{M-1} (X^k)^T + \frac{1}{M} \sum_{k=0}^{M-1} \overline{X}\,\overline{X}^T$$

$$= E[XX^T] - \overline{X}\,\overline{X}^T - \overline{X}\,\overline{X}^T + \overline{X}\,\overline{X}^T$$

from which we obtain

$$Cov(X) = E[XX^T] - \overline{X}\,\overline{X}^T \tag{8.5}$$

Definition 8.8

The *Karhunen-Loève transform (KLT)* is given by

$$[F] = T[f]$$

where the elements of $T = [\gamma_0 \ldots \gamma_{N-1}]^T$ are the eigenvectors of the covariance matrix $Cov([f])$.

Observe that

$$T\overline{X} = T\frac{1}{M}\sum_{k=0}^{M-1} X^k = \frac{1}{M}\sum_{k=0}^{M-1} TX^k = \overline{TX}$$

Therefore,

$$Cov([f]) = E[[f][f]^T] - \overline{[f]}\,\overline{[f]}^T$$

can be transformed into

$$
\begin{aligned}
T\,Cov([f])T^T &= T\,(E[[f][f]^T] - \overline{[f]}\,\overline{[f]}^T)T^T\\
&= E[T[f][f]^T T^T] - T\overline{[f]}\,\overline{[f]}^T T^T\\
&= E[T[f](T[f])^T] - \overline{T[f]}\,\overline{T[f]}^T
\end{aligned}
$$

which yields

$$Cov([F]) = Cov(T[f]) = E[T[f](T[f])^T] - \overline{T[f]}\,\overline{T[f]}^T = T\,Cov([f])\,T^T$$

Moreover, because the rows of the transformation matrix T are eigenvectors of $Cov(X)$ and an eigenvalue λ_i corresponds to each eigenvector γ_i, we have (see Section 8.8)

$$Cov([f])\gamma_i = \lambda_i\gamma_i$$

and therefore, after all eigenvectors are included, we obtain

$$
\begin{aligned}
Cov([f])T^T &= \lambda_i[\gamma_0 \ldots \gamma_{N-1}] = [\lambda_0\gamma_0 \ldots \lambda_{N-1}\gamma_{N-1}]\\
&= [\gamma_0 \ldots \gamma_{N-1}]\begin{bmatrix} \lambda_0 & \cdots & 0 \\ \vdots & \ddots & \vdots \\ 0 & \cdots & \lambda_{N-1} \end{bmatrix}\\
&= [\gamma_0 \ldots \gamma_{N-1}]\,\mathrm{diag}(\lambda_0, \ldots, \lambda_{N-1})
\end{aligned}
$$

That is,

$$Cov([f])T^T = T^T\mathrm{diag}(\lambda_0, \ldots, \lambda_{N-1})$$

or

$$T\,Cov([f])\,T^T = Cov([F]) = \mathrm{diag}(\lambda_0, \ldots, \lambda_{N-1})$$

where the diagonal matrix $\mathrm{diag}(\lambda_0, \ldots, \lambda_{N-1})$ is composed of eigenvalues of $Cov([f])$ such that each eigenvector γ_i from T corresponds to an eigenvalue λ_i. This means that the vector elements of the transform matrix $[F]$ are *uncorrelated*.

To summarize, the process of finding the transform $[F]$ for a vector of samples $[f]$ goes through the following steps:

- find the covariance matrix $Cov([f])$
- find the eigenvalues and then eigenvectors of $Cov([f])$ and create the transformation matrix T out of normalized eigenvectors
- find the transform vector $[F]$

Example 8.1

Let us transform with the KLT the following matrix of samples

$$X = \begin{bmatrix} 1 & 2 & 1 & 0 \\ 2 & -1 & 1 & 2 \end{bmatrix}$$

Before we start, the matrix is divided into a sequence of blocks, as in

$$[f^0] = \begin{bmatrix} 1 \\ 2 \end{bmatrix}, \; [f^1] = \begin{bmatrix} 2 \\ -1 \end{bmatrix}, \; [f^2] = \begin{bmatrix} 1 \\ 1 \end{bmatrix}, \; [f^3] = \begin{bmatrix} 0 \\ 2 \end{bmatrix}$$

where each $[f^k]$ is considered a realization of a random vector $[f]$. To find the covariance matrix for $[f]$, we use Equation (8.5)

$$\overline{[f]} = \frac{1}{4} \sum_{k=0}^{3} [f^k] = \begin{bmatrix} 1 \\ 1 \end{bmatrix}$$

$$\overline{[f]}\,\overline{[f]}^T = \begin{bmatrix} 1 \\ 1 \end{bmatrix} [1 \; 1] = \begin{bmatrix} 1 & 1 \\ 1 & 1 \end{bmatrix}$$

$$E[[f][f]^T] = \frac{1}{4} \sum_{k=0}^{3} [f^k][f^k]^T$$

$$= \frac{1}{4}\left(\begin{bmatrix} 1 \\ 2 \end{bmatrix} [1 \; 2] + \begin{bmatrix} 2 \\ -1 \end{bmatrix} [2 \; -1] + \begin{bmatrix} 1 \\ 1 \end{bmatrix} [1 \; 1] + \begin{bmatrix} 0 \\ 2 \end{bmatrix} [0 \; 2] \right)$$

$$= \frac{1}{4}\begin{bmatrix} 6 & 1 \\ 1 & 10 \end{bmatrix}$$

$$Cov([f]) = E[[f][f]^T] - \overline{[f]}\,\overline{[f]}^T = \begin{bmatrix} 0.5 & -0.75 \\ -0.75 & 1.5 \end{bmatrix}$$

To find the eigenvalues, we solve the characteristic equation

$$|Cov([f]) - \lambda I| = 0$$

$$\det\left(\begin{bmatrix} 0.5 & -0.75 \\ -0.75 & 1.5 \end{bmatrix} - \lambda \begin{bmatrix} 1 & 0 \\ 0 & 1 \end{bmatrix}\right) = \begin{vmatrix} 0.5 - \lambda & -0.75 \\ -0.75 & 1.5 - \lambda \end{vmatrix}$$

$$= (0.5 - \lambda)(1.5 - \lambda) - 0.5625$$

$$= \lambda^2 - 2\lambda - 0.1875$$

Therefore, $\lambda = 0.0986$, $\lambda_1 = 1.9014$, from which we can find the eigenvectors; the first eigenvector γ_0 is found from the relation

$$(Cov([f]) - \lambda_0 I)\gamma_0 = \begin{bmatrix} 0.4014 & -0.7500 \\ -0.7500 & 1.4014 \end{bmatrix} \begin{bmatrix} \gamma_{00} \\ \gamma_{10} \end{bmatrix} = \begin{bmatrix} 0 \\ 0 \end{bmatrix}$$

so that the eigenvector

$$\gamma_0 = \begin{bmatrix} 1.8685 \\ 1 \end{bmatrix}$$

Similarly,

$$\gamma_1 = \begin{bmatrix} -0.5352 \\ 1 \end{bmatrix}$$

After normalization,

$$\frac{\gamma_0}{\|\gamma_0\|} = \frac{1}{\sqrt{1.8685^2 + 1^2}} \begin{bmatrix} 1.8685 \\ 1 \end{bmatrix} = \begin{bmatrix} 0.8816 \\ 0.4719 \end{bmatrix}$$

Similarly,

$$\frac{\gamma_1}{\|\gamma_1\|} = \begin{bmatrix} -0.4719 \\ 0.8817 \end{bmatrix}$$

This yields the following transformation matrix

$$T = \begin{bmatrix} 0.8816 & 0.4719 \\ -0.4719 & 0.8817 \end{bmatrix}$$

which is orthogonal. That is, $TT^{-1} = TT^T = I$, and the following transform matrices $[F] = T[f]$

$$[F^0] = T[f^0] = \begin{bmatrix} 1.8254 \\ 1.2915 \end{bmatrix}, [F^1] = T[f^1] = \begin{bmatrix} 1.2915 \\ -1.8254 \end{bmatrix},$$

$$[F^2] = T[f^2] = \begin{bmatrix} 1.3535 \\ 0.4098 \end{bmatrix}, [F^3] = T[f^3] = \begin{bmatrix} 0.9438 \\ 1.7634 \end{bmatrix}$$

Thus, the sample matrix X

$$X = \begin{bmatrix} 1 & 2 & 1 & 0 \\ 2 & -1 & 1 & 2 \end{bmatrix}$$

is transformed into the matrix

$$Y = \begin{bmatrix} 1.8254 & 1.2915 & 1.3535 & 0.9438 \\ 1.2915 & -1.8254 & 0.4098 & 1.7634 \end{bmatrix}$$

Because $Cov([F]) = TCov([f])T^T$, we obtain

$$Cov([F]) = \begin{bmatrix} 0.8816 & 0.4719 \\ -0.4719 & 0.8817 \end{bmatrix} \begin{bmatrix} 0.5 & -0.75 \\ -0.75 & 1.5 \end{bmatrix} \begin{bmatrix} 0.8816 & -0.4719 \\ 0.4719 & 0.8817 \end{bmatrix}$$

$$= \begin{bmatrix} 0.9860 & 0.0001 \\ 0.0001 & 1.9015 \end{bmatrix}$$

Note that the diagonal elements are almost equal to the eigenvalues 0.986 and 1.9014 found for the matrix $Cov([f])$, and the nondiagonal elements are almost zeros. The discrepancies are due to rounding to four decimal places. The original values of vectors $[f^k]$ can be recovered by applying the inverse of the transformation matrix $T^{-1} = T^T$ to the transform $[F]$

$$[f^0] = T^T[F^0] = \begin{bmatrix} 0.9998 \\ 2.0001 \end{bmatrix}, [f^1] = T^T[F^1] = \begin{bmatrix} 2.0001 \\ -1.0000 \end{bmatrix}$$

$$[f^2] = T^T[F^2] = \begin{bmatrix} 0.9999 \\ 1.0000 \end{bmatrix}, [f^3] = T^T[F^3] = \begin{bmatrix} -0.0001 \\ 2.0001 \end{bmatrix}$$

By requiring the recalculation of the covariance matrix for each set of samples, the KLT is adaptive and thus optimal; this, however, means that finding it is also slow because no general fast algorithm exists to find the KLT and its inverse. Therefore, for practical purposes, suboptimal transforms are utilized, which diagonalize covariance matrix only approximately, and the KLT is used as a point of reference in assessing the effectiveness of other methods.

8.4   The Hadamard Transform

Definition 8.9   A *Hadamard matrix* is a square matrix composed of numbers 1 and -1, whose rows and columns are mutually orthogonal.

This definition does not place any restriction on the size of Hadamard matrices; however, in the context of image compression, a useful subset of Hadamard matrices are those whose orders are powers of 2.

Definition 8.10 A Hadamard matrix H_{2^n} of order $2^n \times 2^n$ is defined by the following recurrence relation

$$H_1 = [1]$$

$$H_{2n} = \begin{bmatrix} H_n & H_n \\ H_n & -H_n \end{bmatrix}$$

Example 8.2 Here are the first three Hadamard matrices of the kind just defined

$$[1], \begin{bmatrix} 1 & 1 \\ 1 & -1 \end{bmatrix}, \begin{bmatrix} 1 & 1 & 1 & 1 \\ 1 & -1 & 1 & -1 \\ 1 & 1 & -1 & -1 \\ 1 & -1 & -1 & 1 \end{bmatrix}, \dots$$

It can be easily shown that for a Hadamard matrix H_k,

its inverse is proportional to the matrix itself $H_k^{-1} = \frac{1}{k} H_k$

the matrix is symmetric, $H_k^T = H_k$

and orthogonal, $H_k^T H_k = k I_k$

for an identity matrix I_k of order k.

Definition 8.11 A *sequency* is the number of times a sign changes on a given row of a Hadamard matrix.

The concept of sequency, due to Harmuth, corresponds to frequency used in the general description of a transform. Thus, the rows of Hadamard matrices can be viewed as equivalents of rectangular waves, as in Figure 8.6. Such waves are called

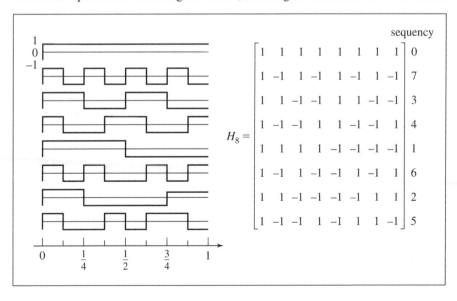

Figure 8.6   Continuous Walsh functions and Hadamard matrix of order 8 reflecting discrete Walsh functions

Walsh functions. Many different orderings of these functions are possible, and the Hadamard matrix shows one such possibility.

Definition 8.12   For a vector $[f] = [x_0 \ x_1 \ldots x_{N-1}]^T$ of $N = 2^n$ real numbers, the one-dimensional *Walsh-Hadamard transform (WHT)* is defined as

$$[F] = \frac{1}{\sqrt{N}} H_N[f] \tag{8.6}$$

where $[F] = [y_0, y_1 \ldots y_{N-1}]^T$ is a vector of the WHT coefficients.

The *inverse Walsh-Hadamard transform* is defined as

$$[f] = \frac{1}{\sqrt{N}} H_N[F]$$

The definition indicates that the Hadamard transform is obtained by using a Hadamard matrix normalized by the inverse of the square root of its order.

Definition 8.13   A two-dimensional $N \times N = 2^n \times 2^n$ *Walsh-Hadamard transform* is given by

$$[F] = \frac{1}{\sqrt{N}} H_N[f] \frac{1}{\sqrt{N}} H_N = \frac{1}{N} H_N[f] H_N$$

and the two-dimensional *inverse WHT* is

$$[f] = \frac{1}{N} H_N[F] H_N$$

Because Hadamard matrices are composed of numbers 1 and -1, no multiplication is necessary in computing WHTs. Except for dividing a result by the normalizing factor, only subtractions and additions can be used: Solving (8.6) requires $O(N^2)$ operations, which can be reduced to $O(N \lg N)$ additions/subtractions (Jain, 1989). Therefore, Hadamard transforms are recommended in situations requiring very fast processing. However, compaction obtained with these transforms is not as good as with other transforms, one reason being that the rows are not ordered by increasing value of sequency.

8.5   The Discrete Fourier Transform

In this and the next sections, only definitions of transforms are presented. The reader interested in justification of these definitions should refer to Chapter 12.

Definition 8.14   The one-dimensional *forward discrete Fourier transform (DFT)* of the sequence $f(0), \ldots, f(N-1)$ is defined as a sequence $F(0), \ldots, F(N-1)$, where

$$F(k) = \frac{1}{\sqrt{N}} \sum_{m=0}^{N-1} f(m) e^{-i2\pi km/N}, \text{ for } k = 0, 1, \ldots, N-1$$

and the *inverse discrete Fourier transform* is defined as

$$f(m) = \frac{1}{\sqrt{N}} \sum_{k=0}^{N-1} F(k) \, e^{i2\pi km/N}, \text{ for } m = 0, 1, \ldots, N-1$$

Definition 8.15   The two-dimensional *forward Fourier transform* of the sequence $f(0,0), \ldots, f(N-1, N-1)$ is defined as a sequence $F(0,0), \ldots, F(N-1, N-1)$, where

$$F(k, l) = \frac{1}{N} \sum_{m=0}^{N-1} \sum_{n=0}^{N-1} f(m, n) e^{-i2\pi(km+ln)/N}, \text{ for } k, l = 0, 1, \ldots, N-1$$

and the *inverse Fourier transform* is given by

$$f(m, n) = \frac{1}{N} \sum_{k=0}^{N-1} \sum_{l=0}^{N-1} F(k, l) e^{i2\pi(km+ln)/N}, \text{ for } m, n = 0, 1, \ldots, N-1$$

Transform kernels are both separable and symmetric; for example, for the forward kernel, we have

$$\frac{1}{N} e^{-i2\pi(km+ln)/N} = \frac{1}{\sqrt{N}} e^{-i2\pi km/N} \frac{1}{\sqrt{N}} e^{-i2\pi ln/N}$$

That is, the forward Fourier transform can be expressed in matrix form as

$$[F] = \frac{1}{N} [e^{-i2\pi km/N}][f][e^{-i2\pi ln/N}]$$

for $k, l, m, n = 0, 1, \ldots, N-1$.

The transform F is usually a complex function, although the function f is real. Therefore, in the case of images, N^2 components of the original image are transformed into $2N^2$ components in the transform image so that each spatial frequency of the original has two corresponding components in the transform, namely, real (magnitude or amplitude) and imaginary (phase). However, it is not necessary to transmit all the $2N^2$ components of the transform image since the function F is conjugate symmetric, which in practical terms means that one-half of the transform plane can be reconstructed from another half, and thus, the transform is uniquely defined by N^2 components. Moreover, a fast Fourier transform (FFT) allows for finding the DFT in $O(N \lg N)$ multiplications/additions in the one-dimensional case and $O(N^2 \lg N)$ in the two-dimensional case. The method, however, requires that the two-dimensional square matrix of samples is of size 2^n for a positive integer n.

Because the DFT transformation kernel is periodic, the DFT is subject to the *Gibbs phenomenon* (*aliasing* or *edge effect*) by producing sharp discontinuities at the block boundaries (for a discussion of this phenomenon, see Chapter 12). This is the result of an abrupt truncation of the infinite Fourier series. One way of solving the problem is by using another transform, the DCT.

8.6 The Discrete Cosine Transform

The discrete cosine transform (DCT) was introduced by Ahmed, Natarajan, and Rao in 1974.

Definition 8.16

The *forward discrete cosine transform* (*FDCT*) of the sequence of samples $f(0), \ldots, f(N-1)$ is defined as a sequence $F(0), \ldots, F(N-1)$, where

$$F(0) = \frac{1}{\sqrt{N}} \sum_{k=0}^{N-1} f(k)$$

$$F(m) = \sqrt{\frac{2}{N}} \sum_{k=0}^{N-1} f(k) \cos \frac{2\pi m(2k+1)}{4N} \text{ for } m = 1, 2, \ldots, N-1$$

and $F(m)$ are the DCT coefficients.

The *inverse discrete cosine transform (IDCT)* is defined as

$$f(k) = \frac{1}{\sqrt{N}} F(0) + \sqrt{\frac{2}{N}} \sum_{m=1}^{N-1} F(m) \cos \frac{2\pi m(2k+1)}{4N} \text{ for } k = 0, 1, \ldots, N-1$$

Definition 8.17

The two-dimensional forward discrete cosine transform of the sequence $f(0, 0), \ldots,$ $f(N-1, N-1)$ is defined as a sequence $F(0, 0), \ldots, F(N-1, N-1)$ where

$$F(m, n) = \frac{2}{N} C(m)C(n) \sum_{k=0}^{N-1} \sum_{l=0}^{N-1} f(k, l) \cos \frac{\pi m(2k+1)}{4N} \cos \frac{\pi n(2l+1)}{4N}$$

for $m, n = 0, 1, \ldots, N-1$ and the corresponding inverse discrete cosine transform is

$$f(k, l) = \frac{2}{N} \sum_{m=0}^{N-1} C(m) \sum_{n=0}^{N-1} C(n) F(m, n) \cos \frac{\pi m(2k+1)}{4N} \cos \frac{\pi n(2l+1)}{4N}$$

for $k, l = 0, 1, \ldots, N-1$ where

$$C(v) = \begin{cases} \frac{1}{\sqrt{2}} & \text{for } v = 0 \\ 1 & \text{otherwise} \end{cases} \tag{8.7}$$

The cosine transformation has a good variation distribution and a low rate of distortion function, which results in an efficient energy compaction. It turns out that the transform coefficients with the largest variances are contained in approximately 25% of the transformed matrix, which is about the same as for the KLT.

8.7   The Discrete Wavelet Transform

Definition 8.18

The one-dimensional *forward discrete wavelet transform (DWT)* of the sequence $f(0), \ldots, f(N-1)$ is defined as

$$F(j, k) = \int_{-\infty}^{\infty} f(x) \psi_{j,k}(x) dx$$

where wavelet function

$$\psi_{j,k}(x) = a_0^{-j/2} \psi(a_0^{-j} x - k\tau_0)$$

for a real-valued function ψ called the *basic wavelet* and constants a_0 and τ_0 that determine sampling intervals. The function f is reconstructed with the formula

$$f(x) = \sum_{j=-\infty}^{\infty} \sum_{k=-\infty}^{\infty} F(j, k) \psi_{j,k}(x)$$

Definition 8.18 is of little practical value. Discrete wavelet transform used in practical applications is the result of an algorithm resulting from multiresolution theory and is presented and exemplified in Chapter 13.

Because of the popularity of DCT and the importance that DWT has acquired in recent years, it is interesting to compare their performance. We have to realize, however, that transforms are used as parts of larger systems. For example, JPEG discussed in Chapter 10 uses DCT in conjunction with quantization and entropy coding. Comparison of performance of systems for compression of still images and video sequences shows that the difference in performance is primarily the result of using different quantizers and entropy coders rather than different transforms. The loss in performance for using DCT instead of DWT for still images is very small, about 1 dB, and for video coding it is even smaller, about 0.5 dB (Xiong et al., 1999).

8.8 Appendix: Matrices

An $N \times M$ matrix is a structure composed of N rows and M columns

$$A = [a_{ij}] = \begin{bmatrix} a_{11} & a_{12} & \cdots & a_{1M} \\ a_{21} & a_{22} & \cdots & a_{2M} \\ \vdots & \vdots & & \vdots \\ a_{N1} & a_{N2} & \cdots & a_{NM} \end{bmatrix}$$

Two $N \times M$ matrices are added by adding their corresponding elements; for example,

$$\begin{bmatrix} a & b & c \\ d & e & f \end{bmatrix} + \begin{bmatrix} p & q & r \\ s & t & u \end{bmatrix} = \begin{bmatrix} a+p & b+q & c+r \\ d+s & e+t & f+u \end{bmatrix}$$

Multiplying a scalar by a matrix translates into multiplying each member of the matrix by this scalar; for instance

$$s \begin{bmatrix} a & b \\ c & d \end{bmatrix} = \begin{bmatrix} as & bs \\ cs & ds \end{bmatrix}$$

The multiplication of a $1 \times M$ row vector by an $M \times 1$ column vector is defined as

$$[r_{11}\, r_{12} \ldots r_{1M}] \begin{bmatrix} c_{11} \\ c_{21} \\ \vdots \\ c_{M1} \end{bmatrix} = r_{11}c_{11} + r_{12}c_{12} + \ldots + r_{M1}c_{M1}$$

The multiplication of an $N \times M$ matrix A by an $M \times P$ matrix B is an $N \times P$ matrix C in which each element c_{ij} is the product of the row i of A and the column j of B; that is,

$$c_{ij} = \sum_{k=1}^{M} a_{ik}b_{kj}$$

For example,

$$\begin{bmatrix} a & b & c & d \\ e & f & g & h \\ i & j & k & l \end{bmatrix} \begin{bmatrix} p & q \\ r & s \\ t & u \\ v & w \end{bmatrix} = \begin{bmatrix} ap+br+ct+dv & aq+bs+cu+dw \\ ep+fr+gt+hv & eq+fs+gu+hw \\ ip+jr+kt+lv & iq+js+ku+lw \end{bmatrix}$$

A *diagonal matrix* is an $N \times N$ square matrix with all elements outside the diagonal equal to zero. An *identity matrix I* is an $N \times N$ diagonal matrix with all diagonal elements equal to one. A square matrix A is *symmetric*, if for all i and j, $a_{ij} = a_{ji}$. That is, in the symmetric matrix, elements on one side of the diagonal are mirror images of elements on the other side.

A matrix A is *invertible* if there exists a matrix A^{-1}, called *inverse of A*, such that

$$A^{-1}A = AA^{-1} = I$$

A *transpose* A^T of a matrix A is the matrix obtained from A by interchanging its rows with columns. For example,

$$A = \begin{bmatrix} a & b & c \\ d & e & f \\ g & h & i \end{bmatrix} \text{ and } A^T = \begin{bmatrix} a & d & g \\ b & e & h \\ c & f & i \end{bmatrix}$$

The *determinant* of matrix A can be defined as follows

$$\det [a] = a$$

$$\det A = a_{i1}(-1)^{i+1}\det M_{i1} + a_{i2}(-1)^{i+2}\det M_{i2} + \ldots + a_{in}(-1)^{i+n}\det M_{in}$$

where the matrix M_{ij}, called a *minor*, is formed by deleting the row i and column j from matrix A. For example,

$$\det \begin{bmatrix} a & b \\ c & d \end{bmatrix} = \begin{vmatrix} a & b \\ c & d \end{vmatrix} = a|d| - b|c| = ad - bc$$

$$\det \begin{bmatrix} a & b & c \\ d & e & f \\ g & h & i \end{bmatrix} = \begin{vmatrix} a & b & c \\ d & e & f \\ g & h & i \end{vmatrix} = a\begin{vmatrix} e & f \\ h & i \end{vmatrix} - b\begin{vmatrix} d & f \\ g & i \end{vmatrix} + c\begin{vmatrix} d & e \\ g & h \end{vmatrix}$$

$$= a(ei - fh) - b(di - fg) + c(dh - eg)$$
$$= aei + bfg + cdh - afh - bdi - ceg$$

Eigenvalues (characteristic values) of a square matrix A are the roots of the polynomial of degree n in λ, called the *characteristic equation* of the matrix A,

$$|A - \lambda I| = 0$$

For example, for the matrix $A = \begin{bmatrix} 1 & 2 \\ 3 & -4 \end{bmatrix}$,

$$\det \left(\begin{bmatrix} 1 & 2 \\ 3 & -4 \end{bmatrix} - \lambda \begin{bmatrix} 1 & 0 \\ 0 & 1 \end{bmatrix} \right) = \begin{vmatrix} 1 - \lambda & 2 \\ 3 & -4 - \lambda \end{vmatrix}$$
$$= (1 - \lambda)(-4 - \lambda) - 6 = \lambda^2 + 3\lambda - 10$$

the characteristic polynomial $\lambda^2 + 3\lambda - 10 = (\lambda - 2)(\lambda + 5)$, and the matrix has two eigenvalues, $\lambda_1 = 2$ and $\lambda_2 = -5$.

Eigenvectors (characteristic vectors) of a square matrix A are the vectors x_i that for the eigenvalues λ_i of the matrix A satisfy the equation

$$\lambda_i x_i = A x_i$$

That is,

$$(A - \lambda_i I)x_i = 0$$

For our matrix A and the first eigenvalue $\lambda_1 = 2$,

$$(A - \lambda_1 I)x_1 = \begin{bmatrix} -1 & 2 \\ 3 & -6 \end{bmatrix} \begin{bmatrix} x \\ y \end{bmatrix} = \begin{bmatrix} 0 \\ 0 \end{bmatrix}$$

for which any multiple of $\begin{bmatrix} 2 \\ 1 \end{bmatrix}$ is a solution; for the second eigenvalue $\lambda_2 = -5$, we have

$$(A - \lambda_2 I)x_2 = \begin{bmatrix} 6 & 2 \\ 3 & 1 \end{bmatrix} \begin{bmatrix} x \\ y \end{bmatrix} = \begin{bmatrix} 0 \\ 0 \end{bmatrix}$$

for which any multiple of $\begin{bmatrix} 1 \\ -3 \end{bmatrix}$ is a solution.

The length of a column vector v is defined as

$$\|v\| = \sqrt{|v_1|^2 + |v_2|^2 + \ldots + |v_M|^2}$$

Two column vectors x, y are *orthogonal* (*perpendicular*) if their scalar product is zero; that is, if

$$x_1 y_1 + x_2 y_2 + \ldots + x_M y_M = 0$$

A vector is *normalized* if it is of length 1; that is, if $\|v\| = 1$. The vector can be normalized by dividing it by its own length; that is, it can be replaced by $\frac{v}{\|v\|}$. Two normalized and orthogonal vectors x, y are *orthonormal*.

If the columns of a square matrix are orthonormal, then the matrix is called *orthogonal* (not orthonormal!). That is, for an orthogonal matrix A,

$$A^T A = A A^T = I$$

$$A^T = A^{-1}$$

Here are some relationships:

$$AI = IA = A$$

$$(AB)^T = B^T A^T$$

$$(AB)^{-1} = B^{-1} A^{-1}$$

$$(A^{-1})^T = (A^T)^{-1}$$

$$\det I = 1$$

$$\det AB = \det A \det B$$

$$\det A^T = \det A$$

A set of vectors $v_1, \ldots, v_k$ is *linearly independent* if

$$c_1 v_1 + \ldots + c_k v_k = 0$$

only if all the coefficients $c_1, \ldots, c_k$ are 0. If any other vector v is a liner combination of $v_1, \ldots, v_k$, that is,

$$v = x_1 v_1 + \ldots + x_k v_k$$

then the vectors $v_1, \ldots, v_k$ are called *basis* of a vector space of which v is an element, or *basis vectors*.

EXERCISES

1. In what respect is a transformation obtained with the logarithm function (Figure 8.1) different from the definition of transformation 8.1?

2. Exactly how many additions and multiplications are performed in (8.3) and (8.4)? Generalize your findings to the case when Y in (8.3) is an $N \times N$ square matrix to

confirm the statement that using separable transforms reduces the number of operations from $O(N^4)$ to $O(N^3)$.

3. Define the one-dimensional forward and inverse DCTs in terms of $C(v)$ given in (8.7).

4. Find the Hadamard and cosine transforms for $[1 \ 1 \ 1 \ 1]^T$, $[2 \ 1 \ 3 \ 2]^T$, $[10 \ 1 \ 8 \ -5]^T$, and then for the same samples arranged as 2×2 matrices—that is, $\begin{bmatrix} 1 & 1 \\ 1 & 1 \end{bmatrix}$, $\begin{bmatrix} 2 & 1 \\ 3 & 2 \end{bmatrix}$, $\begin{bmatrix} 10 & 1 \\ 8 & -5 \end{bmatrix}$. Are there any differences between one-dimensional and two-dimensional transforms for the same samples? If yes, what is the reason? Find also the inverse transforms.

BIBLIOGRAPHY

Ahmed, Nasir, Natarajan, T., and Rao, K. R., Discrete cosine transform, *IEEE Transactions on Computers* C-23 (1974), 90–93 [also in Rao, 1990].

Ahmed, Nasir, and Rao, Kamisetty R., *Orthogonal transforms for digital signal processing*, New York: Springer, 1975.

Gonzalez, Rafael C., and Wintz, Paul, *Digital image processing*, Reading, MA: Addison-Wesley, 1987.

Hadamard, Jacques, Résolution d'une question relative aux determinants, *Bulletin des Sciences Mathématiques et Astronomiques*, ser. 2, 17 (1893), 240-246 [also in Hadamard's *Oeuvres*, Paris: CNRS, 1968, v. 1, 239–245].

Hall, Ernest L., *Computer image processing and recognition*, New York: Academic Press, 1979.

Harmuth, H. F., A generalized concept of frequency and some applications, *IEEE Transactions on Information Theory* IT-14 (1968), 375–382.

Hotelling, Harold, Analysis of a complex of statistical variables into principal components, *Journal of Educational Psychology* 24 (1933), 417–441, 498–520.

Jain, Anil K., *Fundamentals of digital image processing*, Englewood Cliffs, NJ: Prentice Hall, 1989.

Karhunen, Kari, *Über lineare Methoden in der Wahrscheindlichkeitsrechnung*, Helsinki: Kirjapaino, 1947 [transl. by I. Selin, *On linear methods in probability theory*, T-131, 1960, RAND Corp.].

Loève, M[ichel], Functions aléatoires du seconde ordre, in Paul Lévy, *Processus stochastiques et mouvement brownien*, Paris: Hermann, 1965 [1948], 367–420.

Rao, K. Ramamohan (ed.), *Discrete transforms and their applications*, Malabar: Krieger 1990.

Rao, K. R., and Yip, P., *Discrete cosine transform: Algorithms, advantages, applications*, Boston: Academic Press, 1990.

Rosenfeld, Azriel, and Kak, Avinash C., *Digital picture processing*, New York: Academic Press, 1982.

Walsh, J. L., A closed set of normal orthogonal functions, *American Journal of Mathematics* 55 (1923), 5–24.

Xiong, Zixiang, Ramchandran, Kannan, Orchard, Michael T., and Zhang, Ya-Qin, A comparative study of DCT- and wavelet-based image coding, *IEEE Transactions on Circuits and Systems for Video Technology* 9 (1999), 692–695.

Chapter 9

Subband Coding

Subband coding encompasses a class of encoding algorithms that decompose the input signal into several frequency components, or *subbands*, and then encode these components separately. The subbands are generated by using a bank of filters, with each filter passing signals of a specified frequency range (Figure 9.1). The encoder's filter bank is called an *analysis bank*. The division into subbands does not by itself accomplish any compression, but because statistical characteristics of the subbands are different, each subband can be controlled separately; each subband is encoded differently and thus more efficiently than the original signal. The receiver uses a filter bank, called a *synthesis bank*, to re-create the original samples as closely as possible.

All subbands can be of the same width $W_k = W/M$, where W is the total bandwidth and M is the number of subbands. They can also be of variable width, making low-frequency subbands narrower than high-frequency subbands. Such an arrangement is important for audio signals and for images because in these cases, lower frequencies are well preserved and these frequencies are more important for hearing and viewing these signals. However, even in these cases, the same widths can be used for

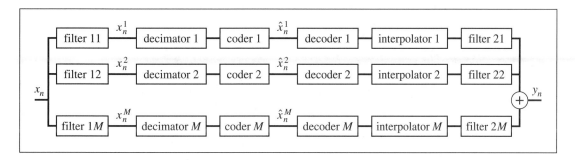

Figure 9.1 The subband coding system

all subbands, but lower frequency subbands can be allocated more bits, whereby they have more quantization levels and the signals in these subbands would be a finer-grained representation than in other subbands.

9.1 Filters

The first phase in subband coding is the division of a broad range of spectral content into separate bands. To that end, filters that can be either analog or digital are used. However, in digital signal processing, digital filters are usually used.

Generally, digital filters are linear combinations of data.

Example 9.1

A *moving average filter* is a filter used to eliminate noise from data by averaging them. A simple example of such a filter is defined as

$$y_n = \frac{1}{2}(x_{n-1} + x_n)$$

which is a filter that averages the previous and the current sample. Consider the temperature measurements taken over some period of time. A possible noise can be filtered out from the measurements by averaging the neighboring temperatures, whereby a general trend in the temperature change can be more visible, as in Figure 9.2.

The filter from Example 9.1 can be generalized, first, to allow for averaging any number of samples, as in

$$y_n = \frac{1}{N}(x_{n-N+1} + \ldots + x_n)$$

Second, it can be generalized to a filter that allows taking into account not only past samples but also future samples. If the data are stored in a file, this does not pose any problem. Third, generalization can go in the direction of allowing any weights, as in

$$y_n = h_{n-N+1}x_{n-N+1} + \ldots + h_n x_n + \ldots + h_{n+M}x_{n+M} \tag{9.1}$$

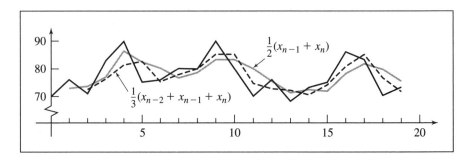

Figure 9.2 Eliminating noise from temperature samples

Although the form (9.1) gives a definition of a filter, it may be the last step in defining it because the coefficients h_k may not be known to start with. Very often, we are interested in defining filters that allow for separating various frequencies. These frequencies are known first, and then the task in designing a filter is to find proper coefficients so that the output of the filter at least approximates the initial requirements. The task is far from simple.

Equation (9.1) is defined in the time domain, but filter specifications are very often given in the frequency domain. Therefore, these specifications have to be translated into the time domain using a *transfer function*. The transfer function H is 2π-periodic; thus, analysis of this function can be restricted to this period, which customarily is the interval $[-\pi, \pi]$. This interval is usually narrowed down to its non-negative part $[0, \pi]$.

Example 9.2

Consider a filter defined as

$$y_n = a x_{n-1} + b x_n + a x_{n+1} \tag{9.2}$$

for which the transfer function (Hamming, 1989)

$$H(2\pi f) = 2a \cos 2\pi f + b \tag{9.3}$$

The graph of H is shown in Figure 9.3a. We want to construct a low-pass filter that passes the signal with frequency $\frac{1}{8}$ and blocks the signal with frequency $\frac{3}{8}$. This filter has the following two conditions imposed on the transfer function:

$$H\left(2\pi \frac{1}{8}\right) = 1 \quad \text{and} \quad H\left(2\pi \frac{3}{8}\right) = 0$$

From this and from (9.3), we find

$$a = \frac{\sqrt{2}}{4}, b = \frac{1}{2}$$

so that

$$H(2\pi f) = \frac{\sqrt{2}}{2} \cos 2\pi f + \frac{1}{2}$$

The graph of the transfer function in Figure 9.3a does indicate that, for the low frequency $\frac{1}{8}$, H is 1 and it is 0 for $f = \frac{3}{8}$. Now we need a formula showing how the filter influences signals (i.e., a formula for x_n that corresponds to a particular frequency). This can be done using $\cos(2\pi f n)$ so that the function

$$\cos\left(2\pi \frac{1}{8} n\right) = \cos\left(\frac{\pi n}{4}\right)$$

generates data that correspond to the frequency $\frac{1}{8}$, and the function

$$\cos\left(2\pi \frac{3}{8} n\right) = \cos\left(\frac{3\pi n}{4}\right)$$

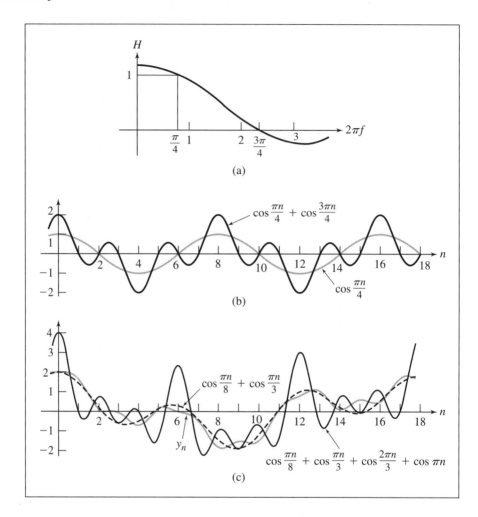

Figure 9.3   **(a) The graph of the transfer function $H(2\pi f) = \frac{\sqrt{2}}{2}\cos 2\pi f + \frac{1}{2}$ from Example 9.2; (b) applying the low-pass filter from Example 9.2 to the samples $x_n = \cos\left(\frac{\pi n}{4}\right) + \cos\left(\frac{3\pi n}{4}\right)$, and (c) to the samples $x_n = \cos\left(\frac{\pi n}{8}\right) + \cos\left(\frac{\pi n}{3}\right) + \cos\left(\frac{2\pi n}{3}\right) + \cos\left(\pi n\right)$**

can be used to sample the data corresponding to frequency $\frac{3}{8}$. To see how the filter works, let us use data defined as

$$x_n = \cos\left(\frac{\pi n}{4}\right) + \cos\left(\frac{3\pi n}{4}\right)$$

that is, data defined as the sum of both low- and high-frequency samples. After substituting the new values for a and b in (9.2), we have the formula for the filter

$$y_n = \frac{\sqrt{2}}{4}(x_{n-1} + x_{n+1}) + \frac{1}{2}x_n$$

The functions x_n and y_n are both plotted in Figure 9.3b. Note that the plot of the filter y_n is identical to the graph of the function $\cos\left(\frac{\pi n}{4}\right)$; that is, the filter does pass the data of low frequency and blocks the data of high frequency. It should be emphasized that the plots in Figure 9.3b–c are drawn for continuous time to show clearly the changes of the functions x_n and y_n, although these functions are defined only for discrete time—that is, only for the time points $n \in \{0, 1, 2 \ldots\}$.

The characteristics of the filter (9.2) were developed with frequencies $\frac{1}{8}$ and $\frac{3}{8}$ in mind. What happens if samples include other frequencies? The graph of the transfer function H indicates that low frequencies will be retained in a somewhat distorted form, and high frequencies will be to a considerable extent eliminated. For example, for frequency $\frac{1}{16}$, $H\left(2\pi\frac{1}{16}\right) = 1.153$; that is, the presence of this frequency is magnified by some 15%. On the other hand, for a high frequency $\frac{1}{3}$, $H\left(2\pi\frac{1}{3}\right) = .146$; that is, some traces of this frequency, about 15%, are retained. To see this, consider samples defined by

$$x_n = \cos\left(\frac{\pi n}{8}\right) + \cos\left(\frac{\pi n}{3}\right) + \cos\left(\frac{2\pi n}{3}\right) + \cos\left(\pi n\right)$$

As shown in Figure 9.3c, the filter (9.2) gives an output that is very close to the graph of the low frequencies

$$\cos\left(\frac{\pi n}{8}\right) + \cos\left(\frac{\pi n}{3}\right)$$

9.2   Downsampling and Upsampling

In subband coding, each subband includes only a fraction of frequencies from the entire range of frequencies for samples x_n. The samples are sampled at the rate proper for the entire range so that aliasing does not take place. The same sampling rate, however, is not necessary for the subbands because the range of frequencies they include is limited. If only two subbands are used, then each subband includes half of all frequencies. Therefore, the sampling rate can be reduced to half of that used to collect the original samples. For M subbands, usually $1/M$ of the original sampling rate is needed for each subband. If the sampling rate is not reduced, then for M subbands, NM samples would have to be processed for all the subbands, where N is the number of samples before dividing frequencies into subbands. To have only N samples after subbands have been created, only every Mth sample is retained in each subband. The process of retaining only every Mth sample is called *downsampling, subsampling*, or *decimating*.

The receiver of samples belonging to separate subbands wants to re-create the original samples. The re-creation consists in adding corresponding samples from particular subbands. But this addition would render only $1/M$ of the original samples. Therefore, the addition is preceded by expanding the number of samples in each subband to N. This process is called *upsampling* or *oversampling* followed by *interpolation*. Both processes are summarized in Figure 9.4.

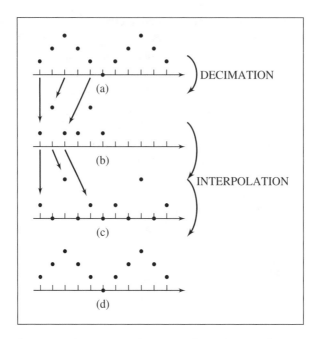

Figure 9.4   The summary of downsampling and upsampling

9.3   Bit Allocation

In bit allocation, the problem is to allocate bits to subbands using a given number of bits so that the overall distortion is minimized. Assume that the input is divided into M subbands of equal size and that the subbands are not overlapping. Thus, the overall distortion is equal to the sum of distortions of all quantizers. If R_k is the number of bits allocated to the subband k to encode samples in this subband and R is the average bit rate per input sample

$$R = \frac{1}{M} \sum_{k=1}^{M} R_k \tag{9.4}$$

then the problem consists of minimizing

$$\sigma_r^2 = \sum_{k=1}^{M} \sigma_{r_k}^2$$

where σ_r^2 is the reconstruction error variance of samples $x_1, \ldots, x_N$,

$$\sigma_r^2 = \frac{1}{N} \sum_{k=1}^{N} (x_k - y_k)^2$$

and y_k is a receiver's reconstruction of a sample x_k. The quantizers' performance can be given (see Exercise 9.3) by the quantization error variance

$$\sigma_q^2 = \varepsilon 2^{-2R} \sigma_x^2$$

for some *quantizer performance factor* ε that depends on the probability distribution and input signal variance σ_x^2. Also,

$$\sigma_q^2 = \frac{1}{N} \sum_{k=1}^{N} (x_k - \hat{x}_k)^2$$

Therefore, assuming that the transmission is error-free, the reconstruction error variance is equal to the quantization error variance, and the total reconstruction error

$$\sigma_r^2 = \sum_{k=1}^{M} \sigma_{r_k}^2 = \sum_{k=1}^{M} \varepsilon 2^{-2R_k} \sigma_{xr_k}^2$$

It is assumed that the factor ε is the same for all subbands. In terms of Lagrange multipliers, the problem is now to solve

$$\frac{\partial}{\partial R_k} \left(\varepsilon \sum_{k=1}^{M} 2^{-2R_k} \sigma_{xr_k}^2 - \lambda \left(R - \frac{1}{M} \sum_{k=1}^{M} R_k \right) \right) = 0$$

from which we obtain

$$R_k = \frac{1}{2} \lg \left(2M\varepsilon \sigma_{xr_k}^2 \ln 2 \right) - \frac{1}{2} \lg \lambda \tag{9.5}$$

This is used to find λ from (9.4),

$$\lambda = \left(\prod_{k=1}^{M} 2\varepsilon M \sigma_{xr_k}^2 \ln 2 \right)^{1/M} 2^{-2R}$$

from which and from (9.5) we have the optimum bit allocation given by

$$R_k = R + \frac{1}{2} \lg \left(\sigma_{xr_k}^2 \Big/ \left(\prod_{k=1}^{M} \sigma_{xr_k}^2 \right)^{1/M} \right) \tag{9.6}$$

Example 9.3   For two subbands, when $M = 2$, we have

$$R_1 = R + \frac{1}{2} \lg \left(\sigma_{xr_1} / \sigma_{xr_2} \right)$$

$$R_2 = R + \frac{1}{2} \lg \left(\sigma_{xr_2} / \sigma_{xr_1} \right) = R - \frac{1}{2} \lg \left(\sigma_{xr_1} / \sigma_{xr_2} \right)$$

It is clear that if the variance of samples in the first subband is greater than in the second subband, $\sigma_{xr_1} > \sigma_{xr_2}$—that is, if the spread of the samples in the first subband is greater than in the second—then more bits are allocated to the first subband than to the second (Figure 9.5).

This example indicates that formula (9.6) allows for noninteger and for negative bit rates, which should not be permitted. In the case of negative values, zero bits are allocated to the corresponding subbands; in our example, $R_2 = 0$. But if the bit rate is increased to zero, then rates of other subbands have to be adjusted so that the average rate R for all subbands remains the same; in our example, $R_1 = 1.5$.

To guarantee an integer bit assignment, a simple algorithm can be used which assigns one bit at a time to the most needy subband (Gersho and Gray, 1992). In each

R	σ_{xr_1}	σ_{xr_2}	R_1	R_2
1.5	20	10	2	1
1.5	20	5	2.5	0.5
1.5	20	2.5	1.5	0
1.5	20	1.25	1.75	−0.5

Figure 9.5   Example values for two subbands

iteration, the algorithm finds the subband with maximum distortion (variance) and assigns to it one bit out of currently available R bits. It does this until all the bits are spent, as shown in this pseudocode:

```
IntegerBitAllocation()
    while R > 0
        find the maximum variance σ²_rk;
        increment the number of bits allocated to subband k;
        decrement R;
```

The algorithm is not optimal, but it gives good solutions.

EXERCISES

1. Apply the moving average filter defined as

$$y_n = \frac{1}{3}(x_{n-2} + x_{n-1} + x_n)$$

to the data in Figure 9.2. What is the output of the filter in comparison with the output in Figure 9.2? What would be the output for the filter averaging N samples?

2. For the filter in Example 9.2, draw a graph of the transfer function when the conditions are
   (a) $H(2\pi 0) = 1$ and $H(2\pi \frac{1}{2}) = 0$
   (b) $H(2\pi \frac{1}{8}) = 1$ and $H(2\pi \frac{1}{4}) = 0$
   (c) $H(2\pi \frac{3}{8}) = 1$ and $H(2\pi \frac{1}{8}) = 0$

3. Show that for a uniform quantizer, the input variance $\sigma_x^2 = \frac{(b-a)}{12}$ and thus $D = \sigma_q^2 = 2^{-2R}\sigma_x^2$. Use the equality $R = \lceil \lg M \rceil$ (give the reason for it).

4. Using formula (9.6), find $R_1, \ldots, R_4$, if $R = 4$, $\sigma_{xr_4}^2 = 1$, and
   (a) $\sigma_{xr_1}^2 = 2\sigma_{xr_2}^2 = 8\sigma_{xr_3}^2 = 16\sigma_{xr_4}^2$
   (b) $\sigma_{xr_1}^2 = 2\sigma_{xr_2}^2 = 4\sigma_{xr_3}^2 = 8\sigma_{xr_4}^2$
   (b) $\sigma_{xr_1}^2 = 4\sigma_{xr_2}^2 = 16\sigma_{xr_3}^2 = 64\sigma_{xr_4}^2$

5. A bit allocation technique presented in Section 9.3 can render fractional bit sizes. To be sure, each sample can be assigned an integer amount of bits. How can the problem of fractional bit sizes be tackled?

BIBLIOGRAPHY

Crochiere, R. E., Sub-band coding, *Bell System Technical Journal* 60 (1981), 1633–1653.

Crochiere, R. E., Webber, S. A., and Flanagan, J. L., Digital coding of speech in subbands, *IEEE International Conference on Acoustics, Speech, and System Processing* (1976), 233–236.

Gersho, Allen, and Gray, Robert M., *Vector quantization and signal compression*, Boston: Kluwer, 1992.

Hamming, Richard W., *Digital filters*, Englewood Cliffs, NJ: Prentice Hall, 1989.

Vaidyanathan, P. P., *Multirate systems and filter banks*, Englewood Cliffs, NJ: Prentice Hall, 1993.

Woods, John W. (ed.), *Subband image coding*, Boston: Kluwer, 1991.

Woods, John W., and O'Neill, Sean, Subband coding of images, *Transactions on Acoustics, Speech, and System Processing* ASSP-34 (1986), 1278–1288.

Chapter 10

Compression of Still Images: JPEG

In 1986, the Joint Photographic Experts Group (JPEG) was formed to standardize algorithms for compression of still images, both monochrome and color. JPEG is a collaborative enterprise between ISO (International Organization for Standardization) and CCITT (Comité Consultatif International de Téléphonie et Télégraphie), and the standard proposed by the committee was published in 1991. The standard is applied to still images, and thereby, it attempts to remove redundancy by using intrapicture coding (i.e., within one picture). The JPEG standard is typically applied to photos, newspaper pictures, computer graphics archiving and transmission over the Web, medical images, satellite weather and surveillance images, and the like.

JPEG defines two classes of encoding and decoding processes, namely, lossy and lossless. The lossy processes are based on the discrete cosine transform (DCT), which allows for a significant compression of images. Images can be compressed by the factor of 20 or more at the price of some distortion of the reconstructed image. The simplest process of this type is the baseline sequential process.

In the lossless processes, the decompressed image should be exactly the same as the image being compressed, and no information should be lost during the compression/decompression process. Processes of that type are not based on the DCT, but rather on some form of differential pulse code modulation (DPCM). The compression ratio is less impressive than in lossy compression, since with lossless techniques, the images are compressed by about 2:1.

JPEG defines four modes of operation and their variants:

1. sequential DCT-based mode
   a. baseline system
   b. extended sequential system
2. progressive DCT-based mode
   a. spectral selection
   b. successive approximation
3. sequential lossless mode
4. hierarchical mode

The first two modes are lossy, and the last can be an extension of a lossy, DCT-based mode or of a lossless mode. In the following sections, we discuss in some detail the baseline system and then briefly present other operation modes.

10.1   The Baseline System

Figure 10.1 presents the major steps of the DCT-based encoding. An image is a large array of pixels, and because of the sheer number of pixels, not all of them are processed at the same time. First, the image is decomposed into 8×8 blocks of pixels, and then these blocks are submitted to the JPEG system to be compressed one by one. The forward cosine transformation transforms each block into a sequence of 64 numbers called DCT coefficients. These 64 coefficients are then quantized using a quantization table also comprised of 64 numbers. The next step is entropy encoding, which is either Huffman coding that uses a Huffman table or arithmetic coding that uses a conditioning table. These tables allow for modeling the images.

Figure 10.1 also depicts major steps of the decoding process, which is basically the reversal of the encoding procedure.

10.1.1   Source Image Format

A source image is a collection of up to 255 *components*, each component being a two-dimensional array of samples (Figure 10.2). Monochrome or gray-scale images are

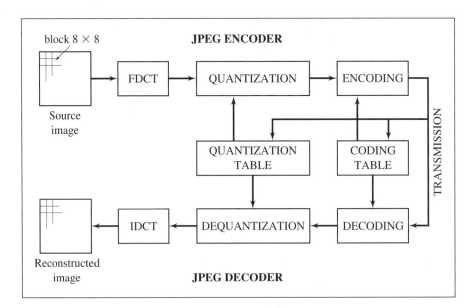

Figure 10.1   The encoding and decoding steps used in JPEG

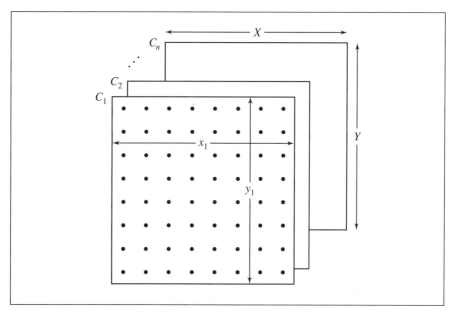

Figure 10.2   A source image with multiple components

composed of only one component. For color images, at least three different sets of components can be used: three components representing red, green, and blue colors (in the RGB representation); four components for cyan, magenta, yellow, and black colors (in the CMYK representation used in the so-called four-color process); or three components for brightness, hue, and saturation (in the luminance-chrominance representation). Components of an image can be considered its layers into which it can be broken down so that they can be easily processed, and after combining these components, the original image can be reconstructed.

Each image component i is an $x_i \times y_i$ array of pixel samples. The maximum of all x_i values defines the dimension X of the entire image, and similarly, the maximum of all y_i values defines dimension Y of the image.

Each component is characterized by a horizontal sampling factor H_i and a vertical sampling factor V_i. These factors define the number of samples in the ith component relative to the other components of the image. The only allowed values for these factors are the numbers 1, 2, 3, or 4. All the sampling factors and the values X and Y are encoded so that the decoder can reconstruct the dimensions x_i and y_i for each component using the following formulas:

$$x_i = \left\lceil X \times \frac{H_i}{H_{max}} \right\rceil \text{ and } y_i = \left\lceil Y \times \frac{V_i}{V_{max}} \right\rceil$$

where H_{max} and V_{max} are the maximum horizontal and vertical sampling factors among all the components of the image.

Each component is sampled separately, and the sampling rate can, in principle, differ from one component to another. In JPEG, however, each component is made up of 8×8 blocks of samples. Each of these blocks is transformed by the FDCT into a set of 64 DCT coefficients. An input sample is a number from the range 0 to 255, and it represents a shade of gray on the gray scale. However, JPEG uses a zero-shift of the input samples so that the range $[0, 255]$ is shifted to the range $[-128, +127]$. (Generally, a range $[0, 2^P - 1]$ of P-bit numbers is shifted to the range $[-2^{P-1}, +2^{P-1} - 1]$, where P depends on the mode of operation.) Through this shift, the precision requirements in the calculation of DCT are reduced.

10.1.2   DCT-based Coding

After sample blocks are prepared, each block is transformed into an array of the 64 DCT coefficients using the formula

$$F(m, n) = \frac{1}{4} C(m)C(n) \sum_{k=0}^{7} \sum_{l=0}^{7} f(k, l) \cos \frac{\pi m(2k + 1)}{16} \cos \frac{\pi n(2l + 1)}{16}$$

for $m, n = 0, 1, \ldots, 7$. The corresponding formula for the inverse discrete cosine transform is

$$f(k, l) = \frac{1}{4} \sum_{m=0}^{7} C(m) \sum_{n=0}^{7} C(n)F(m, n) \cos \frac{\pi m(2k + 1)}{16} \cos \frac{\pi n(2l + 1)}{16}$$

for $k, l = 0, 1, \ldots, 7$, where $C(v) = 1/\sqrt{2}$ for $v = 0$ and $C(v) = 1$ otherwise.

The round-off and truncation effects in computing the 64 DCT coefficients for each block of samples are implementation dependent. Thus, the quality of the output can differ slightly from one implementation to another.

The coefficient located in the upper left corner of a sample block is called the *DC coefficient*. It gives eight times the average of all the samples of one block; because the DC coefficient = $F(0, 0) = 1/8 \sum_k \sum_l f(k, l)$, it has to be divided by 8 to render the true average. It is also the maximum among all coefficients of the block. The frequency for this coefficient is zero in both dimensions (and hence its name, DC for direct current). The remaining 63 coefficients are called *AC coefficients*. The frequency for these coefficients is nonzero in at least one of the two dimensions. Most of the AC coefficients are usually very small. The names of these coefficients are vestiges of the use of DCT to analyze electric currents (i.e., direct and alternate currents).

Because the values $f(k, l) \leq 2^{P-1}$, the largest coefficient, the DC coefficient = $F(0, 0) = 1/8 \sum_k \sum_l f(k, l) \leq (1/8)(64 \times 2^{P-1}) = 2^{P+2}$. Thus, after including the sign, $P + 3$ bits are needed to represent the entire range of the DCT coefficients. Therefore, after discrete cosine transformation has been accomplished, the resulting 8×8 DCT matrix contains larger elements than the original sample matrix. In the new matrix, each entry requires 11-bit precision, whereas each sample was limited to only 8 bits. Clearly, some action needs to be taken to reduce these storage requirements. This next step is quantization.

10.1.3   Quantization

Quantization in JPEG is the process of scaling each DCT coefficient by dividing it by a corresponding quantization value from the quantization table used by the quantizer. The quantized DCT coefficients are then rounded to the nearest integer, as in

$$C(m, n) = \text{round}\big(F(m, n)/Q(m, n)\big) \tag{10.1}$$

In effect, $C(m, n)$ is the normalization of $F(m, n)$ by the quantizer step size $Q(m, n)$ taken from a quantization table Q. In this way, some information is discarded— whereby some compression is already accomplished—but this information is not crucial for adequate restoration of the encoded image.

Dequantization at the decoding stage is the process of rescaling the quantized coefficients to restore as closely as possible the original coefficients. The dequantizer uses the formula

$$D(k, l) = C(k, l) \times Q(k, l)$$

to remove normalization.

The quantizer can use one of the four quantization tables, but JPEG does not supply any default quantization table. Therefore, a particular implementation has to specify such tables taking into account local display devices, specifics of images being processed, and viewing characteristics. Typical examples of quantization tables— provided by the JPEG committee—are given in Figures 10.3 and 10.4. The tables are derived empirically.

Note that the quantization coefficients increase when moving away from the upper left corner of both tables. In this way, finer quantization is achieved for low-frequency coefficients, with coarser quantization for the high-frequency coefficients. Thereby, most of the high-frequency coefficients are suppressed by becoming zeros. Also, as we can see from formula (10.1) for computing a quantized DCT coefficient $C(k, l)$, the quantized coefficients have precision $P + 3 - \lg(Q(m, n))$ if coefficients $Q(m, n)$ before quantization have precision $P + 3$.

To encode gray-scale images, only the luminance table is used. It appears, however, that even for color images most of the information is included in the luminance component.

$i \backslash j$	0	1	2	3	4	5	6	7
0	16	11	10	16	24	40	51	61
1	12	12	14	19	26	58	60	55
2	14	13	16	24	40	57	69	56
3	14	17	22	29	51	87	80	62
4	18	22	37	56	68	109	103	77
5	24	35	55	64	81	104	113	92
6	49	64	78	87	103	121	120	101
7	72	92	95	98	112	100	103	99

Figure 10.3   A luminance quantization table

$i \backslash j$	0	1	2	3	4	5	6	7
0	17	18	24	47	99	99	99	99
1	18	21	26	66	99	99	99	99
2	24	26	56	99	99	99	99	99
3	47	66	99	99	99	99	99	99
4	99	99	99	99	99	99	99	99
5	99	99	99	99	99	99	99	99
6	99	99	99	99	99	99	99	99
7	99	99	99	99	99	99	99	99

Figure 10.4   A chrominance quantization table

After the quantization process for a given block is finished, the resulting quantized coefficients are inserted into the one-dimensional array ZZ in zigzag order (Figure 10.5), which is a pattern described in a technical report by A. G. Tescher in 1978. This pattern of packing the coefficients is chosen because it allows us to put low-frequency coefficients before high-frequency coefficients. With this arrangement, the array elements are in approximately decreasing order, which is significant for the coding stage.

10.1.4   Encoding the Quantized Coefficients

The zigzag sequence order of the quantized coefficients results in long sequences, or *runs*, of zeros in the array ZZ because the high-frequency coefficients are almost always zero, and these runs lend themselves conveniently to *run-length* encoding, which consists in generating codewords for runs of identical symbols.

In the baseline system, the Huffman encoding is used for both DC and AC coefficients with two sets of tables, each set containing one Huffman table for the former

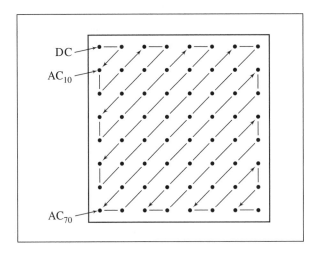

Figure 10.5   The zigzag ordering of the DCT coefficients

and one for the latter coefficients. This limitation means that for interleaved images with three or four components, one set of Huffman tables must be shared between two components.

10.1.4.1 Encoding DC Coefficients

The DC coefficients are encoded using the formula

$$diff = ZZ[0] - pred$$

where the predictor *pred* is the quantized DC value of the most recently coded sample block from the same component. The prediction *pred* is initialized to zero at the beginning of each scan. The difference *diff* is usually small, and therefore, DPCM can be applied efficiently to the coding of DC coefficients.

The difference *diff* is then encoded using the table of Huffman codewords in Figure 10.6. The table includes all the possible difference values *diff* in the baseline system (in the extended system, the table has 16 rows). First, the four-bit-long index SSSS is found with the formula

$$SSSS = \lceil \lg (|diff| + 1) \rceil$$

where SSSS corresponds to one of the twelve categories of difference values. Next, SSSS is used as an index to find in the Huffman table a codeword corresponding to *diff*. A particular codeword depends on the Huffman table used for encoding. JPEG does not have any default Huffman table, but the JPEG report includes an example of such tables, with one for luminance DC difference and one for chrominance DC difference. The table is constructed using a large number of video images, and it is adequate for many applications. The Huffman table for luminance DC difference is shown in Figure 10.7.

Generally, every Huffman codeword consists of at least 2 bits and at most 16 bits. The codewords correspond to categories of difference values, not to particular values.

SSSS	*diff* or AC coefficient	additional bits
0	0	—
1	−1, 1	0, 1
2	−3, −2, 2, 3	00, 01, 10, 11
3	−7, …, −4, 4, …, 7	000, …, 011, 100, …, 111
4	−15, …, −8, 8, …, 15	0000, …, 0111, 1000, …, 1111
5	−31, …, −16, 16, …, 31	00000, …, 01111, 10000, …, 11111
6	−63, …, −32, 32, …, 63	000000, …, 011111, 100000, …, 111111
7	−127, …, −64, 64, …, 127	0000000, …, 0111111, 1000000, …, 1111111
8	−255, …, 128, 128, …, 255	00000000, …, 01111111, 10000000, …, 11111111
9	−511, …, −256, 256, …, 511	000000000, …, 011111111, 100000000, …, 111111111
10	−1023, …, 512, 512, …, 1023	0000000000, …, 0111111111, 1000000000, …, 1111111111
11	−2047, …, −1024, 1024, …, 2047	00000000000, …, 01111111111, 10000000000, …, 11111111111
k	$-2^k + 1, \ldots, -2^{k-1}, 2^{k-1}, \ldots, 2^k - 1$	

Figure 10.6   A table of Huffman codewords for differences of DC coefficients and for AC coefficients

SSSS	Huffman codeword	SSSS	Huffman codeword
0	00	6	1110
1	010	7	11110
2	011	8	111110
3	100	9	1111110
4	101	10	11111110
5	110	11	111111110

Figure 10.7   The Huffman table for luminance DC differences

Therefore, except for when SSSS = 0, the codeword is followed by SSSS additional bits to indicate the sign and magnitude of the difference value being encoded in the following manner:

if *diff* > 0
         append SSSS least significant bits of *diff* to the codeword;
else   append SSSS least significant bits of (*diff* − 1) to the codeword, where
         (*diff* − 1) is given in twos complement representation.

The table in Figure 10.6 gives the additional bits corresponding to each of the *diff* values. For a positive value, the additional bits are the binary representation of *diff*, and for negative values, the additional bits are a portion of the twos complement representation of the number *diff* − 1. Note that the additional bits for positive difference values begin with 1, and for negative values, they begin with 0. Because of the property just mentioned, there is no need to include in the codeword a special bit for sign: the sign bit is implicitly included in the magnitude. The additional bits are appended to the least significant bit of the Huffman codeword, and the most significant bit to the first.

Example 10.1   For *diff* = 12, SSSS = 4, the Huffman codeword = 101 and additional bits = 1100; therefore, the codeword = 1011100. If *diff* = −12, then SSSS and the Huffman codeword are the same as before, but additional bits are the four least significant bits of the twos complement representation of (*diff* − 1) = −13 (i.e., of 11111110011). Hence, the codeword = 1010011.

Note that a significant compression is already accomplished with this division of difference values into categories since the low *diff* values, which are most frequent, are assigned short codewords that are much less than the 11 bits used for the AC coefficients and for the difference values. For example, numbers from category four (i.e., values, for which SSSS = 4) are assigned seven-bit long codewords: three bits for the Huffman codewords and four bits for the unique identifications of the difference.

10.1.4.2   *Encoding AC Coefficients*

After encoding the DC coefficient of a given block, the block's remaining coefficients are encoded in the zigzag order ZZ[1], . . . , ZZ[63]. Because the sequence usually includes long runs of zeros, these runs can be compressed by using run-length coding.

The coding creates a byte RRRRSSSS, where RRRR is the length of a run of zeros and SSSS is the category of the nonzero AC coefficients. To determine the AC categories, the table in Figure 10.6 can also be used with the exception of the first row and after adding to it rows 12 through 15. The table for the AC coefficient categories does not have entry for the category equal to 0 because when SSSS = 0, then SSSS signifies a special symbol. The first special symbol is ZRL, zero run length, used when a run of zeros is greater than 15, in which case the byte RRRRSSSS is equal to binary 11110000, signifying the run of 16 zeros. The second special symbol is EOB, end of block, which means that the remaining elements in the block are zeros; EOB is not included if the last coefficient ZZ[63] is not zero; in this case, RRRRSSSS is equal to binary 00000000.

Although RRRRSSSS is the run-length codeword for a certain run of zeros, it is not this codeword that is transmitted. JPEG uses a table of Huffman codewords for any combination of the run length between 0 and 15 with any number category of the AC coefficients—that is, the table for any pair RRRR/SSSS (run-size/AC coefficient sign and magnitude). Because the baseline system uses 10 (not 11) number categories for the AC coefficients, the table has $16 \times 10 + 2 = 162$ rows, where the two rows correspond to the special symbols EOB and ZRL. Some of the entries in this table are shown in Figure 10.8.

As before, there is also a provision made for the AC coefficients allowing JPEG to encode them uniquely, and this is done in the same way as with the DC differences. To the Huffman codeword corresponding to a particular run-length code RRRRSSSS, additional bits are attached which encode the sign and magnitude of a nonzero AC

RRRR/SSSS	Huffman codeword
0/0 (EOB)	1010
0/1	00
0/2	01
0/3	100
0/4	1011
0/5	11010
:	
2/3	1111110111
:	
4/4	1111111110010111
:	
15/0 (ZRL)	11111111001
15/1	111111111110101
15/2	111111111110110
:	
15/10	111111111111101

Figure 10.8   A table of Huffman codewords for any combination of the runlengths and categories of AC coefficients

coefficient at the end of a particular run. If the coefficient is a positive number, then the additional bits are the binary representation of SSSS least significant bits of the coefficient. For negative coefficients, the additional bits are formed from SSSS least significant bits of the twos complement representation of the number (AC coefficient–1).

Example 10.2   Consider the following example of 63 AC coefficients included in the array ZZ:

ZZ[1 ... 63] = 5 2 0 0 –4 0 0 0 0 15 0 0 0 0 0 0 0 0 0 0 0 0 0 0 –1 0 0 ... 0 0

Let us divide this sequence of coefficients into separate runs and assign to them Huffman codewords and additional bits using Figures 10.6 and 10.8:

ZZ[i ... j]	RRRR/SSSS	Huffman code	additional bits
5	0/3	100	101
2	0/2	01	10
0 0 –4	2/3	1111110111	011
0 0 0 0 15	4/4	1111111110010111	1111
0 0 0 0 0 0 0 0 0 0 0 0 0 0 0	15/0 (ZRL)	11111111001	—
–1	0/1	00	0
0 0 ... 0 0	0/0 (EOB)	1010	—

As the result, the coefficients ZZ[1 ... 63] are encoded with the bit sequence

100 101 01 10 1111110111 011 1111111110010111 1111 11111111001 00 0 1010

which is 61 bits versus $11 \times 63 = 693$ bits occupied by all the AC coefficients.

10.1.5   Multicomponent Images

As mentioned in Section 10.1.1, an image can be composed of several components. The components can be compressed and transmitted separately. For color images, this means that an image is completely reconstructed after all the basic color components are transmitted. Not infrequently, there is a need to transmit the components in parallel when corresponding parts of all the components are transmitted at the same time. This requires interleaving components as they are compressed and transmitted.

First, some definitions. *Data unit* is just one sample in lossless encoding and an 8×8 block of samples in the DCT-based processes. *Minimum coded unit (MCU)* is the smallest group of data being encoded. In the noninterleaved mode, the MCU is just one data unit. In the interleaved mode, the MCU includes interleaved data units from each component. The horizontal and vertical sampling factors for each component divide each of these components into $H_i \times V_i$ arrays (*regions*) of data units, taking the data units left to right and top to bottom from each region. After data units from corresponding regions are included in one MCU, the data units from the next corresponding regions are put into the next MCU, where the order of regions in one component is also defined from left to right and top to bottom. The size of the MCU, however, is limited and is given by the formula

$$\sum_i H_i \times V_i \le 10$$

This restriction means that not all combinations of components and sampling factors are permitted.

Example 10.3

Consider an image of four components $C_1, \ldots, C_4$ in Figure 10.9 with the following horizontal and vertical sampling factors:

$$H_{max} = 2 \qquad\qquad V_{max} = 2$$
$$H_1 = 2 \qquad H_2 = 2 \qquad H_3 = 2 \qquad H_4 = 1$$
$$V_1 = 2 \qquad V_2 = 1 \qquad V_3 = 1 \qquad V_4 = 2$$

with which the size of MCU $= 2 \cdot 2 + 2 \cdot 1 + 2 \cdot 1 + 1 \cdot 2 = 10$, and

$$MCU_1 = C_1(0,0), C_1(0,1), C_1(1,0), C_1(1,1), C_2(0,0), C_2(0,1),$$
$$C_3(0,0), C_3(0,1), C_4(0,0), C_4(1,0)$$

$$MCU_2 = C_1(0,2), C_1(0,3), C_1(1,2), C_1(1,3), C_2(0,2), C_2(0,3),$$
$$C_3(0,2), C_3(0,3), C_4(0,1), C_4(1,1)$$

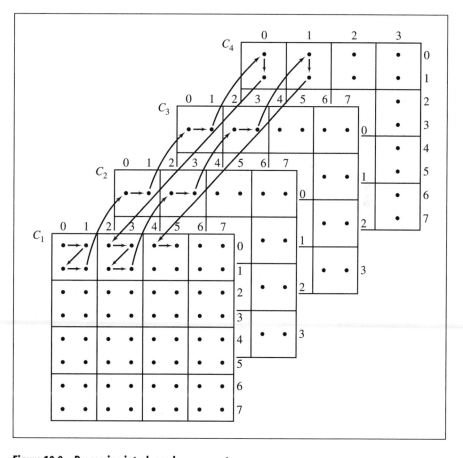

Figure 10.9 Processing interleaved components

10.1.6 Extended Sequential System

The extended sequential system is an enhancement of the baseline system used to provide higher precision and better compression than the baseline system. In this system, adaptive binary arithmetic coding can be used instead of Huffman coding. If Huffman coding is applied, then four Huffman tables can be used for DC coefficients and four for AC coefficients. The pixel samples in the 8×8 blocks have 12 bits, and the quantized DCT coefficients have 15 bits.

10.2 Progressive DCT-Based Mode of Operation

In the progressive mode, an image is encoded in several scans, with each scan improving the quality of the transmitted image. The likeness of the picture improves successively on the receiving side, starting from a very crude and blocky rendition of the image. Successive scans improve the quality of the image until the maximum quality is reached. Progressive increase of image quality can be performed in one of two ways: as in the sequential mode and also in the progressive mode where DC coefficients are coded separately from AC coefficients.

10.2.1 Spectral Selection

In the spectral selection method, only a specified subsequence of the coefficients (a frequency band) from the zigzag sequence is encoded and transmitted. First, only the DC coefficients are sent. Then successively more and more AC coefficients are transmitted, thereby improving the quality of the image.

10.2.2 Successive Approximation

In the successive approximation mode, instead of coding clusters of the DCT coefficients, all of the coefficients are sent, but with a different level of the precision. After transmitting the DC coefficients in the first scan, successive approximation coding starts with using only the most significant bits of each coefficient, and then each scan improves precision by one bit until reaching full precision. The number of most significant bits in the second scan is defined by the so-called point-transform parameter *Al,* which defines by how many bits the coefficients should be shifted right. For positive integers, this operation is tantamount to dividing the coefficients by 2^{Al}.

The two methods are compared in Figure 10.10. An image is a sequence of 8×8 blocks transformed into zigzag arrays of quantized coefficients. As shown on this figure, the spectral selection method transmits the image in horizontal slices, and the successive approximation method sends the image in vertical slices (except for the first scan).

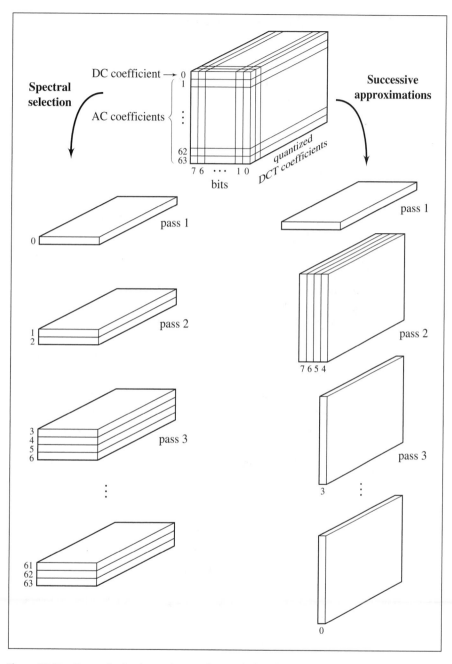

Figure 10.10   Spectral selection and successive approximation methods used in the progressive mode

10.3 **Hierarchical Mode of Operation**

In the hierarchical mode, an image is coded at increasing resolutions, with each resolution increased by the factor of 2 either horizontally, vertically, or in both directions. This mode of operation, also called *pyramidal coding*, is useful for transmitting high-resolution images to devices that require only low resolution (e.g., a monitor whose resolution is significantly smaller than that of a laser printer).

A pyramid can be formed by repeatedly averaging over 2×2 blocks of pixels, as in Figure 10.11. This requires using 33% more data to form the pyramid than for the original picture. A variation of the pyramid method is using sums instead of averages and noticing that from a sum from one level and three of its components from the lower level, the fourth component can be reconstructed (Sloan and Tanimoto, 1979).

Another approach was used by Burt and Adelson (1983), who connected pyramidal coding with the DPCM approach. First, a low-pass filter is applied to the original image I_1 and then downsampled in the rate of one pixel out of four to produce an image I_2, which is a low-resolution version of the original. The result I_2 is upsampled and interpolated to find the rough reconstruction RRI_1 and then the difference image DI_1 between the original I_1 and RRI_1, is computed, encoded, and transmitted. This process can be repeated for each image I_i. Assuming that the original image consists of $2^k \times 2^k$ pixels for some k, the maximum of iterations equals k and is discontinued after the image I_k consists of only $2^0 \times 2^0 = 1$ pixel. Figure 10.12 illustrates this process for a pyramid in Figure 10.11.

If the initial image consists of N pixels, then the process has greater storage requirements since the number of samples operated on by the process equals $N + N/4 + N/4^2 + \ldots \leq 4N/3$ pixels, which is more than in the original picture. This results because after the first iteration, the first downsampled image I_2 requires only $N/4$ pixels, but to reconstruct the original I_1, the difference picture DI_1 has to

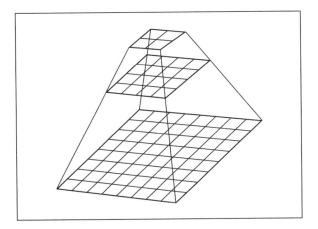

Figure 10.11   Different resolution levels in pyramidal coding

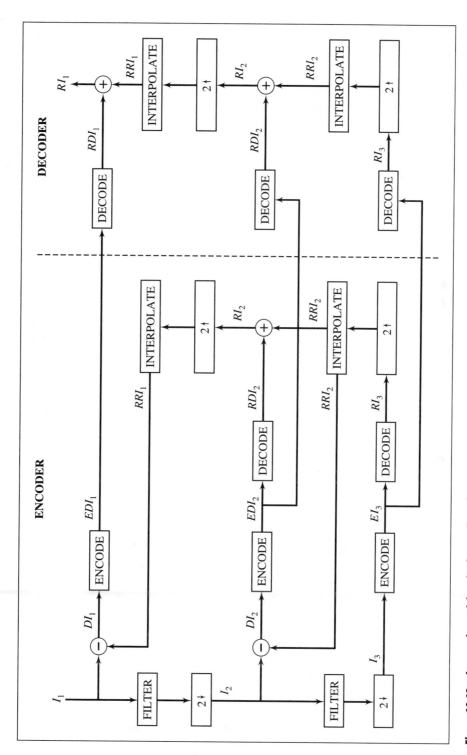

Figure 10.12　An encoder and decoder for two-iteration pyramid coding process

be transmitted as well, which requires $N + N/4$ pixels in total. At the next level, to reconstruct the original I_1 from the second downsampled image, I_3, $N + N/4 + N/4^2$ pixels are necessary. However, the difference images can usually be encoded efficiently, particularly when small-valued samples are eliminated by replacing them with zeros so that long runs of zeros may emerge.

The rule for interpolation used by JPEG is given by

$$x = (a + b)/2$$

where a and b are samples from neighboring positions—whether horizontally or vertically—of the lower-resolution image and x is the interpolated value, as in Figure 10.11. The leftmost column and the top row of the upsampled image match the leftmost column and the top row of the lower-resolution image. The rightmost column and the bottom row of the lower-resolution image are copied to become the values required for the interpolations in the rightmost column and bottom row.

10.4   Sequential Lossless Mode of Operation

To guarantee the exact match between the input and output, JPEG includes a lossless mode of operation that is independent of DCT. The lossless mode uses a simple coding method that predicts the value of a sample based on the values of some of its neighbors. Figure 10.13 shows the position of a sample whose value is being predicted and the positions of its neighbors. Figure 10.14 shows the formulas used in predicting the value of x. The selection value 0 is used only in the hierarchical mode. Selections 1, 2, and 3 are one-dimensional predictors, and the remaining values are two-dimensional predictors. The selection value 1 is used for the first line of samples; the value 2 is used at the beginning of each line. At the beginning of the first line, however, the prediction value 2^{P-1} is used, where P is the precision of the input (this value is 2^{P-Pt-1} if Pt is a nonzero value of a scaling factor called the point-transform shift). The selected two-dimensional predictor is used for all other sample values. The value computed with the chosen predictor is then subtracted from a given sample value, and the difference (divided modulo 2^{16}) is encoded by either the Huffman method or arithmetic coding. The decoder takes this difference and adds it to the prediction.

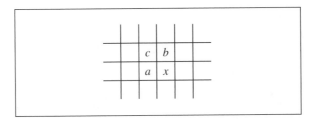

Figure 10.13   The position of a sample x being reconstructed with respect to already reconstructed samples a, b, and c.

Selection value	Prediction
0	no prediction
1	$x = a$
2	$x = b$
3	$x = c$
4	$x = a + b - c$
5	$x = a + (b - c)/2$
6	$x = b + (a - c)/2$
7	$x = (a + b)/2$

Figure 10.14   Formulas used to reconstruct a sample x

10.5   JPEG 2000

JPEG 2000 is a new still-image compression standard that is currently being developed by the International Standards Organization. It is expected to become a standard sometime in the year 2001. JPEG 2000 uses wavelet transformations instead of Fourier transforms. The new standard promises, among other things, to code different parts of an image with differing fidelity; progressive recover an image by fidelity or resolution; switch from image (lossy) to text (lossless) compression during compression since text is often blurred when processed as image; random access to particular sections of an image; and generally, it promises a superior compression performance, particularly for high-compression ratios.

EXERCISES

1. Find codewords for *diff* equal to a. 255, b. –255, c. 3, d. 4, e. 100, f. –100.

2. Encode a sequence of three quantized images ZZ[0 ... 63]:
   (a) –68 13 14 –13 –14 0 0 7 0 0 0 0 –8 0 0 0 0 8 0...0
   (b) –28 1 2 3 4 –1 –2 –3 –4 0...0
   (c) 17 14 –13 30 0 0 –6 0 0 7 0 0 0 0 0 0 0 0 0 0 0 0 0 0 0 3 0 0
       0 0 0 0 0 0 0 0 0 0 0 0 0 0 0 0 –4 0...0

3. In Section 10.3, a variation of pyramid coding was mentioned in which a pyramid is formed by repeatedly finding a sum over 2 × 2 blocks and reconstructing one component on a lower level from the current sum and three components of the lower level. In this way, one-fourth of values can be discarded on each level. Does it reduce the memory requirement for progressive transmission by one-fourth?

BIBLIOGRAPHY

Burt, Peter J., and Adelson, Edward H., The Laplacian pyramid as a compact image code, *IEEE Transactions on Communications* 31 (1983), 532–540.

Kou, Weidong, *Digital image compression: Algorithms and standards*, Boston: Kluwer, 1995.

Pennebaker, William B., and Mitchell, Joan L., *JPEG: Still image data compression standard,* New York: Van Nostrand Reinhold, 1993.

Sloan Kenneth R., and Tanimoto, Steven L., Progressive refinement of raster images, *IEEE Transactions on Computers* 28 (1979), 871–874.

Tescher, Andrew G., *Transform image coding,* Aerospace Corporation Research Report SAMSO-TR-78-127, 1978.

Wallace, Gregory K., The JPEG still picture compression standard, *Communications of the ACM* 34 (1991), 31–44.

Zhang, Manyun, *The JPEG and image data compression algorithms*, Technical report, University of California at Santa Cruz, 1990, UCSC-CRL-90-68.

Chapter 11

Video Image Compression: MPEG

A video sequence is a collection of images taken closely together in time; therefore, in most cases, the differences between adjacent images are not large. Video compression techniques take advantage of the repetition of portions of the picture from one image to another by concentrating on the changes between neighboring images. A widely used standard for video compression is the MPEG system.

11.1 MPEG-1

The work of the MPEG (Moving Picture Experts Group) began in 1988 and was published in a 1990 draft of a standard that is now called MPEG-1. The goal of this system is to compress both audio signals at the rate of up to 192 Kbit/s per channel and video signals at the rate of 1.5 Mbit/s. The system is intended primarily for compressing video pictures so they can be stored on digital storage media, such as compact disks. MPEG-1 can process images with the maximum of 768 pixels per line and 576 lines with the maximum picture rate of 30 pictures/s. But with the constraint of only 396 of 16×16 macroblocks per picture, a 768×576 picture $= 1728$ macroblocks cannot be processed. However, with these constraints, the target specifications were 360×240 pixel resolution and 30 frames/s for NTSC and 360×288 resolution and 25 frames/s for PAL and SECAM; frame rate for film is 24 Hz. MPEG's goal is to compress both audio and video so that the compressed signals require as much space as uncompressed sound. In this way, compact disks used now for storing audio data can be used for storing both sound and video, the latter requiring significantly more space in uncompressed form than the former.

11.1.1 MPEG Video Layers

MPEG is a hierarchy of layers. The outermost layer is the MPEG system layer, which combines audio and video compressed bitstreams into one bitstream. The MPEG bitstream is a sequence of *packs,* which are collections of *packets* that hold compressed audio and video information. The second layer is the video sequence that is a collection of groups of pictures. The groups of pictures layer are a collection composed of at least one picture. Next is a picture layer, with each picture being a sequence of slices. Each slice is a sequence of macroblocks in the raster scan order, and all the macroblocks composing a particular slice have the same shade of gray (Figure 11.1). A macroblock is a collection of four 8×8 DCT blocks of luminance (brightness) samples and two 8×8 blocks of chrominance samples, one for color hue and one for color saturation (Figure 11.2). Note that there are twice as many luminance samples as chrominance samples. This arrangement is due to the fact that the eye does not follow as easily quick spatial changes in chrominance as changes in luminance. Thus, the number of chrominance samples can be smaller than the number of luminance samples.

A video sequence is a collection of groups of pictures. Each *group of pictures* (*GOP*) is a sequence of pictures of three different types. A GOP begins with a picture that belongs to the category of *intracoded pictures* (*I-pictures*) that are coded independently of other types of pictures so that only correlations within the picture are utilized. These pictures serve as a basic reference to encode other types of pictures.

Figure 11.1   A picture composed of five slices. Each square is a macroblock

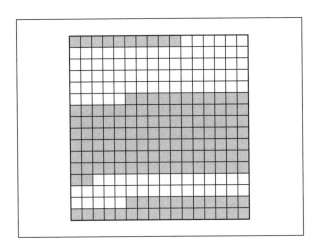

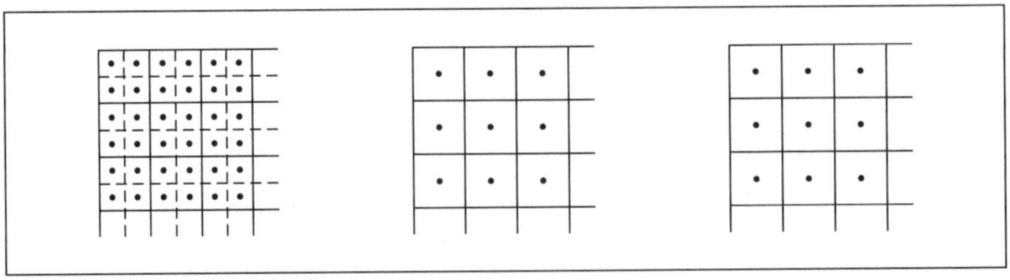

Figure 11.2   Components of a macroblock with dots indicating positions of sample pixels

They allow for viewing a sequence of video pictures starting at or very close to a randomly chosen picture so that each GOP can be decoded independently. However, the compression rate for I-pictures is relatively low. The compression rate of the entire sequence of pictures is improved by using other types of pictures.

The second type of pictures is seldom used *DC-coded pictures* (*D-pictures*) that contain only DC coefficient information. The third type includes *predictive-coded pictures* (*P-pictures*) that are coded based on predictions from preceding I- and P-pictures. And finally, the fourth type includes *bidirectionally predictive-coded pictures* (*B-pictures*) whose coding may be based on both preceding and following I- and P-pictures (Figure 11.3). By referring to a past picture and a future picture for reference, a compression of a B-picture generally can achieve the highest compression rate. If there is a change of scene or an area is uncovered, then predictive coding alone is not of much use, but a reference to a future picture makes compression possible in such cases. Because B-pictures rely on information from future pictures, they are not used in any prediction. Therefore, they can include a high level of distortion because the distortion will not be propagated to other pictures.

It is clear that B-pictures can be decoded only after the decoder knows both the preceding and the future reference pictures. For this reason, the order in which frames are sent is different from the display, as illustrated in Figure 11.3. The display order of pictures forming the GOP is 1, 2, 3, . . . , but pictures are transmitted in the order: 1, 5, 2, 3, 4, 9, 6, 7, 8, 13, 10, 11, 12. For example, the decoder uses I-picture 1 to reconstruct P-picture 5 and then uses the two pictures to reconstruct three B-pictures, 2, 3, and 4, after which it rearranges the sequence to the original order: 1, 2, 3, 4, 5.

It is possible that prediction is limited to some parts of P- and B-pictures or that no prediction is used. In the latter case, only intratechniques are used for coding.

When coding B- and P-pictures, differences are used between the picture being encoded and a reference picture. To ensure that the differences are the same for the

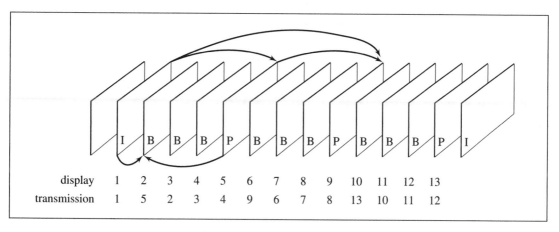

Figure 11.3   Interdependencies between pictures composing a group of pictures in intraframe coding

encoder and decoder, encoded I-pictures are sent to the decoder, but at the same time, they are decoded by the encoder. In this way, the reference I-picture reconstructed by the decoder is the same as the reference I-picture used by the encoder for compression. The coding of I-pictures and the difference arrays for B- and P-pictures are performed similarly as in JPEG. First, blocks of the samples are subjected to discrete cosine transformation, and then the DCT coefficients are quantized with two predefined quantization tables, one for intracoding and one for intercoding. One difference between quantization in JPEG and MPEG lies in the fact that the quantization matrix in MPEG can be scaled by a certain factor that is sent along with the compressed images.

The DCT coefficients of an I-picture are nearly perfectly decorrelated, but there still remains some correlation between the DCT coefficients of the neighboring I-pictures, which is particularly true for the DC coefficients. Therefore, these coefficients are coded separately using the formula

$$diff = DC - pred$$

where the predictor *pred* is a prediction for the *DC* value of the block being coded. The difference values are coded in the same way as in JPEG. First, the size category is coded (a number between 0 and 8) using a DC code table, which is followed by the encoded magnitude and sign. However, MPEG uses different default tables for coding than JPEG.

The coding of the AC coefficients of I-pictures is also done as in JPEG. First, the coefficients are put in zigzag order and then efficiently coded exploiting the presence of runs of zeros for the high-frequency coefficients. To that end, an AC code table of 154 entries is used which includes highly probable combinations of lengths of runs of zeros followed by signs of nonzero AC coefficient values (indicated with a letter s) and the magnitudes (amplitudes) of the nonzero AC coefficients (Figure 11.4). For example,

run/amplitude	codeword
0/1	1s
0/2	0100s
0/3	00101s
0/4	0000110s
0/5	00100110s
:	
2/3	0000001011s
:	
4/1	00110s
:	
30/1	0000000000011100s
31/1	0000000000011011s
EOB	10
ESC	000001

Figure 11.4   Huffman codewords for runlength/amplitude combinations

the zigzag AC sequence ZZ[1 ... 63] = 3 −3 5 0 0 3 0 0 0 0 −1 0... 0 is broken down into the sequence of run/amplitude pairs 0/3 0/−3 0/5 2/3 4/−1 EOB, which is encoded as this stream of bits: 001010 001011 001001100 00000010110 001101 10. All combinations of runs and amplitudes are not in the table. To process other combinations, the escape symbol is issued followed by the explicit encoding of the run-length with six bits and amplitude with eight or sixteen bits (cf. the ELSE category in Weaver-Hankamer algorithm in Section 3.1).

In P- and B-pictures, runs of zero macroblocks are coded with their addresses. Nonzero macroblocks use a six-bit *coded block pattern* (*cbp*) to indicate which of the six blocks composing a macroblock is all zero, and then a variable length codeword is given according to a table of cbp codewords. For example, the cbp 010110 indicates that the second, fourth, and fifth blocks are nonzero, and this fact is coded with the codeword 10001. For nonzero blocks, the runs of zeros are encoded with the table used for coding the AC coefficients of I-pictures.

11.1.2 Motion Compensation and Motion Estimation

A key feature of most video compression techniques is *motion compensation*. In motion compensation, it is assumed that areas of a current picture are translations of areas of another picture. Although other ways of transformation are also possible (e.g., rotation or rescaling), for simplicity only translation is used in MPEG. Compression for a macroblock m_1 being encoded is accomplished by finding in a reference picture a macroblock m_2 that most closely matches m_1 and transmitting the displacement of m_2 relative to the position of m_1. For example, a macroblock m_1 of a B-picture in Figure 11.5 is encoded by reference to a macroblock m_2 of a preceding picture and a macroblock m_3 of a future picture. Because the size of each macroblock is fixed, it is enough to refer to a macroblock location by the position of its upper left corner. If the position of m_1 is (x, y) and the position of m_2 is (x_{m2}, y_{m2}), then the *motion displacement vector*

$$\mathbf{v} = position(m_2) - position(m_1)$$
$$= (horizontal\ displacement,\ vertical\ displacement)$$
$$= (x_{m2} - x, y_{m2} - y)$$

With this convention, a positive horizontal displacement means that the macroblock in the reference picture is to the right of the macroblock being encoded, and a positive vertical displacement means that the reference macroblock is below the current macroblock. In both cases, the reference is made relative to the macroblock being coded. This corresponds to the usual scanning of images: An image is scanned top to bottom and left to right; thus, a positive sign corresponds to being forward in time.

The example in Figure 11.5 illustrates an interesting feature of B-pictures that can use both forward and backward prediction for the same macroblock. In this case,

$$m_1[i][j] = round\big((m_2[i + dx_{m2}][j + dy_{m2}] + m_3[i + dx_{m3}][j + dy_{m3}])/2\big)$$

where dx and dy are horizontal and vertical displacements. In this way, the current pixel is obtained by interpolation from a preceding pixel and a future pixel, which

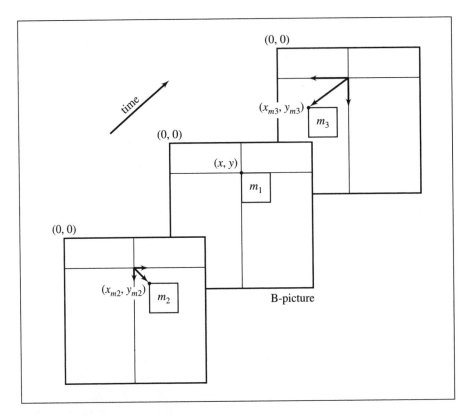

Figure 11.5   Motion displacements for a B-picture

allows for decreasing the impact of noise onto the quality of pictures and dealing with currently uncovered areas that are known only in future pictures, but cannot be predicted from past pictures.

For P-pictures, only forward reference is used. If the current picture in Figure 11.5 is a P-picture, not a B-picture, then only the forward reference is taken into account, and to find values of pixels in m_1, the following formula is used

$$m_1[i][j] = m_2[i + dx_{m2}][j + dy_{m2}]$$

There still remains a crucial question: How can the displacement vectors be determined? The process of finding these vectors is called *motion estimation*. There are many techniques to determine these vectors that can be divided into two classes: pixel-recursive and block matching (Musmann, Pirsch, and Grallert, 1985; Dufaux and Moscheni, 1995). Pixel-recursive techniques are used in situations when the motion vectors change from one pixel to another. In these techniques, the motion vectors of neighboring pixels are used to predict the current motion vector and then iteratively change this estimate to minimize the value of the displaced frame difference. Pixel-recursive algorithms are computationally intensive, and although quite effective, they are not used very often. If the change of these vectors takes place from one area to another, then block matching techniques are more relevant.

MPEG does not prescribe any particular method for motion estimation, but it is very likely that block estimation methods will be primarily used. One problem that has to be solved is the size of the area associated with one motion vector, and in MPEG, this area is a macroblock. Another issue is a criterion problem. A *block matching* technique tries to find for each macroblock m_1 a macroblock m_2 in a reference picture that is its closest match. There may be, however, many different ways of measuring this closeness; one such a measure is the *mean square error (mse;* Jain and Jain, 1981),

$$mse(x, y) = \frac{1}{256} \sum_{i=0}^{15} \sum_{j=0}^{15} (m_1[x + i][y + j] - m_2[x + i + dx_{m2}][y + j + dy_{m2}])^2$$

Another is the *mean absolute distortion (mad;* Koga et al., 1981) defined as

$$mad(x, y) = \frac{1}{256} \sum_{i=0}^{15} \sum_{j=0}^{15} |m_1[x + i][y + j] - m_2[x + i + dx_{m2}][y + j + dy_{m2}]|$$

It has been shown that the squared error criterion gives the best estimates, but *mad* is usually preferred over *mse* because multiplication is replaced by checking a sign. But still, the number of operations is very large. To find the *mad* for two macroblocks m_1 and m_2, there need to be performed 256 subtractions + 256 absolute values + 225 additions + 1 division = 738 operations, without even taking into account additions in index calculation. However, for a particular macroblock m_1, all the macroblocks are checked from a particular area. The area is defined by horizontal and vertical offsets from the position (x, y) of m_1, and in MPEG, the offset can be as large as 64. That is, any macroblock m_2 whose position equals $(x + dx_{m2}, y + dy_{m2})$, where $-64 \leq dx_{m2}, dy_{m2} \leq +63$ (Mitchell et al., 1997, Sec. 11.7), is compared to m_1 using the *mad* measure (see Figure 11.6). In this area of a reference picture, there are $(2 \cdot 64)^2 = 16{,}384$ pixels, each one being a position of a macroblock with which m_1 is to be compared. Therefore, the number of operations to find the closest match for m_1 in this area is $738 \cdot 16{,}384 \approx 12.1$ million. This is just one macroblock of one picture, and there may be as many as 396 macroblocks per picture and 30 pictures per second (as a matter of fact, the combined maximum of number of blocks $\times$ picture rate $\leq 396 \cdot 25 = 9900$). The number of operations is thus overwhelming. To reduce this number, a variety of suboptimal fast algorithms for motion estimation are used.

The process of coding and decoding can now be described as follows (Figure 11.7). Coder, which is an interframe DPCM system, applies a motion estimation technique to a reference picture RP and the current picture CP to produce motion vectors. The vectors and the reference picture are then used to generate a predicted picture PP. The latter is subtracted from the actual current picture to produce a difference picture (prediction error), DP = CP − PP, which is then compressed. The compressed difference picture and the motion vectors are then sent to the decoder. Decoder uses the reference picture RP from its store to generate the predicted picture PP, which is a

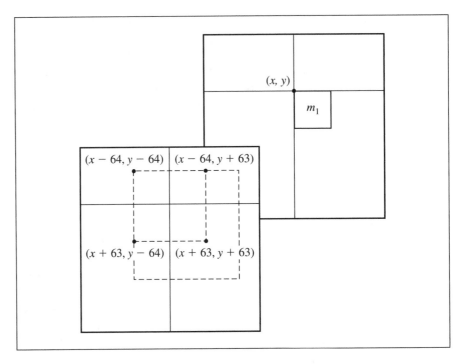

Figure 11.6 Area for finding a closest match for a macroblock m_1; the dotted area indicates where the positions of macroblocks in a reference picture are located; the dotted area and the dashed area indicate where the checked macroblocks are located

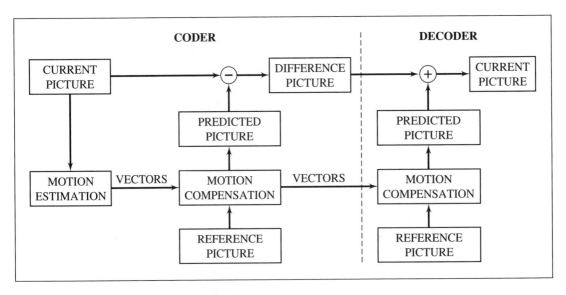

Figure 11.7 Compression of video pictures with motion compensation

motion-compensated reference picture. The latter is then added to the decompressed difference picture to render the original picture, $CP = PP + DP = PP + (CP - PP)$. Also, it should be clear that the decoding process is much quicker than encoding. This is due to the most costly part of the process, namely finding the motion vectors not being required for the decoding. Therefore, computers are commonly equipped with MPEG playback only, with no MPEG recording capacity, because playback can be done in real-time, which is difficult to accomplish for recording without specialized hardware.

11.2   MPEG-2

The discussion in this chapter has been limited to the first MPEG system, called MPEG-1. Capabilities of MPEG-1 were in some respects limited because it was designed for digital storage media applications. MPEG-2, initiated in 1991, is the next generation in the MPEG family for compressing video, and it is designed as a generic standard not to be limited for storage, but also for TV broadcasting, including high-definition TV, on satellite links, videoconferencing, networked data bases, and many other applications. Many capabilities in MPEG-2 are unavailable in MPEG-1. First, in MPEG-1, the sample pixel positioning is fixed, as in Figure 11.2; in MPEG-2, the relative sample positioning can be different. MPEG-2 can also process larger pictures and perform at higher rates than MPEG-1. More important, MPEG-2 can process interlaced video, which cannot be done in MPEG-1. To produce an image on the TV screen, the electron gun excites through an electron beam phosphorous substance on the screen by scanning the screen top to bottom and left to right, processing 525 lines 30 times a second (in color TV, three guns are used for the basic colors). To avoid an image flicker, one picture (*frame*) is a combination of two interlaced parts, or *fields*, each field sent in one-sixtieth of a second. First, one field with odd lines is traced on the screen followed by the second with even lines that are interlaced with, or between the lines of the first frame, as in Figure 11.8.

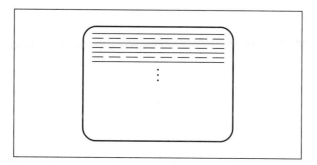

Figure 11.8   A TV picture (frame) shown as a combination of two interlaced fields, one shown with solid lines and one with dashed lines

level	samples/line	lines/frame	frame/s	luminance samples/s	bitrate in Mbits/s
high (MP@ML)	1920	1152	60	62,668,800	80
high-1440 (MP@H14)	1440	1152	60	47,001,600	60
main (MP@ML)	720	576	30	10,368,000	15
low (MP@LL)	352	288	30	3,041,280	4

Figure 11.9   Examples of upper ranges of parameters for four levels in MPEG-2; MP@ML stands for "main profile at main level" and so on

MPEG-2 attempts to be a generic standard to a larger extent than MPEG-1 so that different applications could use only the features appropriate to their requirements. To that end, MPEG-2 defines its range of coding support into *profiles* and *levels*.

MPEG-2 includes definitions of eight different profiles: simple, main, 4:2:2, signal-to-noise scalable, base spatially scalable, enhancement spatially scalable, base high, and enhancement high. The first three are nonscalable profiles. Scalable profiles are not restricted to one resolution and quality. In these profiles, images can be completely decoded from only a part of the bitstream. Most broadcast applications use the main profile.

In addition to profiles that define tools to be used, MPEG-2 has four levels that specify the ranges of some of the parameters used during compression; the levels are called low, main, high-1440, and high. The table in Figure 11.9 includes examples of upper bounds for some of the parameters (Sikora, 1997).

Any MPEG-2 decoder belongs to a particular *conformance class*, or *point*, defined as a combination of a level and a profile. Eight profiles and four levels can render 32 conformance classes, but MPEG-2 allows only 17 (Symes, 1998).

11.3   MPEG-4 and MPEG-7

Although MPEG-2 is a significant improvement over MPEG-1, it is not the last word in video compression. There was also the MPEG-3 project, which was later folded into MPEG-2 after it turned out that the goal of MPEG-3, enabling HDTV, can be accomplished within MPEG-2. A new project, whose Version 2 acquired formal International Standard status in 2000, is MPEG-4, which introduces new coding techniques, new architecture, and new operational models. MPEG-4 audiovisual scenes are composed of hierarchically organized *media objects*. At the lowest level of the hierarchy, there are primitive media objects, such as text, still images (e.g., a fixed background), video objects (a moving vehicle), and audio objects (the sound of the vehicle). Such primitive media objects can be 2D or 3D, natural and synthetic, and MPEG-4's task is to standardize them and thereby to standardize a way to describe an audiovisual scene. A media object is encoded independently of its surroundings or background with descriptive elements that make it possible to operate on the object in an audiovisual scene. Primitive objects are put together to form compound media objects. MPEG-4 thus aims at content-based coding of images and video so that any video objects can be decoded separately. This approach also allows for random access of content in video sequences to pause, fast forward, and perform other operations on stored video objects.

In October 1996, work began on the fourth MPEG standard, called MPEG-7. International Standard status is expected in September 2001.

MPEG-7 consists of three parts: descriptors, description schemes, and a description definition language (DDL). *Descriptors* are the representations of the basic features of audiovisual content, such as the amplitude and frequency of a signal and the number of sources present in a signal. *Description schemes* are structured combinations of descriptors. A central position in the MPEG-7 standard occupies the *description definition language*. The DDL specifies the rules to create description schemes and descriptors and to extend and modify existing description schemes. In particular, it is used to express various relationships (spatial, temporal, structural, and conceptual) between components of description schemes and relationships between description schemes. Material encoded with MPEG-7 can be indexed and queried. The user can, for example, find images that include lines drawn on the screen by the user, return musical pieces that include a few notes played by the user, or show a list of animations that fits a temporal and spatial description.

MPEG-7's objective is to provide a standardized description of multimedia information by its content. That is, predecessors of MPEG-7 are designed to represent audiovisual information, while MPEG-7 is primarily targeted at representing information about the information. Focusing on representing information about the content and not the content itself, MPEG-7 does not replace its MPEG predecessors, but it provides additional functionality which is the standardization of descriptions of multimedia content.

In June 2000, work began on the new standard, MPEG-21. The goal of MPEG-21 is to develop a common multimedia framework to use multimedia resources across different types of networks and devices.

EXERCISES

1. What impact does the size of a macroblock have on motion estimation?

2. It may be reasonable to use in motion estimation a rectangular search area rather than a square (as in Figure 11.6) with the width of the rectangle larger than its height—for instance, 120×60 pixels. Why is this reasonable?

BIBLIOGRAPHY

Bhaskaran, Vasudev, and Konstantinides, Konstantinos, *Image and video compression standards: Algorithms and architectures*, Boston: Kluwer, 1995.

Chiariglione, Leonardo, The development of an integrated audiovisual coding standard: MPEG, *Proceedings of the IEEE* 83 (1995), 151–157.

Dufaux, Frédéric, and Moscheni, Fabrice, Motion estimation techniques for digital TV: A review and a new contribution, *Proceedings of the IEEE* 83 (1995), 858–876.

Furht, Borko, Greenberg, Joshua, and Westwater, Raymond, *Motion estimation algorithms for video compression,* Boston: Kluwer, 1997.

Gharavi, H., and Mills, M., Block matching motion estimation algorithms—new results, *IEEE Transactions on Circuits and Systems* (1989), 649–651.

Haskell, Barry G., Puri, Atul, and Netravali, Arun N., *Digital video: An introduction to MPEG-2*, New York: Chapman & Hill, 1997.

Jain, Jaswant R., and Jain, Anil K., Displacement measurement and its application to interframe image coding, *IEEE Transactions on Communications* 29 (1981), 1799–1808.

Koga, T., Iinuma, K., Hirano, A., Iijima, Y., and Ishiguro, T., Motion-compensated interframe coding for video conferencing, *Proceedings of the National Telecommunications Conference*, New Orleans (1981), G5.3.1–G5.3.5.

LeGall, Didier, MPEG: A video compression standard for multimedia application, *Communications of the ACM* 34 (1994), No. 4, 47–58.

Mitchell, Joan L., Pennebaker, William B., Fogg, Chad E., and LeGall, Didier J. (eds.), *MPEG video compression standard*, New York: Chapman & Hill, 1997.

Musmann, Hans G., Pirsch, Peter, and Grallert, Hans J., Advances in picture coding, *Proceedings of the IEEE* 73 (1985), 523–548.

Reader, Cliff, MPEG4: Coding for content, interactivity, and universal accessibility, *Optical Engineering* 35 (1996), 104–108.

Sikora, Thomas, MPEG digital video standards, *IEEE Signal Processing Magazine*, Sept. 1997, 82–100.

Symes, Peter D., *Video compression*, New York: McGraw-Hill, 1998.

Watkinson, John, *MPEG-2*, Oxford: Focal Press, 1999.

Chapter 12

Fourier Analysis

Fourier series are of extreme importance in theoretical and practical applications. They are widely used in mathematics, physics, chemistry, and engineering. They allow for a convenient analysis of otherwise complicated functions and for solving theoretical and practical problems that would otherwise remain virtually unsolvable.[1]

12.1 Fourier Series

Definition 12.1

We call a function g *periodic with period p,* or *p-periodic,* if $g(x + p) = g(x)$ for all x and the *basic period p* is the smallest period of g (note that any integer multiple np of p is also a period of g). The number $f_0 = 1/p$ is called a *fundamental frequency* of function g.

Example 12.1

Consider the function $a \sin (fx)$. If x denotes time, then $|a|$ is the *amplitude* of the waveform described by the function, f is its *frequency,* and the basic period $p = 2\pi/f$. See Figure 12.1 for a graph of the function $4 \sin 3x$.

A periodic function can be regarded as a superposition of a series of sinusoidal components, and thus, it can be expressed in terms of trigonometric functions. Fourier analysis is interested, among other things, in finding a trigonometric expansion of a periodic function and determining parameters of this expansion.

Definition 12.2

Let a function g satisfy the *Dirichlet conditions*, which are (1) g is a bounded function defined at every point of the fundamental interval $[-\pi, \pi]$; (2) g has only a finite number of discontinuities; and (3) g can have only a finite number of maxima and

---

[1]The importance of Fourier series is very emphatically expressed in the following words: "One might be tempted to paraphrase the famous saying of Victor Hugo that if he were asked to destroy all literature but keep one single book, he would preserve the Book of Job. Similarly, if we were asked to abandon all mathematical discoveries save one, we would hardly fail to vote for the Fourier series as the candidate for survival," Cornelius Lanczos, *Applied analysis*, Englewood Cliffs, NJ: Prentice Hall 1956, p. vii.

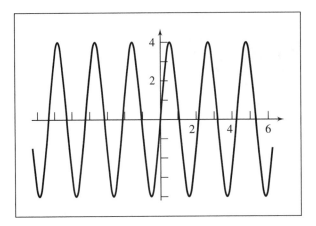

Figure 12.1   Graph of the function 4 sin 3x

minima in this interval. The function g can be expanded in the interval $[-\pi, \pi]$; into the *Fourier series,* which is an infinite sum of sines and cosines (its harmonic components or harmonics) of the form

$$g(x) = \frac{1}{2}a_0 + \sum_{k=1}^{\infty} (a_k \cos kx + b_k \sin kx) \tag{12.1}$$

or equivalently, in the complex form,

$$g(x) = \sum_{k=-\infty}^{\infty} c_k e^{ikx} \tag{12.2}$$

where $c_0 = \frac{1}{2}a_0, c_k = \frac{1}{2}(a_k - ib_k), c_{-k} = \frac{1}{2}(a_k + ib_k)$, for $k > 0$. Coefficients a_k, b_k, and c_k are called *Fourier coefficients.*

The series (12.1) includes sinusoidal components for all possible frequencies k (all possible multiples of the fundamental frequency). Note that for a periodic function g with period 2π—that is, when $g(x) = g(x + 2\pi)$—the series in (12.1) is also a periodic function.

The coefficients a_k and b_k represent unknown amplitudes. As it turns out, the function g itself can be used in evaluating these coefficients. To evaluate a_k and b_k, we integrate the series (12.1) from $-\pi$ to π,

$$\int_{-\pi}^{\pi} g(x)dx = \int_{-\pi}^{\pi} \left(\frac{1}{2}a_0 + \sum_{k=1}^{\infty} (a_k \cos kx + b_k \sin kx) \right) dx$$

$$= \int_{-\pi}^{\pi} \frac{1}{2}a_0 \, dx + \sum_{k=1}^{\infty} \left(a_k \int_{-\pi}^{\pi} \cos k \, dx + b_k \int_{-\pi}^{\pi} \sin kx \, dx \right)$$

$$= \int_{-\pi}^{\pi} \frac{1}{2}a_0 \, dx = \pi a_0$$

thus,

$$a_0 = \frac{1}{\pi} \int_{-\pi}^{\pi} g(x)dx$$

Remembering that

$$\int_{-\pi}^{\pi} \sin nx \, dx = \int_{-\pi}^{\pi} \cos nx \, dx = 0 \quad \text{for } n = 1, 2, \dots$$

$$\int_{-\pi}^{\pi} \sin nx \cos mx \, dx = \int_{-\pi}^{\pi} \cos nx \cos mx \, dx = \int_{-\pi}^{\pi} \sin nx \sin mx \, dx = 0 \quad \text{for } n \neq m,$$

and $\int_{-\pi}^{\pi} \sin^2 nx \, dx = \int_{-\pi}^{\pi} \cos^2 nx \, dx = \pi \quad \text{for } n = 1, 2, \dots$

then after multiplying (12.1) by $\cos kx$ and integrating it, we obtain

$$\int_{-\pi}^{\pi} g(x) \cos nx \, dx = \int_{-\pi}^{\pi} \left(\frac{1}{2} a_0 + \sum_{k=1}^{\infty} (a_k \cos kx + b_k \sin kx) \right) \cos nx \, dx$$

$$= \frac{1}{2} a_0 \int_{-\pi}^{\pi} \cos nx \, dx$$

$$+ \sum_{k=1}^{\infty} \left(a_k \int_{-\pi}^{\pi} \cos kx \cos nx \, dx + b_k \int_{-\pi}^{\pi} \sin kx \cos nx \, dx \right)$$

$$= \pi a_n$$

so that

$$a_k = \frac{1}{\pi} \int_{-\pi}^{\pi} g(x) \cos kx \, dx$$

This formula also includes the case for a_0, (which is why in (12.1) a_0 is divided by 2). Similarly, multiplying (12.1) by $\sin nx$ and then integrating it renders

$$b_k = \frac{1}{\pi} \int_{-\pi}^{\pi} g(x) \sin kx \, dx$$

Also

$$c_k = \frac{1}{2\pi} \int_{-\pi}^{\pi} g(x) e^{-ikx} \, dx$$

Note that $c_0 = \frac{1}{2\pi} \int_{-\pi}^{\pi} g(x) \, dx$. That is, it is the average (mean) value of the function g on the interval $[-\pi, \pi]$ (This average is also called the DC value.)

Example 12.2   Consider the following function

$$g(x) = \begin{cases} 1 - |x| & \text{for } |x| < 1 \\ 0 & \text{for } 1 \leq |x| \leq \pi \end{cases}$$

For this function, the coefficients a_k of the Fourier series are given as

$$a_k = \frac{1}{\pi} \int_{-\pi}^{\pi} g(n) \cos kx \, dx = \frac{1}{\pi} \left(\int_{-1}^{0} (1 + x) \cos kx \, dx + \int_{0}^{1} (1 - x) \cos kx \, dx \right)$$

Because from integration by parts,

$$\int x \cos kx \, dx = \int x d\left(\frac{\sin kx}{k}\right) = \frac{x \sin kx}{k} - \int \frac{\sin kx}{k} \, dx = \frac{x \sin kx}{k} + \frac{\cos kx}{k^2}$$

then

$$a_k = \frac{1}{\pi}\left(\int_{-1}^{0} \cos kx \, dx + \int_{-1}^{0} x \cos kx \, dx + \int_{0}^{1} \cos kx \, dx - \int_{0}^{1} x \cos kx \, dx\right)$$

$$= \frac{1}{\pi}\left(\frac{\sin kx}{k}\bigg|_{-1}^{0} + \left(\frac{x \sin kx}{k} + \frac{\cos kx}{k^2}\right)\bigg|_{-1}^{0} + \frac{\sin kx}{k}\bigg|_{0}^{1} - \left(\frac{x \sin kx}{k} + \frac{\cos kx}{k^2}\right)\bigg|_{0}^{1}\right)$$

$$= \frac{1}{\pi}\left(-\frac{\sin(-k)}{k} + \frac{1}{k^2} + \frac{\sin(-k)}{k} - \frac{\cos(-k)}{k^2} + \frac{\sin k}{k} - \frac{\sin k}{k} - \frac{\cos k}{k^2} + \frac{1}{k^2}\right)$$

$$= \frac{2}{\pi}\left(\frac{1 - \cos k}{k^2}\right)$$

since $\cos k = \cos(-k)$. To find a_0, we use the formula

$$a_0 = \frac{1}{\pi}\int_{-\pi}^{\pi} g(n)dx = \frac{1}{\pi}\left(\int_{-1}^{0}(1+x)dx + \int_{0}^{1}(1-x)dx\right) = \frac{1}{\pi}$$

The reader can check that

$$b_k = \frac{1}{\pi}\int_{-\pi}^{\pi} g(n)\sin kx \, dx = 0$$

Therefore, the Fourier expansion of our function g is

$$g(x) = \frac{1}{2\pi} + \frac{2}{\pi}\sum_{k=1}^{\infty} \frac{1 - \cos k}{k^2} \cos kx$$

This Fourier series includes all the sinusoidal components of the function g. The first four components are shown in Figure 12.2a–d. Figure 12.2e–h shows the expansion that includes a different number of terms of the sum: The first approximation includes only the first term of the series (Figure 12.2e), the second is obtained by superposition of the first two sinusoids (i.e., it is the sum of the first two terms of the series; Figure 12.2f), and so on.

This example shows an obvious fact that the more components are included in an approximation of a function, the better this approximation is. However, the number of terms needed to obtain a satisfactory approximation can vary from one function to another. In Figure 12.2, the match between the function and its approximation is fairly good, but in Figure 12.3, the match is not very good because the function is not continuous.

For the sake of simplicity in the preceding discussion, only functions meeting Dirichlet conditions in the fundamental interval $[-\pi, \pi]$ have been used. However, this limitation can be lifted so that functions ranging over any finite interval $[-p/2, p/2]$ can have a Fourier expansion. This is accomplished by normalizing the

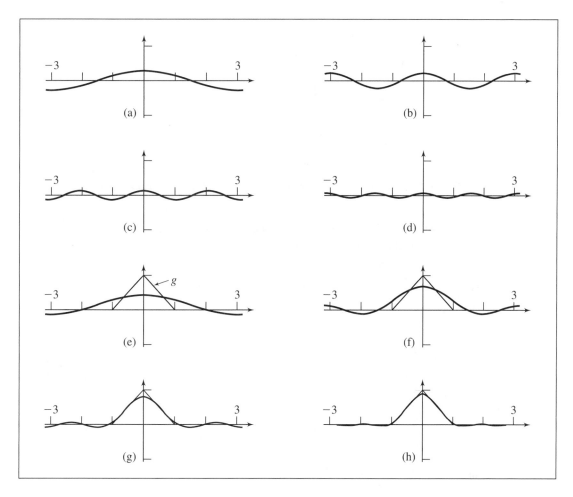

Figure 12.2   Expansion of the function g in Example 12.2 into the Fourier series $\frac{1}{2\pi} + \frac{2}{\pi} \sum_{k=1}^{\infty} \frac{1 - \cos k}{k^2} \cos kx$. **Harmonics of the series: (a)** $\frac{2}{\pi}(1 - \cos 1)\cos x$; **(b)** $\frac{2}{\pi} \frac{1 - \cos 2}{4} \cos 2x$; **(c)** $\frac{2}{\pi} \frac{1 - \cos 3}{9} \cos 3x$; **(d)** $\frac{2}{\pi} \frac{1 - \cos 4}{16} \cos 4x$. **Partial series:**
(e) $\frac{1}{2\pi} + \frac{2}{\pi} \sum_{k=1}^{1} \frac{1 - \cos k}{k^2} \cos kx$; **(f)** $\frac{1}{2\pi} + \frac{2}{\pi} \sum_{k=1}^{2} \frac{1 - \cos k}{k^2} \cos kx$; **(g)** $\frac{1}{2\pi} + \frac{2}{\pi} \sum_{k=1}^{3} \frac{1 - \cos k}{k^2} \cos kx$; **(h)** $\frac{1}{2\pi} + \frac{2}{\pi} \sum_{k=1}^{4} \frac{1 - \cos k}{k^2} \cos kx$

range of g through the transformation $x = \frac{py}{2\pi}$ so that the function $h(y) = g(x) = g\left(\frac{py}{2\pi}\right)$ is 2π-periodic:

$$h(y + 2\pi) = g\left(\frac{p(y + 2\pi)}{2\pi}\right) = g\left(\frac{py}{2\pi} + p\right) = g\left(\frac{py}{2\pi}\right) = h(y)$$

Then, by using Fourier expansion for the function h, we have

$$h(y) = \frac{1}{2}a_0 + \sum_{k=1}^{\infty} (a_k \cos ky + b_k \sin ky)$$

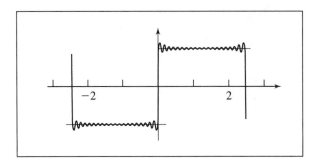

Figure 12.3 Expansion into the Fourier series of the function g in Example 12.3 for $p = 5$

and with the substitution $y = \frac{2\pi x}{p}$, the Fourier expansion of function g for the interval $[-p/2, p/2]$ becomes

$$g(x) = \frac{1}{2} a_0 + \sum_{k=1}^{\infty} \left(a_k \cos \frac{2\pi k x}{p} + b_k \sin \frac{2\pi k x}{p} \right) = \sum_{k=-\infty}^{\infty} c_k e^{i 2\pi k x/p}$$

where

$$a_0 = \frac{2}{p} \int_{-p/2}^{p/2} g(x) dx$$

$$a_k = \frac{2}{p} \int_{-p/2}^{p/2} g(x) \cos \frac{2\pi k x}{p} dx$$

$$b_k = \frac{2}{p} \int_{-p/2}^{p/2} g(x) \sin \frac{2\pi k x}{p} dx$$

$$c_k = \frac{1}{p} \int_{-p/2}^{p/2} g(x) e^{-i 2\pi k x/p} dx$$

It can be shown that similar formulas can be used for the interval $[0, p]$; in this case, the coefficients become

$$a_0 = \frac{2}{p} \int_0^p g(x) dx$$

$$a_k = \frac{2}{p} \int_0^p g(x) \cos \frac{2\pi k x}{p} dx$$

$$b_k = \frac{2}{p} \int_0^p g(x) \sin \frac{2\pi k x}{p} dx \qquad (12.2)$$

$$c_k = \frac{1}{p} \int_0^p g(x) e^{-i 2\pi k x/p} dx$$

Example 12.3

Let us find a Fourier expansion of the following p-periodic function:

$$g(x) = \begin{cases} -1 & \text{for } -p/2 \le x < 0 \\ 1 & \text{for } 0 \le x \le p/2 \end{cases}$$

The Fourier coefficients are given by these formulas:

$$a_k = \frac{2}{p} \int_{-p/2}^{p/2} g(x) \cos \frac{2\pi kx}{p} \, dx = \frac{2}{p} \left(-\int_{-p/2}^{0} \cos \frac{2\pi kx}{p} \, dx + \int_{0}^{p/2} \cos \frac{2\pi kx}{p} \, dx \right)$$

$$= \frac{2}{p} \left(-\frac{p \sin (2\pi kx/p)}{2\pi k} \Big|_{-p/2}^{0} + \frac{p \sin (2\pi kx/p)}{2\pi k} \Big|_{0}^{p/2} \right) = 0$$

$$b_k = \frac{2}{p} \int_{-p/2}^{p/2} g(x) \sin \frac{2\pi kx}{p} \, dx = \frac{2}{p} \left(-\int_{-p/2}^{0} \sin \frac{2\pi kx}{p} \, dx + \int_{0}^{p/2} \sin \frac{2\pi kx}{p} \, dx \right)$$

$$= \frac{2}{p} \left(\frac{p \cos (2\pi kx/p)}{2\pi k} \Big|_{-p/2}^{0} - \frac{p \cos (2\pi kx/p)}{2\pi k} \Big|_{0}^{p/2} \right)$$

$$= \frac{1}{\pi x}(2 - \cos(-k\pi) - \cos k\pi) = \frac{2}{\pi k}(1 - (-1)^k) = \begin{cases} \frac{4}{\pi k} & \text{if } k \text{ is odd} \\ 0 & \text{if } k \text{ is even} \end{cases}$$

Therefore,

$$g(x) = \frac{1}{2} a_0 + \sum_{k=1}^{\infty} \left(a_k \cos \frac{2\pi kx}{p} + b_k \sin \frac{2\pi kx}{p} \right) = \frac{4}{\pi} \sum_{k=1}^{\infty} \frac{\sin (2\pi(2k-1)x/p)}{2k-1}$$

The graph of the Fourier series that includes 20 terms of the sum when the period p of g is equal to 5 is shown in Figure 12.3.

12.2   The Fourier Transform

Up to this point, we have discussed only functions defined on a finite interval. It was a great achievement of Fourier to show that the decomposition into harmonic components can be performed on functions defined for all the numbers in $[-\infty, +\infty]$. This can be accomplished by extending the range $[-p/2, p/2]$ into infinity. However, if we allow p to approach infinity, then the frequency $1/p$ approaches zero. Therefore, all possible frequencies for such a function could not be numbered using integers since the set of these components becomes continuous. Whereas a periodic function was represented as an infinite sum of oscillations defined at frequencies equal to the multiples of the fundamental frequency, functions defined for all real numbers will require using an integral over the continuous range of frequencies, which will lead us to the concept of the Fourier transform.

What exactly is an impact of the growth of period p toward infinity on coefficients c_k of Fourier series (12.1)? From the formula for c_k,

$$c_k = \frac{1}{p} \int_{-p/2}^{p/2} g(x) e^{-i2\pi kx/p} \, dx$$

we have

$$pc_k = \int_{-p/2}^{p/2} g(x) e^{-i2\pi kx/p} \, dx$$

We can also assume that all these integrals are finite; that is, g is *absolutely integrable* so that for some M

$$pc_k = \int_{-p/2}^{p/2} g(x) e^{-i2\pi kx/p} \, dx \le M$$

Now if p goes toward infinity, c_k has to decrease so that

$$\lim_{p \to \infty} pc_k = \int_{-\infty}^{\infty} g(x)e^{-i2\pi kx/p} \, dx$$

At the same time, k has to go to infinity if a particular frequency $f_k = k/p$ is to remain constant. Therefore,

$$\lim_{p \to \infty} pc_k = \int_{-\infty}^{\infty} g(x)e^{-i2\pi kx/p} \, dx = \int_{-\infty}^{\infty} g(x)e^{-i2\pi f_k x} \, dx$$

Now, by passing from the discrete to continuous domain by allowing any continuous frequency, we have

$$\lim_{p \to \infty} pc_k = \int_{-\infty}^{\infty} g(x)e^{-i2\pi f x} \, dx$$

This rather informal reasoning leads us to the definition of the Fourier transform.

Definition 12.3   A *Fourier transform G* of a function g, for which $\int_{-\infty}^{\infty} |g(x)| \, dx < \infty$, is defined by the *Fourier integral* as

$$G(f) = \int_{-\infty}^{\infty} g(x)e^{-i2\pi f x} \, dx$$

The original function g can be recovered from its transform G using this formula

$$g(x) = \int_{-\infty}^{\infty} G(f)e^{i2\pi f x} \, df$$

Due to the similarity of the two last formulas, g is also called an *inverse Fourier transform* of G.

Comment   Sometimes other definitions are used. To retain symmetry between the two transforms, they are defined in the form

$$G_1(\omega) = \frac{1}{\sqrt{2\pi}} \int_{-\infty}^{\infty} g(x)e^{-i\omega x} \, dx$$

$$g(x) = \frac{1}{\sqrt{2\pi}} \int_{-\infty}^{\infty} G_1(\omega)e^{i\omega x} \, d\omega$$

Other commonly used definitions are

$$G_2(\omega) = \int_{-\infty}^{\infty} g(x)e^{-i\omega x} \, dx$$

$$g(x) = \frac{1}{2\pi} \int_{-\infty}^{\infty} G_2(\omega)e^{i\omega x} \, d\omega$$

where angular frequency ω (given in radians per second) is used rather than rotational frequency f (given in hertz).

The Fourier transform of function g shows the spectrum of g—that is, the amount of frequency f in function g for each real number f. In this way, instead of sinusoids of discrete frequencies used in the Fourier expansion of a function, in the Fourier transform, all frequencies are present.

Example 12.4   Consider the rectangle pulse function

$$g(x) = \begin{cases} c & \text{for } |x| < r \\ 0 & \text{otherwise} \end{cases}$$

Its Fourier transform is given by

$$G(f) = \int_{-\infty}^{\infty} g(x)e^{-i2\pi fx}\, dx = \int_{-r}^{r} c\, e^{-i2\pi fx}\, dx = \frac{c}{-i2\pi f}e^{-i2\pi fx}\Big|_{-r}^{r}$$

$$= \frac{c}{-i2\pi f}(e^{-i2\pi fr} - e^{i2\pi fr}) = \frac{c}{-i2\pi f}(-i2\sin(2\pi fr))$$

That is,

$$G(f) = 2cr\frac{\sin(2\pi fr)}{2\pi fr}$$

Both the function g and its transform G are shown in Figure 12.4.

The definition of Fourier transform can be extended to n dimensions, but in the context of image compression, the two-dimensional Fourier transform is of interest to us.

Definition 12.4   A two-dimensional *Fourier transform G* of a function g, for which $\int_{-\infty}^{\infty}\int_{-\infty}^{\infty} |g(x, y)|\, dx\, dy < \infty$, is defined as

$$G(u, v) = \int_{-\infty}^{\infty}\int_{-\infty}^{\infty} g(x, y)e^{-i2\pi(ux+vy)}\, dx\, dy$$

and the two-dimensional *inverse Fourier transform* is given by

$$g(x, y) = \int_{-\infty}^{\infty}\int_{-\infty}^{\infty} G(u, v)e^{i2\pi(ux+vy)}\, du\, dv$$

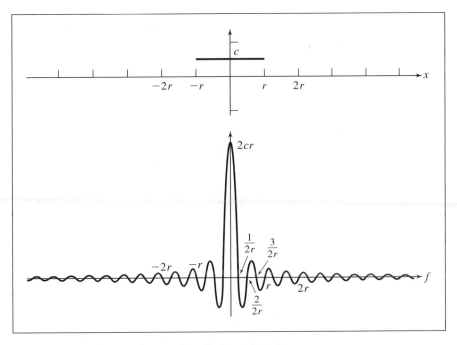

Figure 12.4   Function *g* and its transform *G* in Example 12.4

Example 12.5

Consider the two-dimensional rectangle pulse function (rectangular aperture)

$$g(x, y) = \begin{cases} c & \text{for } |x| < r_1 \text{ and } |y| < r_2 \\ 0 & \text{otherwise} \end{cases}$$

Its Fourier transform is given by

$$G(u, v) = \int_{-\infty}^{\infty} \int_{-\infty}^{\infty} g(x, y) e^{-i2\pi(ux+vy)} \, dx \, dy = c \int_{-r_1}^{r_1} e^{-i2\pi ux} \, dx \int_{-r_2}^{r_2} e^{-i2\pi vy} \, dy$$

$$= c \left(\frac{1}{-i2\pi u} e^{-i2\pi ux} \Big|_{-r_1}^{r_1} \right) \left(\frac{1}{-i2\pi v} e^{-i2\pi vy} \Big|_{-r_2}^{r_2} \right)$$

$$= \frac{c}{-i2\pi u} (e^{-i2\pi u r_1} - e^{i2\pi u r_1}) \frac{c}{-i2\pi v} (e^{-i2\pi v r_2} - e^{i2\pi v r_2})$$

$$= \frac{c}{4\pi^2 uv} (-i2 \sin(2\pi u r_1))(-i2 \sin(2\pi v r_2))$$

That is,

$$G(u, v) = 4c r_1 r_2 \frac{\sin(2\pi u r_1)}{2\pi u r_1} \frac{\sin(2\pi v r_2)}{2\pi v r_2}$$

Both the function g and its transform G are shown in Figure 12.5.

12.3   The Discrete Fourier Transform

To enable computational processing of Fourier transforms, we have to use a discrete approximation of continuous Fourier transformation in the form of a discrete Fourier transform.

Assume that the function g has nonzero values only in the interval $[-p/2, p/2]$; in this case,

$$G(f) = \int_{-\infty}^{\infty} g(x) e^{-i2\pi f x} \, dx = \int_{-p/2}^{p/2} g(x) e^{-i2\pi f x} \, dx$$

Because g is zero outside $[-p/2, p/2]$, then by applying the sampling theorem (see Section 12.4) to the transform G, we can infer that G can be completely reconstructed from its values at points k/p

$$G\left(\frac{k}{p}\right) = \int_{-p/2}^{p/2} g(x) e^{-i2\pi x k/p} \, dx \text{ for } k = 0, \ldots, Wp - 1$$

If the interval $[0, p]$ is also divided into N equal subintervals to represent times at which continuous-time signal g is sampled and the integral is replaced by the Riemann sum, then

$$G\left(\frac{k}{p}\right) \approx \sum_{m=0}^{N-1} g\left(\frac{mp}{N}\right) e^{-i2\pi km/N} \frac{p}{N} \text{ for } k = 0, \ldots, Wp - 1$$

Because $e^{-i2\pi m} = 1$, $e^{-i2\pi(k+N)m/N} = e^{-i2\pi km/N} \cdot e^{-i2\pi m} = e^{-i2\pi km/N}$, and consequently, $G(\frac{k}{W}) = G(\frac{k+N}{W})$; Therefore, all the necessary information is included in the sequence $G(\frac{0}{W}), \ldots, G(\frac{N-1}{W})$. This leads to the following definition.

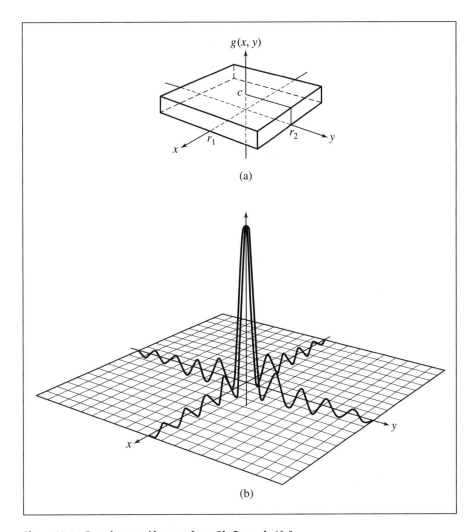

Figure 12.5   Function *g* and its transform *G* in Example 12.5

Definition 12.5

An *N-point discrete Fourier transform* (*DFT*) is a finite sequence of real or complex numbers $G(0), \ldots, G(N-1)$ representing the discrete frequency sequence corresponding to a finite sequence of real or complex numbers $g(0), \ldots, g(N-1)$ representing a discrete time sequence as follows:

$$G(k) = \sum_{m=0}^{N-1} g(m)e^{-i2\pi km/N}, \text{ for } k = 0, \ldots, N-1$$

A corresponding *inverse discrete Fourier transform* is defined as the sum

$$g(m) = \frac{1}{N} \sum_{k=0}^{N-1} G(k)e^{i2\pi km/N}, \text{ for } m = 0, \ldots, N-1$$

There are N complex numbers $G(k)$, and each such number requires N additions. Therefore, finding a discrete Fourier transform requires $O(N^2)$ operations. There exist, however, algorithms to find the discrete Fourier transform faster than in N^2 time. One such algorithm was developed by Cooley and Tukey in 1965 and is called a *fast Fourier transform*.

Because a Fourier transform is a complex function, it is more convenient to represent it in the form of two spectra (see Section 12.5 and Figure 12.9).

Definition 12.6

The *amplitude spectrum* of function g is the magnitude function $|G|$ defined as

$$|G(k)| = \sqrt{(\text{Re}(G(k)))^2 + (\text{Im}(G(k)))^2}$$

and the *phase spectrum* is a set $\{\theta_k: k = 0, 1, 2, \ldots\}$, where

$$G(k) = |G(k)| e^{i\theta_k}$$

Example 12.6

Consider a sequence of four samples, $g = \{1, 2, 3, 4\}$; the DFT coefficients are found by the following computations

$$G(0) = \sum_{m=0}^{3} g(m)e^0 = g(0) + g(1) + g(2) + g(3) = 1 + 2 + 3 + 4 = 10$$

$$G(1) = \sum_{m=0}^{3} g(m)e^{-i\pi 2m/4} = 1e^0 + 2e^{-i\pi/2} + 3e^{-i\pi} + 4e^{-i3\pi/2}$$
$$= 1 - 2i - 3 + 4i = -2 + 2i$$

$$G(2) = \sum_{m=0}^{3} g(m)e^{-i\pi 4m/4} = 1e^0 + 2e^{-i\pi} + 3e^{-i2\pi} + 4e^{-i3\pi}$$
$$= 1 - 2 + 3 - 4 = -2$$

$$G(3) = \sum_{m=0}^{3} g(m)e^{-i\pi 6m/4} = 1e^0 + 2e^{-i3\pi/2} + 3e^{-i3\pi} + 4e^{-i9\pi/2}$$
$$= 1 + 2i - 3 - 4i = -2 - 2i$$

The amplitude spectrum is given by

$$|G(0)| = 10, \; |G(1)| = \sqrt{(-2)^2 + 2^2} = 2\sqrt{2}, \; |G(2)| = 2, \; |G(3)| = 2\sqrt{2}$$

and the phase spectrum by

$$\theta_0 = 0, \; \theta_1 = 3\pi/4, \; \theta_2 = \pi, \; \theta_3 = 5\pi/4$$

The samples, the Fourier transform, and the spectra are shown in Figure 12.6a–d.

The original four samples are reconstructed with the inverse transformation

$$g(0) = \frac{1}{4}\sum_{k=0}^{3} G(k)e^0 = \frac{1}{4}(G(0) + G(1) + G(2) + G(3)) = 1$$

$$g(1) = \frac{1}{4}\sum_{k=0}^{3} G(k)e^{i\pi 2k/4} = \frac{1}{4}(10e^0 + (-2 + 2i)e^{i\pi/2} - 2e^{i\pi} + (-2 - 2i)e^{i3\pi/2})$$

$$= \frac{1}{4}(10 + (-2 + 2i)i + 2 - (-2 - 2i)i) = \frac{1}{4}(10 - 2i - 2 + 2 + 2i + 2) = 2$$

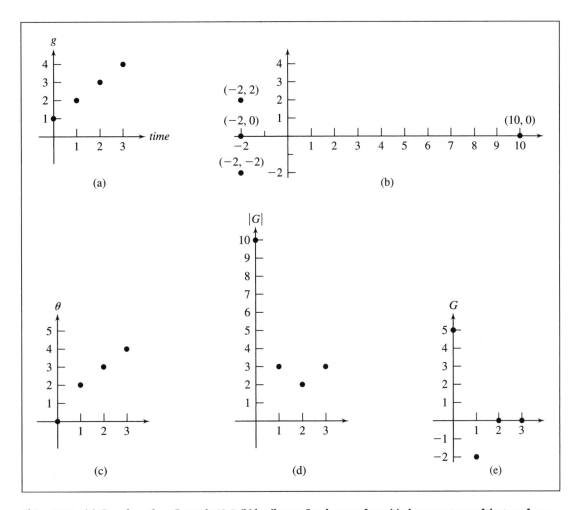

Figure 12.6   (a) Function *g* from Example 12.5, (b) its discrete Fourier transform, (c) phase spectrum of the transform, (d) its amplitude spectrum, and (e) discrete cosine transform spectrum of *g* (Example 12.8)

$$g(2) = \frac{1}{4} \sum_{k=0}^{3} G(k)e^{i\pi 4k/4} = \frac{1}{4}(10e^0 + (-2 + 2i)e^{i\pi} - 2e^{i2\pi} + (-2 - 2i)e^{i3\pi})$$

$$= \frac{1}{4}(10 - (-2 + 2i) - 2 - (-2 - 2i) = 3$$

$$g(3) = \frac{1}{4} \sum_{k=0}^{3} G(k)e^{i\pi 6k/4}$$

$$= \frac{1}{4}(10e^0 + (-2 + 2i)e^{i3\pi/2} - 2e^{i3\pi} + (-2 - 2i)e^{i9\pi/2})$$

$$= \frac{1}{4}(10 - (-2 + 2i)i + 2 + (-2 - 2i)i = 4$$

Definition 12.7

A two-dimensional *discrete Fourier transform G* of a function *g* is defined as

$$G(k, l) = \sum_{m=0}^{M-1} \sum_{n=0}^{N-1} g(m, n) e^{-i2\pi(km/M + ln/N)}$$

for $k = 0, 1, 2, \ldots, M - 1$ and $l = 0, 1, 2, \ldots, N - 1$. The two-dimensional *discrete inverse Fourier transform* is given by

$$g(m, n) = \frac{1}{MN} \sum_{k=0}^{M-1} \sum_{l=0}^{N-1} G(k, l) e^{i2\pi(km/M + ln/N)}$$

for $m = 0, 1, 2, \ldots, M - 1$ and $n = 0, 1, 2, \ldots, N - 1$. If $M = N$, that is, if data are sampled in a square,

$$G(k, l) = \frac{1}{N} \sum_{m=0}^{N-1} \sum_{n=0}^{N-1} g(m, n) e^{-i2\pi(km + ln)/N}$$

and

$$g(m, n) = \frac{1}{N} \sum_{k=0}^{N-1} \sum_{l=0}^{N-1} G(k, l) e^{i2\pi(km + ln)/N}$$

12.3.1   The Discrete Cosine Transform

If the function *g* has only nonzero values in a certain interval *I*, then it can be extended beyond this interval by making it *I*-periodic—that is, by repeating it indefinitely outside the interval. This is important for applying the Fourier transform to the function *g*. It is critical, however, in which way the function is extended, because if it is extended so that the extension includes discontinuities, then the outcome of such an extension is a subject of the *Gibbs phenomenon*. If the extended function is approximated with the Fourier series, then oscillating spikes develop at the points of discontinuities. It turns out that these spikes do not disappear after adding more and more terms of the series. The spikes become narrower but not smaller with respect to height. That is, extending the Fourier series does not result in a nice approximation at the points of discontinuities (Figure 12.7c-d). To avoid this problem, the function should be extended by using its mirror image (the so-called even extension; cf. Exercise 12.5), as in Figure 12.7e, whose Fourier extension very quickly and smoothly converges to the function *g*.

Example 12.7

Consider the function $g(x) = x + 1$ as in Figure 12.7a and its extension into the function 12.7b. The extended function has sharp discontinuities at the interval boundaries. The Fourier expansion of the extended function is found with formulas (12.2) to be

$$2.5 - \sum_{n=1}^{\infty} \frac{3}{\pi n} \sin \frac{2\pi n x}{3}$$

When drawn with 20 and 40 harmonic components (12.7c–d), the series does not get smoother at the discontinuities since the spikes still remain, although they become nar-

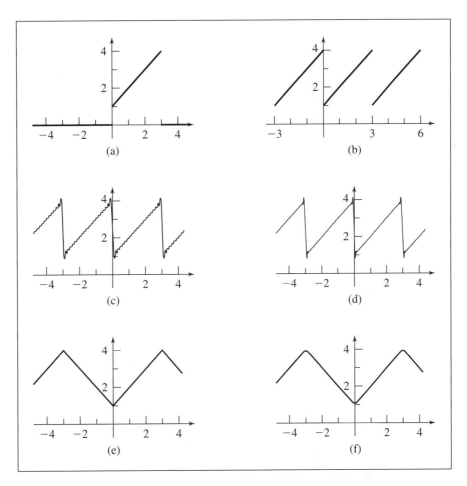

Figure 12.7   Graphs illustrating the Gibbs phenomenon: reconstructing function
(a) $g = x + 1$ defined in interval $[0, 3]$ and (b) extended to a function with period 3; Fourier series
$2.5 - \frac{3}{\pi n} \sum\limits_{n=1}^{\infty} \sin \frac{2\pi nx}{3}$ of the extended function is shown with (c) 20 and (d) 40 harmonic
components; (e) even extension of function g and (f) its Fourier expansion with 20 harmonic
components

rower. However, when the function g is extended as in 12.7e so that no discontinuities arise, the Fourier expansion of the extended function g can be found to be

$$2.5 + \sum_{n=1}^{\infty} \frac{6}{(\pi n)^2} (\cos n\pi - 1) \cos \frac{\pi nx}{3} = 2.5 - \sum_{\substack{n=1 \\ n \text{ is odd}}}^{\infty} \frac{12}{(\pi n)^2} \cos \frac{\pi nx}{3}$$

since $\cos n\pi = (-1)^n$ and $(-1)^n - 1 = -2$ for odd ns and zero otherwise. (Note that this time the period of the extended function is 6, not 3; however, it can be shown that in the case of even extension,

$$g(x) = \frac{1}{2} a_0 + \sum_{k=1}^{\infty} \left(a_k \cos \frac{\pi kx}{p} \right)$$

where

$$a_k = \frac{2}{p} \int_0^p g(x) \cos \frac{\pi k x}{p} \, dx$$

and $p = 3$, not 6.) Figure 12.7e–f shows how smoothly the series approximates the function g.

A similar problem arises in applications of DFT for data compression; namely, the DFT does not compress very well in the presence of discontinuities (energy of samples is dispersed over transform coefficients). To avoid this problem, DFT is replaced by another transform that looks at the samples as though they were doubled by adding to a sequence of samples another sequence of the same sequence in the reverse order (i.e., adding the mirror image of the original sequence).

We form the mirror image of a sequence of samples $g(m)$ for $m = 0, \ldots, N - 1$ by reflecting the existing samples about the point $N - \frac{1}{2}$ so that the extended sequence of samples is defined by

$$g_e(m) = \begin{cases} g(m) & \text{for } m = 0, \ldots, N - 1 \\ g(2N - 1 - m) & \text{for } m = N, \ldots, 2N - 1 \end{cases}$$

Now the Fourier transformation is applied to $g_e(m)$ for $m = 0, \ldots, 2N - 1$, which renders

$$G_e(k) = \sum_{m=0}^{2N-1} g_e(m) e^{-i2\pi km/2N} = \sum_{m=0}^{N-1} g(m) e^{-i2\pi km/2N} + \sum_{m=N}^{2N-1} g_e(m) e^{-i2\pi km/2N}$$

for $k = 0, \ldots, 2N - 1$. A new variable $s = 2N - 1 - m$ changes from $N - 1$ to 0 as m changes from N to $2N - 1$, whereby $g_e(2N - 1 - m) = g(s)$, and thus

$$G_e(k) = \sum_{m=0}^{N-1} g(m) e^{-i2\pi km/2N} + \sum_{s=0}^{N-1} g(s) e^{-i2\pi k(2N-1-s)/2N}$$

Because the name of the variable is irrelevant, we can use m again instead of s. The exponential term in the second sum can also be broken down into two parts so that

$$G_e(k) = \sum_{m=0}^{N-1} g(m) e^{-i2\pi km/2N} + \sum_{m=0}^{N-1} g(m) e^{-i2\pi k2N/2N} e^{i2\pi k(m+1)/2N}$$

$$= \sum_{m=0}^{N-1} g(m) (e^{-i2\pi km/2N} + e^{i2\pi k(m+1)/2N})$$

because $e^{-i2\pi k} = 1$. Multiplying both sides by $e^{-i\pi k/2N}$ renders

$$e^{-i\pi k/2N} G_e(k) = \sum_{m=0}^{N-1} g(m) (e^{-i2\pi km/2N} e^{-i\pi k/2N} + e^{i2\pi k(m+1)/2N} e^{-i\pi k/2N})$$

$$= \sum_{m=0}^{N-1} g(m) (e^{-i\pi k(2m+1)/2N} + e^{i\pi k(2m+1)/2N})$$

$$= \sum_{m=0}^{N-1} g(m) 2 \cos \frac{\pi k(2m + 1)}{2N}, \text{ for } k = 0, \ldots, 2N - 1$$

with the help of Euler's identity Section 12.5. The discrete cosine transform $G(k)$ is derived from $G_e(k)$ by dividing the latter by $e^{-i\pi k/2N}$ for $k = 0, \ldots, N - 1$ and setting it to zero for $k = N, \ldots, 2N - 1$. After we take into account the normalization, we obtain the following definition.

Definition 12.8

A *forward discrete cosine transform* (*FDCT*) is a finite sequence of real or complex numbers $G(0), \ldots, G(N - 1)$ defined on a finite sequence of real or complex numbers $g(0), \ldots, g(N - 1)$ as follows:

$$G(0) = \frac{1}{\sqrt{N}} \sum_{m=0}^{N-1} g(m)$$

$$G(k) = \sqrt{\frac{2}{N}} \sum_{m=0}^{N-1} g(m) \cos \frac{\pi k(2m+1)}{2N} \quad \text{for } k = 1, 2, \ldots, N-1$$

where $G(k)$ are the DCT coefficients.

The *inverse discrete cosine transform* (*IDCT*) is defined as

$$g(m) = \frac{1}{\sqrt{N}} G(0) + \sqrt{\frac{2}{N}} \sum_{k=1}^{N-1} G(k) \cos \frac{\pi k(2m+1)}{2N} \quad \text{for } k = 0, 1, \ldots, N-1$$

Example 12.8

Consider a sequence of four samples, $g = \{1, 2, 3, 4\}$ from Example 12.7. Remembering that $\cos \frac{\pi}{8} = \frac{\sqrt{2+\sqrt{2}}}{2}$ and $\cos \frac{3\pi}{8} = \frac{\sqrt{2-\sqrt{2}}}{2}$, the coefficients of DCT are

$$G(0) = \frac{1}{2} \sum_{m=0}^{3} g(m) = \frac{1}{2}(1 + 2 + 3 + 4) = 5$$

$$G(1) = \frac{\sqrt{2}}{2} \sum_{m=0}^{3} g(m) \cos \frac{\pi(2m+1)}{8}$$

$$= \frac{\sqrt{2}}{2} \left(\cos \frac{\pi}{8} + 2 \cos \frac{3\pi}{8} + 3 \cos \frac{5\pi}{8} + 4 \cos \frac{7\pi}{8} \right)$$

$$= \frac{\sqrt{2}}{2} \left(-3 \frac{\sqrt{2+\sqrt{2}}}{2} - \frac{\sqrt{2-\sqrt{2}}}{2} \right) = -2.2305$$

$$G(2) = \frac{\sqrt{2}}{2} \sum_{m=0}^{3} g(m) \cos \frac{\pi 2(2m+1)}{8}$$

$$= \frac{\sqrt{2}}{2} \left(\cos \frac{\pi}{4} + 2 \cos \frac{3\pi}{4} + 3 \cos \frac{5\pi}{4} + 4 \cos \frac{7\pi}{4} \right) = 0$$

$$G(3) = \frac{\sqrt{2}}{2} \sum_{m=0}^{3} g(m) \cos \frac{\pi 3(2m+1)}{8}$$

$$= \frac{\sqrt{2}}{2} \left(\cos \frac{3\pi}{8} + 2 \cos \frac{9\pi}{8} + 3 \cos \frac{15\pi}{8} + 4 \cos \frac{21\pi}{8} \right)$$

$$= \frac{\sqrt{2}}{2} \left(\frac{\sqrt{2+\sqrt{2}}}{2} - 3 \frac{\sqrt{2-\sqrt{2}}}{2} \right) = -0.1585$$

The graph of DCT G is shown in Figure 12.6e. Note that the amplitudes $G(2)$ and $G(3)$ are insignificantly small in comparison with the first two amplitudes. Therefore, most of the information concerning the samples is concentrated in the transform coefficients $G(0)$ and $G(1)$, whereas for the DFT and for the same samples (Figure 12.6d), $|G(2)|$ and $|G(3)|$ are of the same magnitude as $|G(1)|$. Thus, the information concerning the samples is distributed more evenly between the coefficients, which means that all four DFT coefficients are of comparable importance. For data compression, however, as discussed in Chapter 9, the more coefficients are equal to or almost equal to zero, the better for the compression.

Definition 12.9

A two-dimensional forward discrete cosine transform of an $N \times N$ matrix of samples is defined as an $N \times N$ matrix whose elements are numbers

$$G(k, l) = \frac{2}{N} C(k)C(l) \sum_{m=0}^{N-1} \sum_{n=0}^{N-1} g(m, n) \cos \frac{\pi k(2m + 1)}{2N} \cos \frac{\pi l(2n + 1)}{2N}$$

and the corresponding inverse discrete cosine transform is a matrix whose elements

$$g(m, n) = \frac{2}{N} \sum_{k=0}^{N-1} C(k) \sum_{l=0}^{N-1} C(l)G(k, l) \cos \frac{\pi k(2m + 1)}{2N} \cos \frac{\pi l(2n + 1)}{2N}$$

where

$$C(v) = \begin{cases} \frac{1}{\sqrt{2}} & \text{for } v = 0 \\ 1 & \text{otherwise} \end{cases}$$

12.4   The Sampling Theorem

Theorem 12.1

If a function g contains no frequency greater than W and the time step $T = \frac{1}{2W}$ (i.e., g is sampled at points of time spaced $\frac{1}{2W}$ seconds apart, whereby the sampling rate $\frac{1}{T} = 2W$ is the double of the limit frequency W), then g can be completely determined at any point of time by using the interpolation formula

$$g(x) = \sum_{k=-\infty}^{\infty} g\left(\frac{k}{2W}\right) \frac{\sin \pi(2Wx - k)}{\pi(2Wx - k)}$$

Proof. The restriction for g to have no frequency greater than W means that for the Fourier transform of g

$$G(f) = \int_{-\infty}^{\infty} g(x)e^{-i2\pi f x} \, dx$$

$G(f) = 0$ for $|f| \geq W$ so that it can be expanded on the interval $[-W, W]$ into the Fourier series

$$G(f) = \sum_{k=-\infty}^{\infty} c_k e^{i2\pi k f/2W}$$

where

$$c_k = \frac{1}{2W} \int_{-W}^{W} G(f) e^{-i2\pi k f/2W} \, df$$

Also, g is the inverse Fourier transform,

$$g(x) = \int_{-\infty}^{\infty} G(f) e^{i2\pi f x} df = \int_{-W}^{W} G(f) e^{i2\pi f x} df$$

which for $x = k/2W$ becomes

$$g\left(\frac{k}{2W}\right) = \int_{-W}^{W} G(f) e^{i2\pi f k/2W} df$$

and therefore,

$$c_k = \frac{1}{2W} g\left(\frac{-k}{2W}\right)$$

which means that if the function g is determined at points $\ldots, -\frac{2}{2W}, -\frac{1}{2W}, 0, \frac{1}{2W}, \frac{2}{2W}, \ldots$, then the coefficients c_k are uniquely determined. Thus, the transform G can be found for each frequency f, which in turn allows us to find the value of g at each point of time.

Consider now how to recover the value of g at any point of time using only sampled values.

$$g(x) = \int_{-W}^{W} G(f) e^{i2\pi f x} df = \int_{-W}^{W} \sum_{k=-\infty}^{\infty} c_k e^{i2\pi k f/2W} e^{i2\pi f x} df$$

$$= \frac{1}{2W} \int_{-W}^{W} \sum_{k=-\infty}^{\infty} g\left(-\frac{k}{2W}\right) e^{i2\pi k f/2W} e^{i2\pi f x} df$$

If we change the order of summation and integration to allow for termwise integration, we have

$$g(x) = \frac{1}{2W} \sum_{k=-\infty}^{\infty} g\left(-\frac{k}{2W}\right) \int_{-W}^{W} e^{i\pi f (k/W + 2x)} df$$

$$= \frac{1}{2W} \sum_{k=-\infty}^{\infty} g\left(-\frac{k}{2W}\right) \frac{e^{i\pi f (k/W + 2x)}}{i\pi(k/W + 2x)} \Big|_{-W}^{W}$$

$$g(x) = \sum_{k=-\infty}^{\infty} g\left(\frac{k}{2W}\right) \frac{\sin \pi(2Wx + k)}{\pi(2Wx + k)} = \sum_{k=-\infty}^{\infty} g\left(\frac{k}{2W}\right) \frac{\sin \pi(2Wx - k)}{\pi(2Wx - k)}$$

This indicates that each sampled value is weighted with the function $\sin x/x$ that peaks at the sampled points. That is, each sample $g(s)$ can be thought of as a generator of the function $\sin x/x$ that has the maximum at s and is equal to zero at all other sample points (Figure 12.8).

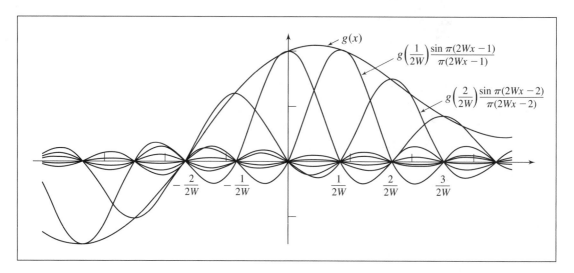

Figure 12.8   Reconstructing a function g with the function $\sin x / x$

12.5   Appendix: Complex Numbers and Euler's Identity

It is known from calculus that e^x, $\sin x$, and $\cos x$ have the following expansion into the power series, where x can be a real or complex number:

$$e^x = 1 + \frac{x}{1!} + \frac{x^2}{2!} + \frac{x^3}{3!} + \cdots$$

$$\cos x = 1 - \frac{x^2}{2!} + \frac{x^4}{4!} - \cdots$$

$$\sin x = \frac{x}{1!} + \frac{x^3}{3!} + \frac{x^5}{5!} + \cdots$$

Substitution of ix for x, where $i = \sqrt{-1}$ is an imaginary number, gives us the expansion

$$e^{ix} = 1 + \frac{ix}{1!} + \frac{(ix)^2}{2!} + \frac{(ix)^3}{3!} + \cdots$$

$$= \left(1 - \frac{x^2}{2!} + \frac{x^4}{4!} - \cdots\right) + i\left(\frac{x}{1!} + \frac{x^3}{3!} + \frac{x^5}{5!} + \cdots\right)$$

$$= \cos x + i \sin x$$

The equation

$$e^{ix} = \cos x + i \sin x$$

is called *Euler's identity*. If this identity is used for $-x$, then we have

$$e^{-ix} = \cos x - i \sin x$$

because $\cos -x = \cos x$ and $\sin -x = -\sin x$. Adding the two identities gives us

$$\cos x = \frac{e^{ix} + e^{-ix}}{2}$$

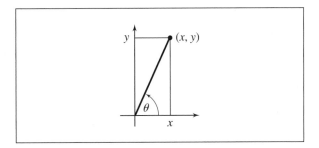

Figure 12.9   The trigonometric form of a complex number

and subtracting the first from the second gives us

$$\sin x = \frac{e^{ix} - e^{-ix}}{2i}$$

These formulas are very convenient because they allow for an easy conversion of trigonometric functions that are real valued into complex valued exponential functions.

Any complex number z can be represented in the form

$$z = x + iy$$

where $x = \mathrm{Re}(z)$ is its real part and $y = \mathrm{Im}(z)$ is the imaginary part or in the form of a pair (x, y) that represents a point on the Cartesian plane (Figure 12.9). The position of this point is uniquely determined by the values of x and y or by the length of the line r that connects this point with the origin of the coordinate system and the angle θ between the line and the x axis, where

$$r = |x + iy| = \sqrt{x^2 + y^2}$$
$$\theta = \arctan \frac{y}{x}$$

whereby the number z can be shown as

$$z = |x + iy| \, e^{i\theta}$$

EXERCISES

1. Using Definition 12.2, express a_k and b_k in terms of c_k.

2. Expand into Fourier series the following functions periodic on $[-\pi, \pi]$:

   a. $\sin^2 x$; b. $|\sin x|$; c. x^2; d. $x(\pi - |x|)$; e. $|x|$; f. x;

   g. 1 for $x \in (-.25, .25)$ and 0 otherwise.

3. A function g is called *even* if $g(x) = g(-x)$; g is called *odd* if $-g(x) = g(-x)$. Show that if function g is even, then in (12.1), coefficients $b_k = 0$ and if it is odd, then coefficients $a_k = 0$.

4. Find the relations between the three definitions of the Fourier transform, G, G_1, and G_2 mentioned in the Comment following Definition 12.3.

5. The Fourier transform G and the inverse Fourier transform g form a *transform pair*, or $g(x) \leftrightarrow G(y)$. Show that the following relations hold for transform pairs:

   a.   scaling: $g(ax) \leftrightarrow \frac{1}{|a|} G(\frac{y}{a})$ and $\frac{1}{|a|} g(\frac{x}{a}) \leftrightarrow G(ay)$

   b.   shifting: $g(x - a) \leftrightarrow G(y)e^{-iay}$ and $g(x)e^{-iax} \leftrightarrow G(y + a)$

   c.   linearity: $ag + bh \leftrightarrow aG + bH$ if $h(x) \leftrightarrow H(y)$

6. Find Fourier transforms of the following functions:

   a. $e^{-ax^2/2}$; b. $e^{-a|x|}$; c. $\frac{1}{x^2 + a^2}$; d. $\frac{1}{x} \sin ax$

7. Find DFT and DCT for the following sequences:

   a. $g = \{2, 2, 2, 2, 0, 0, 0, 0\}$; b. $\{2, 2, 0, 0, 0, 0, 0, 0, 2, 2\}$; c. $\{2, 2, 0, 0, 2, 2, 0, 0\}$;

   d. $\{2, 2, 2, 2, 2, 2, 2, 2\}$

BIBLIOGRAPHY

Champeney, David C., *Fourier transforms and their physical applications*, London: Academic Press, 1973.

Cooley, James W., and Tukey, John W., An algorithm for the machine calculation of complex Fourier series, *Mathematics of Computation,* 19 (1965), 297–301.

Folland, Gerald B., *Fourier analysis and its applications*, Pacific Grove, CA: Wadsworth, 1992.

Hancock, John C., *An introduction to the principles of communication theory*, New York: McGraw-Hill, 1961.

Oliver, B. M., Pierce, J. R., and Shannon, C. E., The philosophy of PCM, *Proceedings of the IRE* 36 (1948), 1324–1331.

Phillips, Charles L., and Parr, John M., *Signals, systems, and transforms*, Upper Saddle River, NJ: Prentice Hall, 1999.

Stuart, R. D., *An introduction to Fourier analysis*, London: Methuen, 1961.

Walker, James S., *Fast Fourier transforms*, Boca Raton, FL: CRC Press, 1996.

Chapter 13

Wavelets

The Fourier transform represents signals as the sum of sines and cosines that have infinite duration, and thus, it requires complete past and future knowledge about a signal to determine its value at a particular frequency ω. Therefore, the Fourier transform is useful for signals with statistical properties that are constant over time or space. It is less suitable, however, as the representation of nonstationary signals, whose statistical properties change with time. Because the Fourier transform is a function independent of time, it does not reflect frequencies that vary in time. For example, the higher and more limited in time a function is, such as a spike, the more high-frequency harmonics are needed to represent the signal. But all these harmonics are infinite in time, so that for the time when the function equals zero, the harmonics must cancel each other. Short-time Fourier transform addresses the problem of locality of functions by introducing a window with which the analyzed function is scaled.

Definition 13.1

The *short-time Fourier transform (STFT, windowed Fourier transform)* of function f is defined by

$$F_w(\omega, \tau) = \frac{1}{\sqrt{2\pi}} \int_{-\infty}^{\infty} f(x) e^{-iax} w(x - \tau) dx$$

where τ is a *shift* (translation) *parameter*, $w \in L^2(R)$ represents a well-localized in time *window function*, and $L^2(R)$ is a set of all square integrable real functions—that is, functions for which $\int f^2(x) dx < \infty$. When the window function is a Gaussian,

$$w_\alpha(x) = \frac{1}{2\sqrt{\pi\alpha}} e^{-\frac{x^2}{4\alpha}}$$

$\alpha > 0$, STFT transform becomes the *Gabor transform* (Gabor, 1946).

The window is shifted along the time axis to compute the transform at various positions τ. Multiplying the window function by a signal before computing the Fourier transform amounts to restricting the frequencies to the time covered by the window. However, STFT is not an ideal solution. One problem is the size of the window that is fixed and cannot be adapted to the changing characteristics of the signal. Therefore, the rendering of low frequencies (i.e., wavelengths longer than the window width) is inadequate; on the other hand, the long window gives very poor localization of high frequencies.

If Δ_w is a radius of the window function w, then the *Heisenberg uncertainty principle* states that for the Fourier transform W of w,

$$\Delta_w \Delta_W \geq \frac{1}{4\pi}$$

with equality only for the Gabor transform. The inequality limits the STFT time and frequency resolutions; that is, time and frequency cannot be measured at any precision level at the same time, and in particular, very high frequencies cannot be localized to very small time windows. Such time-varying signals can be better represented as the sum of basis functions that are localized in time. The solution is offered by wavelet analysis.

Wavelet analysis is a scale-independent means of analyzing signals. It uses short windows at high frequencies and long windows at low frequencies. The notion of *scale* is introduced as an alternative to frequency, which leads to the *time-scale* representation. In STFT, a signal is mapped into a time-frequency plane, whereas in wavelet transform, it is mapped into a time-scale plane.

In wavelet analysis, a basic function (analyzing function) called *basic wavelet* or *mother wavelet* is used as a window or a scale. But at the same time, all possible scalings of basic wavelet are used as basis functions derived from it. These basis functions, called *wavelets*, are generated by translating (shifting) and dilating (scaling, i.e., stretching or shrinking) the basic wavelet in time.

13.1   Wavelet Transforms

Definition 13.2   The *inner product (scalar product)* of two functions f and g, f, g: $[p, q] \rightarrow$ R is defined by

$$\langle f, g \rangle = \int_p^q f(x)g(x)dx$$

The *norm* of a function f is defined as

$$\| f \| = \int_{-\infty}^{\infty} |f(x)|^2 \, dx$$

Two functions f and g are *orthogonal* when $\langle f, g \rangle = 0$. A function f is *normalized* when $\| f \| = 1$.

Definition 13.3   *The continuous wavelet transform (CWT; integral wavelet transform)* of function f, introduced by Grossman and Morlet (1984), is defined by

$$CWT(a, \tau) = \frac{1}{\sqrt{a}} \int_{-\infty}^{\infty} f(x)\psi \left(\frac{x - \tau}{a} \right) dx$$

where a real-valued function ψ is a basic wavelet, τ is a shift parameter, and a is a scale parameter.

The basic wavelet generates a set of wavelet basis functions

$$\psi_{a, \tau}(x) = \frac{1}{\sqrt{a}} \psi \left(\frac{x - \tau}{a} \right)$$

For low-frequency wavelets, $a > 1$, while for high-frequency wavelets, $a < 1$. In this way, the definition of CWT can be given more succinctly:

$$CWT(a, \tau) = \langle f, \psi_{a,\tau} \rangle$$

The scaling parameter is a normalization factor that guarantees that the norms of functions $\psi_{a,\tau}$ are equal because

$$\left\| \psi\left(\frac{x - \tau}{a}\right) \right\| = \sqrt{\int_{-\infty}^{\infty} \left| \psi\left(\frac{x - \tau}{a}\right) \right|^2 dx} = \sqrt{a} \| \psi(x) \|$$

$CWT(a, \tau)$ represents the detail contained in the signal f at the scale a. This is particularly apparent in the multiresolution analysis discussed later.

Definition 13.4   When the wavelet function ψ meets the *admissibility condition*

$$C_\psi = \int_{-\infty}^{\infty} \frac{|\Psi(\omega)|^2}{|\omega|} d\omega < \infty$$

where Ψ is the Fourier transform of ψ, then the *inverse continuous wavelet transform* is given by

$$f(x) = \frac{1}{C_\psi} \int_0^\infty \int_{-\infty}^\infty CWT(a, \tau)\psi_{a,\tau}(x)d\tau \frac{da}{a^2}$$

If $\psi(t)$ decays to zero at infinity, the admissibility condition implies that

$$\int_{-\infty}^\infty \psi(x)dx = 0$$

that is, the basic wavelet has zero mean. This also means that ψ must be a wave that goes up and down the x axis.

It is a computational imperative that parameters a and τ be discrete. This leads to a definition of a discrete wavelet transform (a wavelet series expansion) (Daubechies, 1990).

Definition 13.5   A *discrete wavelet transform (DWT)* is defined by

$$DWT(j, k) = \int_{-\infty}^\infty f(x)\psi_{j,k}(x)dt$$

where

$$\psi_{j,k}(x) = \frac{1}{\sqrt{a_0^j}} \psi\left(\frac{x}{a_0^j} - k\tau_0\right)$$

so that $\psi_{0,0} = \psi(x)$. Constants a_0 and τ_0 determine the sampling intervals. The function f is reconstructed with

$$f(x) = \sum_{j=-\infty}^\infty \sum_{k=-\infty}^\infty DWT(j,k)\psi_{j,k}(x)$$

Commonly, binary scalings $a = 2^j$ (i.e., $a_0 = 2$) and dyadic translations $\tau = k2^j$ (i.e., $\tau_0 = 1$) are used so that

$$\psi_{j,k}(x) = \frac{1}{\sqrt{2^j}} \psi\left(\frac{x}{2^j} - k\right)$$

$$DWT(j, k) = \int_{-\infty}^\infty f(x)\psi_{jk}(t) = \frac{1}{\sqrt{2^j}} \int_{-\infty}^\infty f(x)\psi\left(\frac{x}{2^j} - k\right)$$

(13.1)

The double infinite series is not usually a problem in reconstructing function f. If f is limited in time, then the terms in the series with large parameters k are small or disappear, and for large parameters j, basic wavelets become very broad or narrow so that the terms with such j's also become negligible (Chui, 1992; a semidiscrete CWT for which $a = 2^j$ and τ is any real number was investigated first by Mallat and Hwang, 1992).

Example 13.1

The *Haar wavelets* constitute the simplest system of wavelets (Haar, 1910). The mother wavelet is defined as

$$\psi_H(x) = \begin{cases} 1 & 0 \leq x < .5 \\ -1 & .5 \leq x < 1 \\ 0 & \text{otherwise} \end{cases}$$

and wavelets are defined as

$$\psi_{j,k}(x) = 2^{-j/2}\psi_H(2^{-j}x - k) = \begin{cases} 1 & k2^j \leq x < k2^j + 2^{j-1} \\ -1 & k2^j + 2^{j-1} \leq x < (k+1)2^j \\ 0 & \text{otherwise} \end{cases}$$

Some of these wavelets are shown in Figure 13.1.

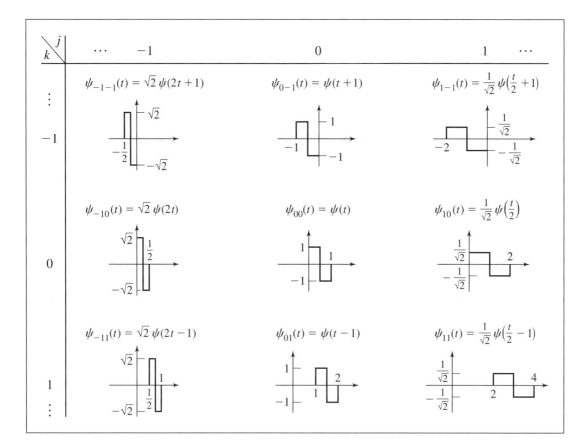

Figure 13.1   Haar wavelets

13.2   Multiresolution Analysis

Fast wavelet transform made wavelet transforms practicable. It is an algorithm for finding a discrete wavelet transform and was introduced by Mallat and his multiresolution theory (Mallat, 1989).

Mallat's multiresolution theory analysis begins with a basic function ϕ called a *scaling function* instead of a basic wavelet ψ and is used to generate ψ. The translated and dilated versions of ϕ are defined by

$$\phi_{j,k}(x) = \frac{1}{\sqrt{2^j}} \, \phi\left(\frac{x}{2^j} - k\right)$$

Scaling functions $\phi_{j,k}$ are shifted and dilated versions of the basic scaling function $\phi = \phi_{0,0}$ and are used to sample signals at various times and scales. If ϕ is a function of some width W centered near 0, then $\phi_{j,k}$ are functions of width $2^j W$ centered near $k2^j$.

Definition 13.6   An infinite sequence $\{V_j\}$ of linear function spaces is called a *multiresolution analysis* associated with a scaling function ϕ when

13.6.1. the spaces are nested: $\{0\} \subset \ldots \subset V_1 \subset V_0 \subset V_{-1} \subset \ldots \subset L^2(R)$

13.6.2. $f(x) \in V_j$ iff $f(2x) \in V_{j-1}$

13.6.3. functions $\phi_k(x) = \phi(x - k)$ form an orthonormal basis of V_0; that is, the functions ϕ_k are orthogonal and normalized

It is clear from the definition of $\phi_{j,k}$ given earlier that $\phi_{0,k}(x) = \phi(x - k)$. Thus, $\phi_{0,k} \in V_0$ for all integers k, due to 13.6.3, and the set $\{\phi_{j,k}: k \in Z = \{\ldots, -1, 0, 1, \ldots\}\}$ is an orthonormal basis for V_j, due to 13.6.2.

Because $V_0 \subset V_{-1}$ and $\phi(x) = \phi_{0,0}(x)$, what belongs to V_0 also belongs to V_{-1}, and therefore, $\phi(x)$ can be expressed as a linear combination of the basis $\{\phi_{-1,k}: k \in Z\} = \{\sqrt{2}\phi(2x - k): k \in Z\}$ of space V_{-1}—that is, as a sum

$$\phi(x) = \sqrt{2} \sum_{k=-\infty}^{\infty} h_k \phi(2x - k) \tag{13.2}$$

which is the *two-scale relation* (because it involves x and $2x$) of the scaling function ϕ and a two-scale sequence $\{h_k: k \in Z\}$; this recursive formula is also called a *dilation equation*.

Define space W_0 all of whose elements are orthogonal to all elements of V_0 and such that

$$V_{-1} = W_0 \oplus V_0$$

That is, W_0 is an orthogonal complement of V_0 in V_{-1} (i.e., $W_0 \cap V_0 = \{0\}$) or, more generally, when

$$V_{j-1} = W_j \oplus V_j$$

W_j is an orthogonal complement of V_j in V_{j-1} so that

$$L^2(R) = \ldots \oplus W_1 \oplus W_0 \oplus W_{-1} \oplus \ldots$$

This is an orthogonal sum since the spaces W_j are mutually orthogonal (in contrast to spaces V_j, which are nested). Each function $f \in L^2(R)$ has a unique orthogonal decomposition

$$f(x) = \ldots + f_1(x) + f_0(x) + f_{-1}(x) + \ldots$$

where $f_j \in W_j$. That is, each component $f_j(x)$ of function f has a unique representation in terms of the wavelet series.

It can be proven that there is a function $\psi(x)$ whose translates $\psi(x - k)$ form an orthogonal basis of space W_0, and it is given by a two-scale relation

$$\psi(x) = \sqrt{2} \sum_{k=-\infty}^{\infty} g_k \phi(2x - k) \tag{13.3}$$

a two-scale sequence $\{g_k : k \in Z\}$, analogous to (13.2) for the scaling function N. Because the spaces W_j are obtained from W_0 by dilation, $W_j = \{f(2^j x) : f(x) \in W_0\}$, and the basis for each W_j is given by the sequence of wavelets $\{\psi_{j,k} : j \in Z\}$, where $\psi_{j,k} = 2^{-j/2} \psi(2^{-j}x - k)$, which is the same as the wavelets given by (13.1). Furthermore, the basis functions $\phi_{j,k}$ of V_j together with basis functions $\psi_{j,k}$ of W_j form a basis for space V_{j-1}.

Multiresolution analysis concerns square integrable functions, but the functions have to be adjusted to the spaces V_j and W_j for which scaling functions and wavelets form the bases. This is done through the orthogonal projection.

Definition 13.7

The *orthogonal projection* g of f in a space S is a function that is the closest representation of f in S. Each function in $L^2(R)$ is represented in V_j with an orthogonal projection P:

$$Pf = \sum \langle f, \phi_{j,k} \rangle \phi_{j,k}$$

That is, space V_j is the set of all approximations at the resolution 2^{-j} for the functions in $L^2(R)$.

Since spaces V_j and W_j are orthogonal to each other, then so are functions ϕ and ψ, $\langle \phi, \psi \rangle = 0$. Therefore,

$$\langle \phi, \psi \rangle = 2 \sum_j \sum_k g_j h_k \langle \phi_{-1,j}, \phi_{-1,k} \rangle = 2 \sum_k g_k h_k = 0$$

so that the choice

$$g_k = (-1)^k h_{1-k} \tag{13.4}$$

gives correct solutions; for N coefficients $h_0, \ldots, h_{N-1}$, where N is an even number and the remaining h coefficients are equal to zero, the choice can be

$$g_k = (-1)^k h_{N-1-k} \tag{13.5}$$

Example 13.2

Define V_j as the space of Haar functions that are all piecewise constant functions in $L^2(R)$—that is, functions that are constant over intervals of length 2^j, $[2^j k, 2^j(k + 1))$, $k \in Z$. All functions in V_0 are constant on intervals $[k, k + 1)$ so that they are also constant over intervals $[k/2, (k + 1)/2)$, and consequently, they also belong to the space V_{-1} (Figure 13.2).

The Haar scaling function for these function spaces is the function

$$\phi_H(x) = \begin{cases} 1 & \text{for } 0 \le x < 1 \\ 0 & \text{otherwise} \end{cases}$$

and

$$\phi_{j,k}(x) = 2^{-j/2}\phi_H(2^{-j}x - k) = \begin{cases} 1 & \text{for } k2^j \le x < (k+1)2^j \\ 0 & \text{otherwise} \end{cases}$$

(Figure 13.3). The sequence of functions $\{\phi_{j,k} : k \in Z\}$ is an orthonormal basis of a function space V_j of Haar functions (Exercise 13.1).

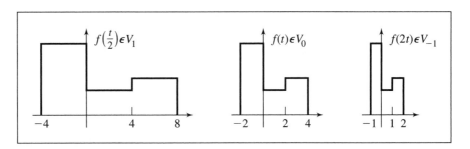

Figure 13.2   Dependencies between spaces V_j

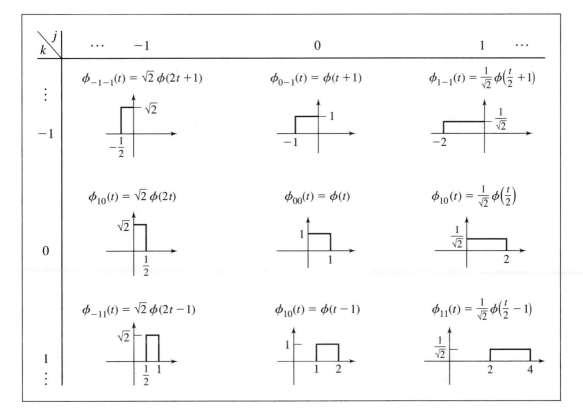

Figure 13.3   Haar scaling functions

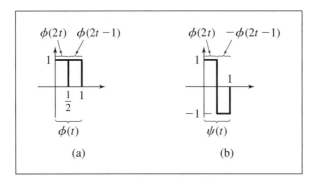

Figure 13.4   Connections between Haar wavelets and scaling functions

It is clear that

$$\phi_H(x) = \phi_H(2x) + \phi_H(2x - 1)$$

(Figure 13.4a), and thus (13.2) is satisfied for $h_0 = h_1 = \frac{1}{\sqrt{2}}$. Moreover,

$$\psi_H(x) = \phi_H(2x) - \phi_H(2x - 1)$$

(Figure 13.4b), and thus (13.3) is satisfied for $g_0 = h_1 = \frac{1}{\sqrt{2}}$, $g_1 = -h_0 = -\frac{1}{\sqrt{2}}$.

Example 13.3   A system of orthonormal wavelets that are compactly supported (i.e., they are zero outside an interval) was constructed by Ingrid Daubechies (1988). It turns out that Haar wavelets are a special case of Daubechies wavelets.

There is no analytic formula that allows for constructing such wavelets. Daubechies scaling functions and wavelets are limits of constructs generated by recursive dilation equations (13.2) and (13.3). A particular Daubechies system depends on the number of nonzero coefficients h_i and g_i. For

$$h_0 = \frac{1 + \sqrt{3}}{4\sqrt{2}}, \ h_1 = \frac{3 + \sqrt{3}}{4\sqrt{2}}, \ h_2 = \frac{3 - \sqrt{3}}{4\sqrt{2}}, \ h_3 = \frac{1 - \sqrt{3}}{4\sqrt{2}}$$

different approximations of the scaling function are presented in Figure 13.5a–e. With coefficients

$$g_0 = \frac{1 - \sqrt{3}}{4\sqrt{2}}, \ g_1 = -\frac{3 - \sqrt{3}}{4\sqrt{2}}, \ g_2 = \frac{3 + \sqrt{3}}{4\sqrt{2}}, \ g_3 = -\frac{1 + \sqrt{3}}{4\sqrt{2}}$$

the corresponding Daubechies wavelet D4 found with equation (13.3) is given in Figure 13.5f.

With (13.4) we have

$$\psi(x) = \sqrt{2} \sum_{k=-\infty}^{\infty} (-1)^k h_{1-k} \phi(2x - k) \tag{13.6}$$

$$\psi_{j,k}(x) = 2^{-j/2} \psi(2^{-j}x - k) = 2^{-j/2}\sqrt{2} \sum_{n} g_n \phi(2^{-j+1}x - 2k - n)$$

$$= \sum_{n} g_n \phi_{j-1, 2k+n}(x) = \sum_{n} g_{n-2k} \phi_{j-1,n}(x)$$

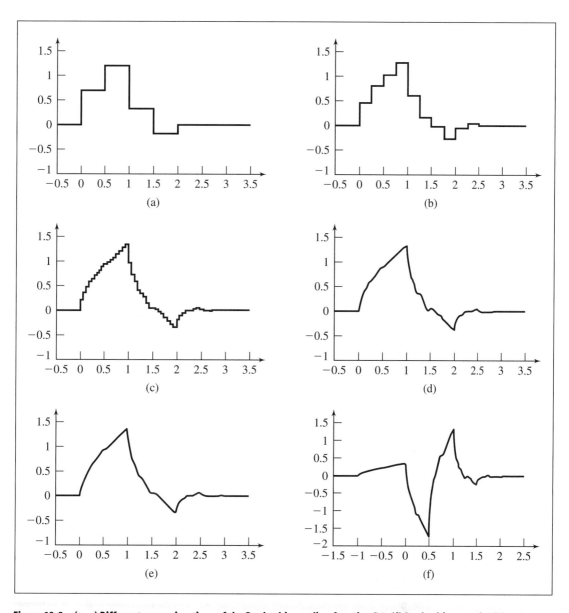

Figure 13.5   (a–e) Different approximations of the Daubechies scaling function D4; (f) Daubechies wavelet D4

and thus,

$$\langle f, \psi_{j,k} \rangle = \int f(t)\psi_{j,k}(t)dt = \int f(t)\sum_n g_{n-2k}\phi_{j-1,n}(t)dt = \sum_n g_{n-2k}\langle f, \phi_{j-1,n}\rangle$$

Similarly,

$$\phi_{j,k}(x) = 2^{-j/2}\phi(2^{-j}x - k) = \sum_n h_{n-2k}\phi_{j-1,n}(x)$$

Therefore,

$$\langle f, \phi_{j,k} \rangle = \sum_n h_{n-2k} \langle f, \phi_{j-1,n} \rangle$$

Let $c_{j,k} = \langle f, \phi_{j,k} \rangle$ and $d_{j,k} = \langle f, \psi_{j,k} \rangle$. Then

$$c_{j,k} = \langle f, \phi_{j,k} \rangle = \sum_n h_{n-2k} \langle f, \phi_{j-1,n} \rangle = \sum_n h_{n-2k} c_{j-1,k} \tag{13.7}$$

and

$$d_{j,k} = \langle f, \psi_{j,k} \rangle = \sum_n g_{n-2k} \langle f, \phi_{j-1,n} \rangle = \sum_n g_{n-2k} c_{j-1,k} \tag{13.8}$$

Formulas (13.7) and (13.8) are instrumental in *decomposition* of the coefficients c_j into a low-resolution version c_{j-1} and detail d_{j-1}. This process allows us to construct finer resolution of a function f from its coarser resolution and the differences between these resolutions. This process can be applied recursively to c_{j-1} so that the original coefficients can be expressed by a hierarchy

$$\ldots \leftarrow c_j \leftarrow c_{j-1} \leftarrow c_{j-2}$$
$$\nearrow \qquad \nearrow$$
$$\ldots \quad d_i \qquad d_{j-1}$$

The process of recovering c_{j-1} from c_j and d_j is called *reconstruction*. Because $V_{j-1} = V_j \oplus W_j$, then for a function $f \in V_{j-1}, f = v + w$ for $v \in V_j$ and $w \in W_j$, so that

$$c_{j-1,k} = \langle f, \phi_{j-1,k} \rangle = \langle v + w, \phi_{j-1,k} \rangle = \langle v, \phi_{j-1,k} \rangle + \langle w, \phi_{j-1,k} \rangle$$

$$= \left\langle \sum_n c_{j,n} \phi_{j,n}, \phi_{j-1,n} \right\rangle + \left\langle \sum_n d_{j,n} \psi_{j,n}, \phi_{j-1,n} \right\rangle$$

$$= \sum_n c_{j,n} \langle \phi_{j,n}, \phi_{j-1,n} \rangle + \sum_n d_{j,n} \langle \psi_{j,n}, \phi_{j-1,n} \rangle$$

$$= \sum_n c_{j,n} \left\langle \sum_m h_{m-2n} \phi_{j-1,m}, \phi_{j-1,k} \right\rangle + \sum_n d_{j,n} \left\langle \sum_m g_{m-2n} \phi_{j-1,m}, \phi_{j-1,k} \right\rangle$$

$$= \sum_n h_{k-2n} c_{j,n} + \sum_n g_{k-2n} d_{j,n}$$

because $\langle \phi_{j-1,m}, \phi_{j-1,k} \rangle = 1$ for $m = k$ and 0 otherwise. That is, the reconstruction formula is

$$c_{j-1,k} = \sum_n h_{k-2n} c_{j,n} + \sum_n g_{k-2n} d_{j,n} \tag{13.9}$$

The process of reconstructing coefficients c is summarized in this schematic diagram:

$$\ldots \rightarrow c_j \rightarrow c_{j-1} \rightarrow c_{j-2}$$
$$\nearrow \qquad \searrow$$
$$\ldots \quad d_i \qquad d_{j-1}$$

The sequence $c_0, d_0, d_1, \ldots, d_{j-1}$, from which the original coefficients c^j can be recovered, is called a wavelet transform.

We can see that coefficients h_k are sufficient to find the wavelet transform; in particular, there is no need to know the scaling function or mother wavelet to accomplish the task. As a matter of fact, fast wavelet transform is the way of determining the wavelet transform without referring to the wavelet at all. What we need are the tables of h_k (and g_k) values to perform the computations. Scaling function and mother wavelet, to be sure, were used to determine these values, but afterwards, these functions are no longer needed.

Example 13.4

Consider the piecewise constant function $f = \{8, 6, 4, 2, 1, 2, 3, 4\}$ for intervals $[0, 1), \ldots, [6, 7)$ and $f(x) = 0$ for $x < 0$ and $x \geq 7$. Considered as a member of the Haar space V_0, the function can be represented in the basis $\{\phi_{0,k} : k \in Z\}$ of the space V_0 as

$$f(t) = \sum c_{0,k}\phi_{0,k} = c_{0,0}\phi_{0,0} + \ldots + c_{0,7}\phi_{0,7}$$

$$= 8\phi_{0,0} + 6\phi_{0,1} + 4\phi_{0,2} + 2\phi_{0,3} + 1\phi_{0,4} + 2\phi_{0,5} + 3\phi_{0,6} + 4\phi_{0,7}$$

(13.10)

with remaining coefficients $c_{0,k} = 0$. Coefficients $c_{0,0}, \ldots, c_{0,7}$ are simply the original values of the function f because f is the weighted sum of the basis functions $\phi_{0,k}$ of space V_0 with these values as weights. That is, f is pieced together in V_0 from the basis functions weighted with numbers $\{8, 6, 4, 2, 1, 2, 3, 4\}$ (Figure 13.6a).

Next, because $V_0 = V_1 \oplus W_1$, f is shown as a combination of bases of spaces V_1 and W_1 (i.e., bases $\{\phi_{1,k} : k \in Z\}$ and $\{\psi_{1,k} : k \in Z\}$):

$$f(x) = \sum c_{1,k}\phi_{1,k} + \sum d_{1,k}\psi_{1,k}$$

$$= c_{1,0}\phi_{1,0} + \ldots + c_{1,3}\phi_{1,3} + d_{1,0}\psi_{1,0} + \ldots + d_{1,3}\psi_{1,3}$$

$$f(x) = \frac{1}{\sqrt{2}}(14\phi_{1,0} + 6\phi_{1,1} + 3\phi_{1,2} + 7\phi_{1,3} + 2\psi_{1,0} + 2\psi_{1,1} - \psi_{1,2} - \psi_{1,3})$$

(13.11)

with the remaining coefficients $c_{1,k}$ and $d_{1,k} = 0$ because

$$c_{1,0} = h_0 c_{0,0} + h_1 c_{0,1} \qquad\qquad d_{1,0} = g_0 c_{0,0} + g_1 c_{0,1}$$

$$= \frac{1}{\sqrt{2}}8 + \frac{1}{\sqrt{2}}6 = \frac{14}{\sqrt{2}} \qquad\qquad = \frac{1}{\sqrt{2}}8 - \frac{1}{\sqrt{2}}6 = \frac{2}{\sqrt{2}}$$

$$c_{1,1} = h_0 c_{0,2} + h_1 c_{0,3} \qquad\qquad d_{1,1} = g_0 c_{0,2} + g_1 c_{0,3}$$

$$= \frac{1}{\sqrt{2}}4 + \frac{1}{\sqrt{2}}2 = \frac{6}{\sqrt{2}} \qquad\qquad = \frac{1}{\sqrt{2}}4 - \frac{1}{\sqrt{2}}2 = \frac{2}{\sqrt{2}}$$

$$c_{1,2} = h_0 c_{0,4} + h_1 c_{0,5} \qquad\qquad d_{1,2} = g_0 c_{0,4} + g_1 c_{0,5}$$

$$= \frac{1}{\sqrt{2}}1 + \frac{1}{\sqrt{2}}2 = \frac{3}{\sqrt{2}} \qquad\qquad = \frac{1}{\sqrt{2}}1 - \frac{1}{\sqrt{2}}2 = -\frac{1}{\sqrt{2}}$$

$$c_{1,3} = h_0 c_{0,6} + h_1 c_{0,7} \qquad\qquad d_{1,3} = g_0 c_{0,6} + g_1 c_{0,7}$$

$$= \frac{1}{\sqrt{2}}3 + \frac{1}{\sqrt{2}}4 = \frac{7}{\sqrt{2}} \qquad\qquad = \frac{1}{\sqrt{2}}3 - \frac{1}{\sqrt{2}}4 = -\frac{1}{\sqrt{2}}$$

Note that because each scaling function $\phi_{1,0}, \ldots, \phi_{1,3}$ and wavelet $\psi_{1,0}, \ldots, \psi_{1,3}$ include the coefficient $\frac{1}{\sqrt{2}}$, the first four terms in the sum representing function f in (13.11) are simple averages, and the last four terms are differences between these averages and terms in the sum representing function f in (13.10). This is illustrated in Figure 13.6b. For example, the sum $\frac{1}{\sqrt{2}}(14\phi_{1,0} + 2\psi_{1,0})$ reconstructs the original values of f in the interval $[0, 2)$: $1 = \frac{1}{\sqrt{2}}2\psi_{1,0}$ is added to $7 = \frac{1}{\sqrt{2}}14\phi_{1,0}$ in the interval $[0, 1)$ to

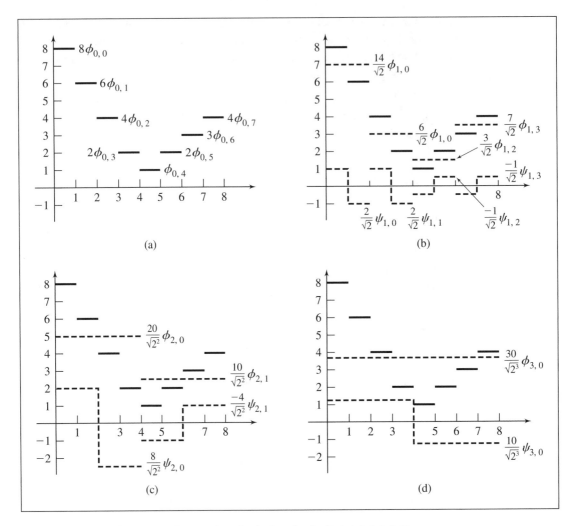

Figure 13.6   Generating fast wavelet transform for the function $f = \{8, 6, 4, 2, 1, 2, 3, 4\}$

reconstruct the original value of 8 for f for this interval, and $-1 = \frac{1}{\sqrt{2}} 2\psi_{1,0}$ is added to 7 in the interval $[1, 2)$ to reconstruct the original value of 6 for f for this interval.

In the next step, because $V_1 = V_2 \oplus W_2$ (i.e., $V_0 = V_2 \oplus W_2 \oplus W_1$), f is shown as a combination of bases of spaces V_2, W_2, and W_1—that is, bases $\{\phi_{2,k}: k \in Z\}$, $\{\psi_{2,k}: k \in Z\}$, and $\{\psi_{1,k}: k \in Z\}$:

$$f(x) = \sum c_{2,k}\phi_{2,k} + \sum d_{2,k}\psi_{2,k} + \sum d_{1,k}\psi_{1,k}$$
$$= c_{2,0}\phi_{2,0} + c_{2,1}\phi_{2,1} + d_{2,0}\psi_{2,0} + d_{2,1}\psi_{2,1} + d_{1,0}\psi_{1,0} + \ldots + d_{1,3}\psi_{1,3}$$
$$= \frac{1}{\sqrt{2^2}}(20\phi_{2,0} + 10\phi_{2,1} + 8\psi_{2,0} - 4\psi_{2,1}) + \frac{1}{\sqrt{2}}(2\psi_{1,0} + 2\psi_{1,1} - \psi_{1,2} - \psi_{1,3})$$

because

$$c_{2,0} = h_0 c_{1,0} + h_1 c_{1,1}$$
$$= \frac{1}{\sqrt{2}} \frac{14}{\sqrt{2}} + \frac{1}{\sqrt{2}} \frac{6}{\sqrt{2}} = \frac{20}{\sqrt{2^2}};$$

$$d_{2,0} = g_0 c_{1,0} + g_1 c_{1,1}$$
$$= \frac{1}{\sqrt{2}} \frac{14}{\sqrt{2}} - \frac{1}{\sqrt{2}} \frac{6}{\sqrt{2}} = \frac{8}{\sqrt{2^2}}$$

$$c_{2,1} = h_0 c_{1,2} + h_1 c_{1,3}$$
$$= \frac{1}{\sqrt{2}} \frac{3}{\sqrt{2}} + \frac{1}{\sqrt{2}} \frac{7}{\sqrt{2}} = \frac{10}{\sqrt{2^2}};$$

$$d_{2,1} = g_0 c_{1,2} + g_1 c_{1,3}$$
$$= \frac{1}{\sqrt{2}} \frac{3}{\sqrt{2}} - \frac{1}{\sqrt{2}} \frac{7}{\sqrt{2}} = \frac{4}{\sqrt{2^2}}$$

Now $c_{2,0} \phi_{2,0}$ represents the average of f in the interval $[0, 4)$, which encompasses four intervals of the original definition of function f (Figure 13.6c). The differences between this average and the values of f in the four intervals are encoded in both $d_{2,0}\psi_{2,0}$ and $c_{1,0}\phi_{1,0}$ for the first two intervals, $[0, 1)$ and $[1, 2)$, and in $d_{2,0}\psi_{2,0}$ and $c_{1,1}\phi_{1,1}$ for the next two intervals, $[2, 3)$ and $[3, 4)$.

Finally, because $V_2 = V_3 \oplus W_3$ (i.e., $V_0 = V_3 \oplus W_3 \oplus W_2 \oplus W_1$), f is shown as a combination of bases of spaces V_3, W_3, W_2, and W_1—that is, bases $\{\phi_{3,k} : k \in Z\}$, $\{\psi_{3,k} : k \in Z\}$, $\{\psi_{2,k} : k \in Z\}$, and $\{\psi_{1,k} : k \in Z\}$:

$$f(x) = \sum c_{3,k}\phi_{3,k} + \sum d_{3,k}\psi_{3,k} + \sum c_{2,k}\psi_{2,k} + \sum c_{1,k}\psi_{1,k}$$
$$= c_{3,k}\phi_{3,0} + d_{3,0}\psi_{3,0} + d_{2,0}\psi_{2,0} + d_{2,1}\psi_{2,1} + d_{1,0}\psi_{1,0} + \ldots + d_{1,3}\psi_{1,3}$$
$$= \frac{1}{\sqrt{2^3}}(20\phi_{3,0} + 10\psi_{3,0}) + \frac{1}{\sqrt{2^2}}(8\psi_{2,0} - 4\psi_{2,1})$$
$$+ \frac{1}{\sqrt{2}}(2\psi_{1,0} + 2\psi_{1,1} - \psi_{1,2} - \psi_{1,3})$$

because

$$c_{3,0} = h_0 c_{2,0} + h_1 c_{2,1} = \frac{1}{\sqrt{2}} \frac{20}{\sqrt{2^2}} + \frac{1}{\sqrt{2}} \frac{10}{\sqrt{2^2}} = \frac{30}{\sqrt{2^3}};$$

$$d_{3,0} = g_0 c_{2,0} + g_1 c_{2,1} = \frac{1}{\sqrt{2}} \frac{20}{\sqrt{2^2}} - \frac{1}{\sqrt{2}} \frac{10}{\sqrt{2^2}} = \frac{10}{\sqrt{2^3}}$$

The process can be summarized in the following diagram:

$$c_j: \quad \frac{1}{\sqrt{2^3}}\{30\} \leftarrow \frac{1}{\sqrt{2^2}}\{20, 10\} \leftarrow \frac{1}{\sqrt{2}}\{14, 6, 3, 7\} \leftarrow \{8, 6, 4, 2, 1, 2, 3, 4\}$$

$$d_j: \quad \frac{1}{\sqrt{2^3}}\{10\} \quad \frac{1}{\sqrt{2^2}}\{8, -4\} \quad \frac{1}{\sqrt{2}}\{2, 2, -1, -1\}$$

and the final Haar wavelet transform is the sequence $\left\{ \frac{30}{\sqrt{2^3}}, \frac{10}{\sqrt{2^3}}, \frac{8}{\sqrt{2^2}}, -\frac{4}{\sqrt{2^2}}, \frac{2}{\sqrt{2}}, \frac{2}{\sqrt{2}}, -\frac{1}{\sqrt{2}}, -\frac{1}{\sqrt{2}} \right\} = \{10.6066, 3.5355, 4, -2, 1.4142, 1.4142, -0.7071, -0.7071\}$.

The coefficients $c_{j,k}$ can be recovered by application of (13.9). For example,

$$c_{2,0} = h_0 c_{3,0} + g_0 d_{3,0} = \frac{1}{\sqrt{2}} \frac{30}{\sqrt{2^3}} + \frac{1}{\sqrt{2}} \frac{10}{\sqrt{2^3}} = \frac{20}{\sqrt{2^2}}$$

$$c_{2,1} = h_1 c_{3,0} + g_1 d_{3,0} = \frac{1}{\sqrt{2}} \frac{30}{\sqrt{2^3}} - \frac{1}{\sqrt{2}} \frac{10}{\sqrt{2^3}} = \frac{10}{\sqrt{2^2}}$$

which can be summarized in the diagram:

$$c_j: \quad \frac{1}{\sqrt{2^3}}\{30\} \rightarrow \frac{1}{\sqrt{2^2}}\{20, 10\} \rightarrow \frac{1}{\sqrt{2}}\{14, 6, 3, 7\} \quad \rightarrow \{8, 6, 4, 2, 1, 2, 3, 4\}$$

$$d_j: \quad \frac{1}{\sqrt{2^3}}\{10\} \qquad \frac{1}{\sqrt{2^2}}\{8, -4\} \qquad \frac{1}{\sqrt{2}}\{2, 2, -1, -1\}$$

This example indicates that the elements of the Haar wavelet transform are highly skewed: The largest values are at the beginning, and the remaining values are small. To accomplish lossy compression, these small values can be disregarded by replacing them with zeros so that runs of zeros appear, which can be efficiently encoded. For example, if the Haar wavelet transform { 10.6066, 3.5355, 4, –2, 1.4142, 1.4142, –0.7071, –0.7071} is reduced to { 10.6066, 3.5355, 4, –2, 1.4142, 1.4142, 0, 0}, then the original function values f = {8, 6, 4, 2, 1, 2, 3, 4} can still be recovered with (13.9) as {8, 6, 4, 2, 1.5, 1.5, 3.5, 3.5}.

Multiresolution analysis can be generalized to higher dimensions, particularly to two dimensions, which is important because images are two-dimensional matrices.

First, with the tensor product $\otimes$ we define the functional space $F \otimes G = \{(f \otimes g)(x, y) = f(x)g(y): f \in F \text{ and } g \in G\}$.

The definition

$$\Phi_{j,k,m} = \phi_{j,k}(x)\phi_{j,m}(y)$$

determines the orthonormal basis of scale functions for two-dimensional spaces V_j^2 and the hierarchy

$$\ldots V_1^2 \subset V_0^2 \subset V_{-1}^2 \ldots$$

in which each space V_j^2 has an orthogonal complement W_j^2 in V_{j-1}^2. Therefore,

$$V_{j-1}^2 = V_{j-1} \otimes V_{j-1} = (V_j \oplus W_j) \otimes (V_j \oplus W_j)$$
$$= (V_j \otimes V_j) \oplus ((W_j \otimes V_j) \oplus (V_j \otimes W_j) \oplus (W_j \otimes W_j)) = V_j^2 \otimes W_j^2$$

which indicates that three wavelets should be defined for the three components of W_j^2:

$$\Psi_{j,k,m,1}(x, y) = \phi_{j,k}(x)\psi_{j,m}(y)$$

$$\Psi_{j,k,m,2}(x, y) = \psi_{j,k}(x)\phi_{j,m}(y)$$

$$\Psi_{j,k,m,3}(x, y) = \psi_{j,k}(x)\psi_{j,m}(y)$$

Schematically, this can be represented by the diagram in Figure 13.7. This diagram also suggests the process of finding the wavelet transform. The two-dimensional decomposition is achieved by alternating between one-dimensional decompositions of rows and columns. First, all rows are decomposed, then all columns, and then again rows and columns but only in the upper left quadrant of the submatrix being currently processed. The original matrix can be easily restored by reversing the process.

Example 13.5   A 2 × 2 sample matrix is first processed rowwise and then columnwise to give a two-dimensional Haar wavelet transform:

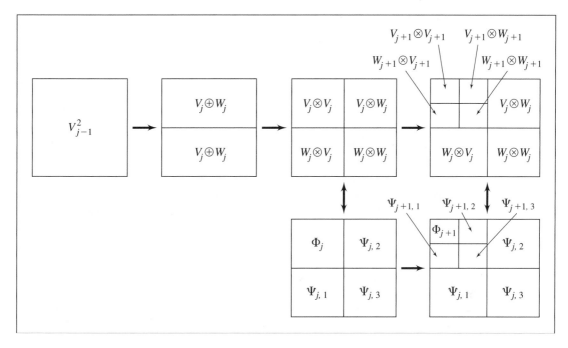

Figure 13.7   Generating a two-dimensional wavelet transform

$$\begin{bmatrix} 2 & 3 \\ 4 & 7 \end{bmatrix} \rightarrow \begin{bmatrix} \dfrac{2+3}{\sqrt{2}} & \dfrac{2-3}{\sqrt{2}} \\ \dfrac{4+7}{\sqrt{2}} & \dfrac{4-7}{\sqrt{2}} \end{bmatrix} \rightarrow \begin{bmatrix} \dfrac{2+3+4+7}{\sqrt{2^2}} & \dfrac{(2-3)+(4-7)}{\sqrt{2^2}} \\ \dfrac{(2+3)-(4+7)}{\sqrt{2^2}} & \dfrac{(2-3)-(4-7)}{\sqrt{2^2}} \end{bmatrix} \rightarrow \begin{bmatrix} 8 & -2 \\ -3 & 1 \end{bmatrix}$$

The advantages of such processing can be observed for larger sample matrices, in particular, when samples do not differ by much from one another. Consider this matrix and its decomposition:

$$\begin{bmatrix} 3 & 4 & 5 & 4 \\ 4 & 3 & 3 & 2 \\ 1 & 2 & 1 & 2 \\ 4 & 3 & 2 & 1 \end{bmatrix} \rightarrow \begin{bmatrix} 8 & -1 & -\dfrac{1}{\sqrt{2}} & \dfrac{1}{\sqrt{2}} \\ 6 & 1 & \dfrac{1}{\sqrt{2}} & \dfrac{1}{\sqrt{2}} \\ 3 & 0 & -\dfrac{1}{\sqrt{2}} & -\dfrac{1}{\sqrt{2}} \\ 5 & 2 & \dfrac{1}{\sqrt{2}} & \dfrac{1}{\sqrt{2}} \end{bmatrix} \rightarrow \begin{bmatrix} 11 & 1 & 0 & \dfrac{1}{\sqrt{2}} \\ 3 & -1 & 0 & \dfrac{1}{\sqrt{2}} \\ \sqrt{2} & -\sqrt{2} & -1 & 0 \\ -\sqrt{2} & -\sqrt{2} & -1 & -1 \end{bmatrix}$$

$$\rightarrow \begin{bmatrix} 6\sqrt{2} & 5\sqrt{2} & 0 & \dfrac{1}{\sqrt{2}} \\ \sqrt{2} & 2\sqrt{2} & 0 & \dfrac{1}{\sqrt{2}} \\ \sqrt{2} & -\sqrt{2} & -1 & 0 \\ -\sqrt{2} & -\sqrt{2} & -1 & -1 \end{bmatrix} \rightarrow \begin{bmatrix} 7 & 7 & 0 & \dfrac{1}{\sqrt{2}} \\ 5 & 3 & 0 & \dfrac{1}{\sqrt{2}} \\ \sqrt{2} & -\sqrt{2} & -1 & 0 \\ -\sqrt{2} & -\sqrt{2} & -1 & -1 \end{bmatrix}$$

After eliminating small coefficients, the reconstructed matrix is a very good approximation of the original:

$$
\begin{bmatrix}
7 & 7 & 0 & 0 \\
5 & 3 & 0 & 0 \\
\sqrt{2} & -\sqrt{2} & 0 & 0 \\
-\sqrt{2} & -\sqrt{2} & 0 & 0
\end{bmatrix}
\rightarrow
\begin{bmatrix}
3.5 & 3.5 & 4.5 & 4.5 \\
3.5 & 3.5 & 2.5 & 2.5 \\
1.5 & 1.5 & 1.5 & 1.5 \\
3.5 & 3.5 & 1.5 & 1.5
\end{bmatrix}
\tag{13.12}
$$

Usually, calculations of some c and d coefficients for a finite number of samples refer to c and d coefficients that are outside the range of the coefficients already computed. For example, according to decomposition formula (13.7), the D4 coefficient $c_{1,3} = h_0 c_{0,6} + h_1 c_{0,7} + h_2 c_{0,8} + h_3 c_{0,9}$, but until that point, only coefficients $c_{0,0}, \ldots, c_{0,7}$ exist; there are no coefficients $c_{0,8}$ and $c_{0,9}$. One way to alleviate the problem is to extend the existing coefficients with zeros, which is tantamount to the statement that no extension is needed because, for example, $c_{1,3} = h_0 c_{0,6} + h_1 c_{0,7} + h_2 c_{0,8} + h_3 c_{0,9} = h_0 c_{0,6} + h_1 c_{0,7}$. Another method consists of making the sequence of coefficients periodic. This begins with coefficients $c_{0,k}$ (i.e., with the original samples), which automatically renders the subsequent sequences $c_1, c_2, \ldots$ of coefficients periodic as well.

Example 13.6

Consider the sequence of samples $f = \{8, 6, 4, 2, 1, 2, 3, 4\}$ for which D4 wavelet transform should be determined. We have the first set of coefficients, $\{c_{0,0}, c_{0,1}, c_{0,2}, c_{0,3}, c_{0,4}, c_{0,5}, c_{0,6}, c_{0,7}\} = \{8, 6, 4, 2, 1, 2, 3, 4\}$, which is extended to a periodic sequence $\{\ldots, c_{0,0}, c_{0,1}, c_{0,2}, c_{0,3}, c_{0,4}, c_{0,5}, c_{0,6}, c_{0,7}, c_{0,0}, c_{0,1}, \ldots\} = \{\ldots, 8, 6, 4, 2, 1, 2, 3, 4, 8, 6, \ldots\}$. Using this extended sequence, we find

$$c_{1,0} = h_0 c_{0,0} + h_1 c_{0,1} + h_2 c_{0,2} + h_3 c_{0,3}$$
$$= \frac{1}{4\sqrt{2}}((1 + \sqrt{3})8 + (3 + \sqrt{3})6 + (3 - \sqrt{3})4 + (1 - \sqrt{3})2) = \frac{40 + 8\sqrt{3}}{4\sqrt{2}}$$

$$c_{1,1} = h_0 c_{0,2} + h_1 c_{0,3} + h_2 c_{0,4} + h_3 c_{0,5}$$
$$= \frac{1}{4\sqrt{2}}((1 + \sqrt{3})4 + (3 + \sqrt{3})2 + (3 - \sqrt{3}) + (1 - \sqrt{3})2) = \frac{15 + 3\sqrt{3}}{4\sqrt{2}}$$

$$c_{1,2} = h_0 c_{0,4} + h_1 c_{0,5} + h_2 c_{0,6} + h_3 c_{0,7}$$
$$= \frac{1}{4\sqrt{2}}((1 + \sqrt{3}) + (3 + \sqrt{3})2 + (3 - \sqrt{3})3 + (1 - \sqrt{3})4) = \frac{20 + 4\sqrt{3}}{4\sqrt{2}}$$

$$c_{1,3} = h_0 c_{0,6} + h_1 c_{0,7} + h_2 c_{0,8} + h_3 c_{0,9} = h_0 c_{0,6} + h_1 c_{0,7} + h_2 c_{0,0} + h_3 c_{0,1}$$
$$= \frac{1}{4\sqrt{2}}((1 + \sqrt{3})3 + (3 + \sqrt{3})4 + (3 - \sqrt{3})8 + (1 - \sqrt{3})6) = \frac{45 - 7\sqrt{3}}{4\sqrt{2}}$$

$$d_{1,0} = g_0 c_{0,0} + g_1 c_{0,1} + g_2 c_{0,2} + g_3 c_{0,3}$$
$$= \frac{1}{4\sqrt{2}}((1 - \sqrt{3})8 - (3 - \sqrt{3})6 + (3 + \sqrt{3})4 - (1 + \sqrt{3})2) = 0$$

$$d_{1,1} = g_0 c_{0,2} + g_1 c_{0,3} + g_2 c_{0,4} + g_3 c_{0,5}$$
$$= \frac{1}{4\sqrt{2}}((1 - \sqrt{3})4 - (3 - \sqrt{3})2 + (3 + \sqrt{3}) - (1 + \sqrt{3})2) = \frac{-1 - 3\sqrt{3}}{4\sqrt{2}}$$

$$d_{1,2} = g_0 c_{0,4} + g_1 c_{0,5} + g_2 c_{0,6} + g_3 c_{0,7}$$
$$= \frac{1}{4\sqrt{2}}((1 - \sqrt{3}) - (3 - \sqrt{3})2 + (3 + \sqrt{3})3 - (1 + \sqrt{3})4) = 0$$

$$d_{1,3} = h_0 c_{0,6} + h_1 c_{0,7} + h_2 c_{0,8} + h_3 c_{0,9} = h_0 c_{0,6} + h_1 c_{0,7} + h_2 c_{0,0} + h_3 c_{0,1}$$
$$= \frac{1}{4\sqrt{2}}((1 - \sqrt{3})3 - (3 - \sqrt{3})4 + (3 + \sqrt{3})8 - (1 + \sqrt{3})6) = \frac{9 + 3\sqrt{3}}{4\sqrt{2}}$$

The sequence $\{c_{1,0}, c_{1,1}, c_{1,2}, c_{1,3}\}$ is extended to the periodic sequence $\{\ldots, c_{1,0}, c_{1,1}, c_{1,2}, c_{1,3}, c_{1,0}, c_{1,1}, \ldots\}$ with which we compute

$$
\begin{aligned}
c_{2,0} &= h_0 c_{1,0} + h_1 c_{1,1} + h_2 c_{1,2} + h_3 c_{1,3} \\
&= \frac{1}{(4\sqrt{2})^2}\big((1 + \sqrt{3})(40 + 8\sqrt{3}) + (3 + \sqrt{3})(15 + 3\sqrt{3}) \\
&\qquad + (3 - \sqrt{3})(20 - 4\sqrt{3}) + (1 - \sqrt{3})(45 - 7\sqrt{3})\big) \\
&= \frac{64 - 3\sqrt{3}}{8}
\end{aligned}
$$

$$
\begin{aligned}
c_{2,1} &= h_0 c_{1,2} + h_1 c_{1,3} + h_2 c_{1,4} + h_3 c_{1,5} = h_0 c_{1,2} + h_1 c_{1,3} + h_2 c_{1,0} + h_3 c_{1,1} \\
&= \frac{56 + 3\sqrt{3}}{8}
\end{aligned}
$$

$$
d_{2,0} = g_0 c_{1,0} + g_1 c_{1,1} + g_2 c_{1,2} + g_3 c_{1,3} = \frac{1 - 14\sqrt{3}}{8}
$$

$$
\begin{aligned}
d_{2,1} &= g_0 c_{1,2} + g_1 c_{1,3} + g_2 c_{1,4} + g_3 c_{1,5} = g_0 c_{1,2} + g_1 c_{1,3} + g_2 c_{1,0} + g_3 c_{1,1} \\
&= \frac{-1 + 22\sqrt{3}}{8}
\end{aligned}
$$

Finally, the sequence $\{c_{2,0}, c_{2,1}\}$ is extended to the periodic sequence $\{\ldots, c_{2,0}, c_{2,1}, c_{2,0}, c_{2,1}, \ldots\}$ to determine

$$
\begin{aligned}
c_{3,0} &= h_0 c_{2,0} + h_1 c_{2,1} + h_2 c_{2,2} + h_3 c_{2,3} = h_0 c_{2,0} + h_1 c_{2,1} + h_2 c_{2,0} + h_3 c_{2,1} \\
&= \frac{15}{\sqrt{2}}
\end{aligned}
$$

$$
\begin{aligned}
d_{3,0} &= g_0 c_{2,0} + g_1 c_{2,1} + g_2 c_{2,2} + g_3 c_{2,3} = g_0 c_{2,0} + g_1 c_{2,1} + g_2 c_{2,0} + g_3 c_{2,1} \\
&= \frac{4 - 3\sqrt{3}}{4\sqrt{2}}
\end{aligned}
$$

The D4 wavelet transform $\{c_{3,0}, d_{3,0}, d_{2,0}, d_{2,1}, d_{1,0}, d_{1,1}, d_{1,2}, d_{1,3}\}$ equals

$$
\left\{ \frac{15}{\sqrt{2}}, \frac{4 - 3\sqrt{3}}{4\sqrt{2}}, \frac{1 - 14\sqrt{3}}{8}, \frac{-1 + 22\sqrt{3}}{8}, \frac{40 - 8\sqrt{3}}{4\sqrt{2}}, \frac{15 + 3\sqrt{3}}{4\sqrt{2}}, \frac{20 - 4\sqrt{3}}{4\sqrt{2}}, \frac{45 - 7\sqrt{3}}{4\sqrt{2}} \right\}
$$

that is, $\{10.6066, 0, -2.9061, 4.6381, 0, -1.0953, 0, 2.5095\}$.

The original samples can be reconstructed by applying the reconstruction formula (13.9). For example,

$$
c_{2,0} = h_0 c_{3,0} + h_2 c_{3,-1} + g_0 c_{3,0} + g_2 c_{3,-1} = h_0 c_{3,0} + h_2 c_{3,0} + g_0 c_{3,0} + g_2 c_{3,0}
$$

$$
c_{2,1} = h_1 c_{3,0} + h_3 c_{3,-1} + g_1 c_{3,0} + g_3 c_{3,-1} = h_1 c_{3,0} + h_3 c_{3,0} + g_1 c_{3,0} + g_3 c_{3,0}
$$

$$
c_{1,0} = h_0 c_{2,0} + h_2 c_{2,-1} + g_0 c_{2,0} + g_2 c_{2,-1} = h_0 c_{2,0} + h_2 c_{2,1} + g_0 c_{2,0} + g_2 c_{2,1}
$$

$$
c_{1,1} = h_1 c_{2,0} + h_3 c_{2,-1} + g_1 c_{2,0} + g_3 c_{2,-1} = h_1 c_{2,0} + h_3 c_{2,1} + g_1 c_{2,0} + g_3 c_{2,1}
$$

$$
c_{1,2} = h_0 c_{2,1} + h_2 c_{2,0} + g_0 c_{2,1} + g_2 c_{2,0}
$$

$$
c_{1,3} = h_1 c_{2,1} + h_3 c_{2,0} + g_1 c_{2,1} + g_3 c_{2,0}
$$

$$
c_{0,0} = h_0 c_{1,0} + h_2 c_{1,-1} + g_0 c_{1,0} + g_1 c_{2,-1} = h_0 c_{1,0} + h_2 c_{1,3} + g_0 c_{1,0} + g_1 c_{2,3}
$$

The process can be applied to images represented by two-dimensional matrices. To compress such images, as in preceding example, small coefficients can be eliminated by replacing them with zeros. For the sample matrix from Example 13.4

$$\begin{bmatrix} 3 & 4 & 5 & 4 \\ 4 & 3 & 3 & 2 \\ 1 & 2 & 1 & 2 \\ 4 & 3 & 2 & 1 \end{bmatrix} \tag{13.13}$$

the two-dimensional D4 wavelet transform

$$\begin{bmatrix} 6.5780 & 6.0703 & 0.3062 & 0.4009 \\ 5.5882 & 3.8137 & 0.5467 & -0.2888 \\ -2.2854 & -0.9833 & -0.7958 & -1.3873 \\ 2.2854 & -1.1127 & 0.7288 & -1.5458 \end{bmatrix} \tag{13.14}$$

is reduced to

$$\begin{bmatrix} 6.5780 & 6.0703 & 0 & 0 \\ 5.5882 & 3.8137 & 0 & 0 \\ -2.2854 & 0 & 0 & -1.3873 \\ 2.2854 & -1.1127 & 0 & -1.5458 \end{bmatrix} \tag{13.15}$$

but this still allows for a good reconstruction:

$$\begin{bmatrix} 2.9782 & 4.2009 & 4.2344 & 4.5865 \\ 4.0028 & 2.9302 & 2.7450 & 2.3220 \\ 0.8471 & 2.5266 & 1.4738 & 1.1535 \\ 3.5804 & 2.8677 & 2.1388 & 1.4135 \end{bmatrix} \tag{13.16}$$

To see how good the reconstruction is, we can use the mean absolute distortion, *mad,* as a discrepancy measure coefficient defined as (cf. Chapter 11)

$$\sum_i \left| (\text{original sample})_i - (\text{reconstructed sample})_i \right|$$

For D4 wavelet transform, the discrepancy between the original matrix (13.13) and the reconstructed matrix (13.16) equals 5.327, whereas for the Haar wavelet transform, the discrepancy between (13.13) and (13.12) equals 8, which is significantly higher than for the D4 reconstruction. This allows for creating longer runs of zeros to have better compression and still reconstruct the original without significant distortion. For example, after reducing D4 wavelet transform from (13.14) to

$$\begin{bmatrix} 6.5780 & 6.0703 & 0 & 0 \\ 5.5882 & 3.8137 & 0 & 0 \\ -2.2854 & 0 & 0 & 0 \\ 2.2854 & 0 & 0 & -1.5458 \end{bmatrix}$$

which has two more zeros than (13.15), the discrepancy between the original (13.13) and the reconstructed matrix is 7.699, which is still better than 8 for the Haar transform.

The problem with periodic extension is that it can introduce discontinuities at the beginning and at the end of the range. The problem can be alleviated by creating a mirror image of the sequence of samples and then extending it into a periodic sample (cf. a similar approach is used to deal with the Gibbs phenomenon with the cosine transform in Section 12.3.1 and Figure 12.7; see also Cohen et al., 1993; Nievergelt, 1999, Ch. 3). Examples of more elaborate wavelet-transform-based compression techniques can be found in Shapiro (1993; embedded zerotree wavelet, or EZW, encoder), Said and Pearlman (1996; set partitioning in hierarchical trees, or SPIHT, method), and Tian and Wells (1998).

EXERCISES

1. Show that the Haar scaling functions $\{\phi_{j,k}: k \in Z\}$ form an orthonormal basis in V_j.

2. Show that the decomposition $f = p + q$ for $f \in V_{j-1}$, $p \in V_j$ and $q \in W_j$ is unique.

3. Show that for an integrable scaling function ϕ such that $\int \phi dt \neq 0$, the dilation equation yields
   (a) $\sum h_k = \sqrt{2}$
   (b) $h_k = \sqrt{2} \int \phi(t)\phi(2t - k)dt$

4. Find the fast wavelet transform, as in Example 13.4, for the function $f_1(x) = f(x + 1)$—that is, for a function whose plot is shifted to the left by one— so that function $f_1 = \{8, 6, 4, 2, 1, 2, 3, 4\}$ for intervals $[-1, 0), \ldots, [5, 6)$ and $f_1(x) = 0$ for $x < -1$ and $x \geq 7$.

5. Find the fast wavelet transform, as in Example 13.4, for the function $f_2(x) = f(2x)$—that is, for a squeezed version of f—so that $f_2 = \{8, 6, 4, 2, 1, 2, 3, 4\}$ for intervals $[0, 0.5), \ldots, [3.5, 4)$ and $f_2(x) = 0$ for $x < 0$ and $x \geq 4$.

6. Find Haar and D4 wavelet transforms for the following functions f:
   a.   [2, 4, 6, 8, 10, 12, 14, 16]   b.   [1, 9, 1, 9, 1, 9, 1, 9]
   c.   [1, 9, 1, 9, 1, 9, 1, 8]   d.   [2, 2, 2, 2, 2, 2, 2, 2]
   e.   [2, 2, 2, 2, 2, 2, 2, 1]   f.   [0, 1, 2, 4, 4, 2, 1, 0].

   Remove from the wavelet transforms the coefficients between –1 and 1 and then reconstruct the function f and compute the *mad*.

BIBLIOGRAPHY

Burrus, C. Sidney, Gopinath, Ramesh A., and Guo, Haitao, *Introduction to wavelets and wavelet transforms*, Upper Saddle River, NJ: Prentice Hall, 1998.

Chan, Y. T., *Wavelet basics*, Boston: Kluwer, 1995.

Chui, Charles K., *An introduction to wavelets*, Boston: Academic Press, 1992.

Cohen, Albert, Daubechies, Ingrid, and Vial, Pierre, Wavelets on the interval and fast wavelet transforms, *Applied and Computational Harmonic Analysis* 1 (1993), 54–81.

Daubechies, Ingrid, Orthonormal bases of compactly supported wavelets, *Communications on Pure and Applied Mathematics* 41 (1988), 909–996.

Daubechies, Ingrid, The wavelet transform, time-frequency localization and signal analysis, *IEEE Transactions on Information Theory* 36 (1990), 961–1005.

Gabor, Dennis, Theory of communications, *Journal of the Institute for Electrical Engineers* 93 (1946), 429–457.

Grossman, Alex, and Morlet, Jean, Decomposition of Hardy functions into square integrable wavelets of constant shape, *SIAM Journal on Mathematics Analysis* 15 (1984), 723–736.

Haar, Alfred, Zur Theorie der orthogonalen Funktionensysteme, *Mathematische Annalen* 69 (1910), 331–371 [also in his *Gesammelte Arbeiten*, Budapest: Akadémiai Kiadó, 1959, 47–87].

Mallat, Stephane, Multiresolution approximations and wavelet orthonormal bases of $L^2(R)$, *Transactions of the American Mathematical Society* 315 (1989), 69–87.

Mallat, Stephane, *A wavelet tour of signal processing*, San Diego, CA: Academic Press, 1999.

Mallat, Stephane, and Hwang, Wen Liang, Singularity detection and processing with wavelets, *IEEE Transactions on Information Theory* 38 (1992), 617–643.

Nievergelt, Yves, *Wavelets made easy*, Boston: Birkhäuser, 1999.

Prasad, Lakshman, and Iyengar, S. S., *Wavelet analysis with applications to image processing*, Boca Raton, FL: CRC Press, 1997.

Said, A., and Pearlman, William A., A newfast and efficient image codec on set partitioning in hierarchical trees, *IEEE Transactions on Circuits and Systems for Video Technology* 6 (1996), 243–250.

Shapiro, Jerome M., Embedded image coding using zerotrees of wavelet coefficients, *IEEE Transactions on Signal Processing* 41 (1993), 3445–3462.

Stollnitz, Eric J., DeRose, Tony D., and Salesin, David H., *Wavelets for computer graphics: Theory and application*, San Francisco: Morgan Kaufmann, 1996.

Tian, J., and Wells, Raymond O., Embedded image coding using wavelet-difference reduction, in Topiwala, P. (ed.), *Wavelet image and video compression*, Norwell: Kluwer, 1998, 289–301.

Appendix

Data Compression Software on the Internet

There are numerous sites on the Internet that offer software for various data compression techniques. Here is a sample of these sites.

Sites with Comprehensive Set of Compression Pointers

http://www.internz.com/compression-pointers.html

http://dogma.net/DataCompression/

http://www.hn.is.uec.ac.jp/~arimura/compression_links.html

http://www.data-compression.com/

http://www.rdrop.com/~cary/html/data_compression.html

News Groups

comp.compression

comp.compression.research

The Huffman, Arithmetic, and Ziv-Lempel Compression

http://www.dc.ee/Files/Programm.Packing

http://www.programmersheaven.com/zone22/cat166/index.htm

The Huffman and Shannon Compression

http://www-stud.fht-esslingen.de/~david/dencode/

http://elvis.rowan.edu/~stone/datacmpr.htm

Arithmetic Coding

ftp://ftp.cpsc.ucalgary.ca/pub/projects/ar.cod/

http://www.cs.mu.oz.au/~alistair/arith_coder/

JPEG

ftp://ftp.uu.net/graphics/jpeg/

ftp://nic.funet.fi/pub/graphics/packages/jpeg/

JJ2000, an Implementation of JPEG 2000:

http://jj2000.epfl.ch/

MPEG

http://www.mpeg.org/MPEG/MSSG/

ftp://ftp.mpeg.org/pub/mpeg/mssg/

ftp://mm-ftp.cs.berkeley.edu/pub/multimedia/mpeg/play/

ftp://ftp.mni.mcgill.ca/pub/mpeg/

References to New Wavelet-Based Software

http://www.wavelet.org

Large WaveLab Library of MatLab Routines

http://playfair.stanford.edu/~wavelab

LastWave, a Wavelet Signal Processing Environment

http://www.cmap.polytechnique.fr/users/www.bacry

A Matlab Toolkit

http://www-dsp.rice.edu/software/RTW

An EZW Coder

http://perso.wanadoo.fr/polyvalens/clemens/ezw/ezw.html

Demo Programs for SPIHT Compression

http://www.cipr.rpi.edu/research/SPIHT/

Name Index

Subject Index